Space in Performance

THEATER: Theory/Text/Performance

Enoch Brater, Series Editor

Recent Titles:

Staging Place: The Geography of Modern Drama by Una Chaudhuri

The Aesthetics of Disturbance: Anti-Art in Avant-Garde Drama by David Graver

Toward a Theater of the Oppressed: The Dramaturgy of John Arden by Javed Malick

Theater in Israel edited by Linda Ben-Zvi

Crucibles of Crisis: Performing Social Change edited by Janelle Reinelt

Fornes: Theater in the Present Tense by Diane Lynn Moroff

Taking It to the Streets: The Social Protest Theater of Luis Valdez and Amiri Baraka by Harry J. Elam Jr.

Hearing Voices: Modern Drama and the Problem of Subjectivity by John H. Lutterbie

Mimesis, Masochism, & Mime: The Politics of Theatricality in Contemporary French Thought edited by Timothy Murray

Approaching the Millennium: Essays on Angels in America edited by Deborah R. Geis and Steven F. Kruger

Rooms with a View: The Stages of Community in the Modern Theater by Richard L. Barr

Staging Resistance: Essays on Political Theater edited by Jeanne Colleran and Jenny S. Spencer

Sightlines: Race, Gender, and Nation in Contemporary Australian Theatre by Helen Gilbert

Edges of Loss: From Modern Drama to Postmodern Theory by Mark Pizzato

Postmodern/Drama: Reading the Contemporary Stage by Stephen Watt

Trevor Griffiths: Politics, Drama, History by Stanton B. Garner Jr.

Memory-Theater and Postmodern Drama by Jeanette R. Malkin

Performing America: Cultural Nationalism in American Theater edited by Jeffrey D. Mason and J. Ellen Gainor

Space in Performance: Making Meaning in the Theatre by Gay McAuley

Mirrors of Our Playing: Paradigms and Presences in Modern Drama by Thomas R. Whitaker

Space in Performance
Making Meaning in the Theatre

Gay McAuley

ANN ARBOR

THE UNIVERSITY OF MICHIGAN PRESS

For
David
Sam and Hannah
with love

Copyright © by the University of Michigan 1999
All rights reserved
Published in the United States of America by
The University of Michigan Press
Manufactured in the United States of America
⊚ Printed on acid-free paper

2002   2001   2000   1999   4   3   2   1

A CIP catalog record for this book is available from the British Library.

Library of Congress Cataloging-in-Publication Data

McAuley, Gay.
    Space in performance : making meaning in the theatre / Gay
McAuley.
        p.   cm. — (Theater—theory/text/performance)
    Includes bibliographical references and index.
    ISBN 0-472-11004-7 (alk. paper)
    1. Theaters—Stage—setting and scenery.   2. Theater architecture.
3. Theater audiences—Psychology.   I. Title.   II. Series.
PN2091.S8   M383   1999
792'.025—dc21   98-58101
                                                              CIP

Acknowledgments

The theatre is a strange phenomenon, always under attack, even (perhaps especially) when at its most popular, attracting generation upon generation of idealistic young people to work long and hard for little material reward, frequently disappointing, even boring, but on occasion providing its spectators with an intensity of experience unmatched by any other art form. My first debt of gratitude is to the artists involved in the many productions I have seen over the last forty years in London, Paris, and in my adopted home of Sydney, and indeed to theatre artists everywhere, for it is their dedication that keeps the theatre alive.

More important even than the artists whose work I have experienced as a spectator in the theatre are those who have permitted me to watch their rehearsals. Observation of the creative process in action has been crucial in developing many of the insights and theoretical perspectives that are detailed in the following pages. The names of all the actors, directors, and designers involved in these productions are listed in the appendix, and to all I extend my appreciation and gratitude. One person must be singled out for special thanks—Rex Cramphorn, who died in 1991 at the tragically early age of fifty. Rex was a highly intelligent director, beloved of actors because he knew that the best theatre emerges from rehearsals in which, as he put it, "the grace of creativity can fall on any member of the group, conferring on him or her the right to lead the work," and one of his greatest skills was in achieving the conditions in which this could occur. He was also happy to open his work process to scrutiny, and it is in no small measure due to his example that so many other actors and directors were persuaded to do likewise. I learned a great deal from Rex, but it was not until I came to write this book that I realized just how central his work has been in my own theatre experience.

I take this opportunity, too, to acknowledge the work done by my colleagues at the University of Sydney's Theatre Workshop, in particular Derek Nicholson, director from 1974 to 1989, and Kim Spinks, dramaturg extraordinaire. This was a period of fruitful collaboration between theatre practitioners and academics, and it produced some marvelous theatre, experimentation in ways of teaching theatre and documenting performance, and many shared insights into the ways in which the theatre functions to create and communicate meaning. I should also like to thank the Faculty of Arts for maintaining funding of these collaborative theatre projects after the demise of the Theatre Workshop, even during periods of great financial stringency for the faculty.

My thanks are due to all the staff at the Centre for Performance Studies—to Tim Fitzpatrick in particular for running the center so efficiently in my absence in 1996 when I was writing this book, to Russell Emerson, who has led me through the intricacies of word processing and who prepared the tables, floor plans, and graphics that illustrate my argument, and to Marjorie Moffat, our indispensable administrator. My thanks also to Peta Tait for reading the chapter on the spectator, to Tony Day for advice and information about Indonesian performance practices, and to Patrice Pavis for the many occasions on my visits to Paris when we have gone to the theatre together and for his illuminating discussions of the practice of performance analysis. I should also like to thank Brunhild Rohle for making possible my short but intensive experience of the work of the Deutsches Theater in 1996.

Raymond de Berquelle photographed many of the productions sponsored by the Theatre Workshop and later the Centre for Performance Studies, and he bore patiently with my demands for analytical photographs even when these resulted in less interesting compositions than he would have produced if free to choose his own angles. All the photographs in chapter 5 were taken by Raymond de Berquelle, and I thank him for permission to reproduce them here. I should also like to thank Derek Nicholson for permission to reproduce his photographs of *The Theatrical Illusion* and *Britannicus* and the British Museum for permission to reproduce the Hogarth and Daumier prints.

The genesis of this book coincided to a large extent with my children's teenage years, and, although my progress seemed so slow to them that they feared at times I would be in my dotage before the book was written, their interest and pride in my work have been one of the unexpected joys of parenthood. My thanks, above all, go to my husband, David, who has always been a tower of strength on the home front, insisting that academic and domestic responsibilities are entirely compatible and ensuring that I keep a balanced view about the relative importance of theatre in the scheme of things.

Contents

1

Introduction: Space as Theatrical Signifier

The theatre is space.
 —Anne Ubersfeld, *L'Ecole du spectateur*

The theatre, as the *Oxford English Dictionary* tells us, is both a place and an art form: "an edifice specially adapted to dramatic representations" and "dramatic performances as a branch of art" (*Shorter OED* [1933] 1970). Indeed, theatre is perhaps the only art form in which the name given to the place where the artistic event occurs, or where the art object is displayed, is the same as that of the art form itself. Popular usage has thus encapsulated for English speakers a perception of the vital connection between physical space and the artistic communication in question that critics and theorists have only recently begun to explore. Interestingly enough, practitioners whose work is so closely bound up with this spatial reality seem sometimes to overlook it when they attempt to define the essential nature of their art.

Brecht, summing up a lifetime's work in the theatre in his *Short Organum* in 1948, wrote: "Theatre consists in this: in making live representations of reported or invented happenings between human beings and doing so with a view to entertainment" (1964, 180). The notion of entertainment brings with it by implication the presence of the spectator, but Brecht's formulation puts the emphasis on enactment, or what he calls "live representations," on narrative, and on the "making" itself, the production and performance process.

For Eric Bentley (1965), too, mimesis is of central importance, and he defines theatre in a quasi-algebraic formula: "A impersonates B, while C looks on." The formula stresses the relational quality of theatre, another very important factor, and indicates that there is a double relationship in play (A to B and A/B to C), but it seems that for Bentley it is the relation between actor and character, reality and fiction, that is the crucial one, because he immediately writes C out of the formula: "That very histrionic object, the mirror, enables any actor to watch himself and thereby become C, the audience. And the mirror on the wall is only one: the mirrors in the mind are many" (1965, 150). I would argue that in thus transforming the spectator into an abstraction and indeed in removing the theatrical act from real space, Bentley moves into a domain beyond theatre.

The keyword in Brecht's definition is *live*, for it is this that distinguishes theatre from the mediated forms of representation of happenings between human beings that are also offered to audiences for their entertainment, and it is through this that his definition intersects with that of Grotowski, writing twenty years later about a very different performance practice: "the theatre is an act carried out *here and now* in the actors' organisms, in front of other men" (1969, 118). Grotowksi is not interested in narrative, mimesis, or enactment but in the immediacy of the act, its physiological reality, situated in the actor's body. The act does, however, require the presence of the spectator, and, although Grotowski's work has since led him to focus exclusively on the performer, in the 1960s he was prepared to define theatre essentially in terms of this relationship: "We can thus define the theatre as 'what takes place between spectator and actor.' All the other things are supplementary— perhaps necessary, but nevertheless supplementary" (32–33). It is significant that in Grotowski's own terms the performance activities undertaken without an audience in mind are termed "paratheatrical" rather than theatrical.

The English language introduces the notion of place in this formulation: for an event to occur, it must "take place," that is, be located somewhere, but Grotowski does not refer explicitly to space as such in this definition. Peter Brook, on the other hand, makes space the primary condition: "I can take any empty space and call it a bare stage. A man walks across this empty space whilst somebody else is watching him, and this is all that is needed for an act of theatre to be engaged" (1968, 9). The minimal "act of theatre" here seems rather random, even arbitrary, notwithstanding the shadowy presence of Brook himself (stage manager or director?), who has transformed the empty space into stage by "taking" and "calling" it. The intentionality that German theorists such as Dietrich Steinbeck and Arno Paul, writing in the 1970s, required of the spectator and that contemporary theorists would argue should be present in both performer and spectator has thus been assumed by the direc-

tor, who perhaps becomes a kind of originary spectator, calling forth the
theatrical moment by his presence, watching both the man who walks
and the person who watches.

Notwithstanding these reservations, the beauty of Brook's definition is that it draws attention to the function of the space itself; the empty
space is here not simply the means of valorizing the actor's presence,
which is the function of Copeau's famous bare platform,[1] but the condition that alone makes possible the simultaneous presence of performer
and watcher. In Richard Southern's attempt to "get at the heart of what
Theatre really is" he uses the metaphor of Peer Gynt peeling the onion to
find its core, a *via negativa* familiar to both Copeau and Grotowski, and
sheds what he calls "accretions" such as movable scenery, auditorium,
stage as raised platform, and finally costume and mask. He concludes:
"Remove these and there will probably fall apart two separate pieces,
leaving nothing inside; those two pieces would be the Player and the
Audience. Take these apart and you can have no theatre" (Southern
1962, 21). For Richard Southern, as for Grotowski and for Brook, theatre
is to be found in the relationship between performer (however defined)
and spectator.

The minimal definitions quoted are fascinating for the terms that are
masked or elided, for what is not said and what is implied as much as for
what is explicitly stated, and they reveal a great deal about the evolution
of theatre practice over the course of this century. Mimesis, or enactment,
is seen as essential by some, merely optional by others, the necessary
intentionality may be that of the spectator or the performer or even that of
the director, but the common thread linking all the formulations and the
practices from which they derive is that theatre is something that takes
place "live" and that it requires the simultaneous presence of both performer and spectator. What they do not say, perhaps because they take it
for granted, is that in order for performer and spectator to come together,
to be present to each other, there must be a space of some sort. Richard
Southern quite rightly removes most of the specifics of the theatre building, seeing them as accretions, but he cannot remove the spatial condition
itself, the condition that Anne Ubersfeld, in the wonderfully concise
phrase that serves as epigraph to this chapter, sees as constitutive of theatre. While theatre can indeed take place anywhere (outdoors, in the
street, on the bare earth), the point is that it must take place somewhere.
In my view, therefore, we should include this third term and acknowledge that, if theatre involves communication between live actors and live

spectators, then they must be present to each other within a given space. This book is an attempt to explore the multiple functions of this spatial reality in the construction and communication of theatrical meaning. The title indicates that my focus is the lived space of performance, space as it is occupied and experienced by performers and spectators.

One of the factors that has helped to clarify critical thinking about the nature of theatrical semiosis has undoubtedly been the development over the course of the twentieth century of a number of different media, each of which has elaborated its own forms of dramatic presentation (first film then radio and, from the 1950s, television). The enormous popularity of film and television drama in particular has severed the symbiotic connection between theatre and drama, in force from the time of Aristotle onward and still evident in the dictionary definitions of theatre that I have already quoted. The impact of this has created new challenges for the theatre and has, at the same time, enabled people to see more clearly what constitutes the specificity of theatre and the ways in which it differs from other dramatic media. While theatre was the only medium through which the drama could be presented it was understandable that there should be a certain slippage between the two, although it was certainly unfortunate that Aristotle's hierarchical distinction between the play and its stage presentation should have been so slavishly followed by critics and scholars for so long.[2]

Aristotle's distinction, interpreted as a valorization of the written and a devalorization of the performed, has been used by all those who were reluctant to engage with the complex reality of performance, whatever their real motivation: the philosophers' disquiet about the nature of acting, the moralists' abhorrence of actors' lifestyles, the authoritarians' traditional fear of whatever escapes their control (as live performance tends to do), or even simply the daunting nature of the methodological problems involved in the task. The result has been that for centuries in universities and schools throughout the Western world drama was studied as a branch of literature with little or no reference to any performance reality. In the twentieth century there has been a significant paradigm shift, theatre studies has been established as an academic discipline in its own right, the nexus between theatre and drama has been broken, due in large part to the emergence of different media each developing drama and the dramatic in its own way, and performance has emancipated itself from dependence on dramatic text to such an extent that commentators and practitioners in the United States can seriously question whether text-based theatre has a future at all.[3]

Antonin Artaud is a key figure in the development of this new thinking about theatre. In his practice, and even more so through his polemical essays, which, though written in the 1930s, had their major impact in the 1960s and 1970s, he argued passionately against the subordination of the theatrical to the literary. It is no coincidence that he was also one of the first to insist on the importance of the physical and of space itself in theatrical semiosis: "I maintain that the stage is a tangible, physical place that needs to be filled and it ought to be allowed to speak its own concrete language" (Artaud [1964] 1970, 27). The consequence of asserting the primacy of the theatrical over the written is necessarily a reevaluation of the physical reality of performance, and that in turn entails rethinking the role of space.

What Artaud perceived so clearly, and what so many of his contemporaries thought to be the ravings of a madman, is now widely acknowledged. The specificity of theatre is not to be found in its relationship to the dramatic, as film and television have shown through their appropriation and massive exploitation of the latter, but in that it consists essentially of the interaction between performers and spectators in a given space. Theatre is a social event, occurring in the auditorium as well as on the stage, and the primary signifiers are physical and even spatial in nature. This perception should not, however, lead us to deny the historical reality, as the more vehement detractors of text-based theatre seem to demand. While the performance of scripted drama, mimesis, enactment, and the representation of fictional actions may no longer be seen as *necessary* components of the theatrical, it is a fact that these have been for hundreds of years an essential part of the theatre's activity and are still the dominant forms in both commercial and state-subsidized theatre practice. In this study I am concerned with traditional text-based theatre as well as with other forms of performance practice. Experience of a wide range of performance (physical theatre, mixed-media production, theatre of image, performance art, street theatre, improvization) has fed into my thinking and theorizing, but I also refer extensively to a corpus of performances drawn from text-based theatre practice. The reason for my choice of these performances is twofold: first, it seemed to me that, if the performances discussed were based on familiar and well known texts, then some of the difficulties involved in communicating the results of performance analysis to people who have not seen the performances in question may be reduced; and, second, because I think it is desirable that the new understanding and appreciation of the theatre experience emerging from this century's avant-garde and alternative performance practices also be used to refocus thinking about the traditional forms.

The physical language of the stage that Artaud proclaimed has proved very difficult to theorize, or even to describe, with any precision. Early attempts by semioticians to do this, while successfully bringing about a new understanding of how meaning is constructed and communicated in the theatre, were undeniably hampered by the literal way in which the linguistic analogy was pursued. The nature of the linguistic models from which semiotic theory was at the time derived (e.g., Saussure's rather rigid notion of the sign; Jakobson's conduit model, which sees meaning traveling unproblematically from emitter to receiver) was also part of the problem. It may be that, notwithstanding the fact that meaning is undoubtedly communicated in a theatrical performance, it is simply not appropriate to describe theatre as a language, even if the term is simply being used as a metaphor or analogy. Henri Lefebvre, for example, sees theatre, music, architecture, painting, and sculpture as "non-verbal signifying sets" and defines these as "characterised by a spatiality which is in fact irreducible to the mental realm" (Lefebvre 1991, 62), in which he sees language to be situated. While Lefebvre's observation has the great merit of drawing attention to the crucial importance of "spatiality" in the theatre experience, one may nevertheless query his confident relegation of language to the "mental realm." More flexible models of language, notably those derived from Michael Halliday's functional/systemic linguistics (Halliday 1978), acknowledge that speech is embodied and gendered, that language is always socially and culturally situated, and that in any transaction the receiver is as active a participant as the sender. This clearly situates language in the social realm and, considering the centrality of such factors in theatrical communication, it could be claimed that, far from language being an appropriate means of modeling theatrical function, it is theatre that can more usefully serve as a heuristic device to illuminate the functioning of language.

Be that as it may, the experience of the early theatre semioticians has made contemporary theorists wary about any linguistic analogy, and I would suggest that even the textual analogy that was so influential in the 1980s needs to be approached with caution. The claim that a theatrical

performance, or a building or even a body or a landscape, can be seen as
a text was liberating in that such phenomena began to be explored and
analyzed in new ways, but the notion of text, even when used metaphorically, reintroduces language and linguistic modes of apprehension as
well as the additional complication of writing. A text is something that
has been written, and, if a performance is seen as a text, then it can be
read. Indeed, *reading* was a keyword in the critical vocabulary of the
time, but reading implies both a controlled linear process (scanning the
page from left to right, top to bottom, word following word from first to
last) and a cerebral connection between reader and text that are misleading in relation to the theatrical event. The reading analogy also puts the
stress on visual apprehension, which is inappropriate in view of the bodily presence of spectators, who use all their senses and whose "organisms," to refer back to Grotowski, are as much in play as those of the performers.

I prefer to see the theatrical event as a dynamic process of communication in which the spectators are vitally implicated, one that forms
part of a series of interconnected processes of socially situated signification and communication, for theatre exists within a culture that it helps
to construct, and it is the product of a specific work process. My interest
in this book is not so much signs and sign systems as functions within
these processes. Starting from the perception of the vital importance of
space in any understanding of the communication that occurs in theatre,
the aim of the book is to explore the many ways in which space functions: the physical places of performance as they exist in the wider social
space of the community, the space of interaction between performers
and spectators, the energized space of the stage when it is occupied and
rendered meaningful by the presence of performers, the organization of
stage and offstage, the fictional places that are represented or evoked
within or in relation to all these physical areas, and, interacting with all
of them, the space of verbal reference.

A major problem in any such study is defining the limits of the
field. Given the centrality of space in theatrical semiosis, it is evident
that the field could extend to include every aspect of the theatre experience, but I have tried to limit my discussions to those features that actually require the specific physical space of the theatre or other place of
performance in order to become fully meaningful. I am not, therefore,
dealing with visual communication per se—aspects such as the performers' appearance, costume, makeup, hairstyle, and facial expression,

while important signifiers, are equally important without the stage on
which they are displayed, as the experience of film has shown. Indeed,
they may be even more important in film due to the possibilities for
close and detailed vision that the camera provides. Vitally important, on
the other hand, is everything to do with the performers' occupation of
the space, their entrances, exits, other movements and gestures, and the
proxemic relationships that these moves and gestures set up between
actors, spectators, objects, and the space itself. These movements and
groupings become meaningful only when situated in the given space,
and they are the major means whereby that space is activated and itself
made meaningful.

It is evident from the foregoing that the emphasis in this study will
not be on theatre buildings as such, whether purpose built theatres,
found or recuperated spaces, or even the charged spaces that get constituted wherever a busker begins to perform and passersby gather around
to watch. There have been several excellent studies of this sort in recent
years, some primarily historical in scope such as those by Richard and
Helen Leacroft (1984), Denis Bablet and Jean Jacquot (1988), and Richard
Southern (1962), others adopting a more overtly semiotic perspective, as
in Marvin Carlson (1989) and, in Iain Mackintosh's delightful study
(1993) of theatre buildings, a book that is both practical and speculative
and is not afraid to deal with intangibles such as enhancing the flow of
energy from spectators to performers and back. Some of these studies
concentrate on the stage space itself and the technology pertaining to its
functioning, others are more interested in the stage/auditorium relationship and the viewing positions that this predicates, some include information on the other public areas within the theatre, and some (as Carlson
does to very good effect) consider the exterior of the theatre building and
its location within the wider social space of the city. My interest here,
however, is not the place in itself but the ways in which space functions
in practice in the performance experience and in the construction of
meaning by spectators.

Marvin Carlson makes the pertinent point that, although we have a
good idea of the shape and appearance of many of the great theatres of
the past, we rarely have a sense of where those theatres were situated
within the urban plan and even less of what this might have meant to
audiences at the time (1989, 10). It can equally be said of most of these
theatres that very little is known about the organization of the backstage
areas. Traditionally private, out of bounds to all save the insiders, the

wings or other access to the stage, the dressing rooms, greenroom, or other social space reserved for the practitioners, and the stage door or practitioners' point of entry to the building are tantalizingly absent from the historical record. If they had been systematically documented, however, they would have constituted a most fascinating repository of indications about the work processes involved in theatre practice, relations between the various practitioners (judged in terms of the amount and the nature of the space they are accorded), and the social esteem (or the lack of it) a given society accords its theatre. The absence of such areas from the purview of so many of the studies that could be termed *building-centered* is an indication of the extent to which these studies are in fact concerned with the building as aesthetic object, rather than with its function in a complex social process.

A great deal of information about spatial function is contained in the written playtext, and such texts can undoubtedly be a source of valuable information about performance practice, especially when read in conjunction with architectural and iconographic records by appropriately trained and skilled readers. Some recent critical works, such as Stanton B. Garner's *Bodied Spaces* (1994) and Una Chaudhuri's *Staging Place* (1995), have explored the treatment of fictional place and its thematic resonance in the work of a number of modern playwrights, and, while these studies do not engage overtly with performance practice, they do reveal the importance of the category of space in theatrical meaning making.

Other text-centered critics make more far-reaching claims for the playtext. Michael Issacharoff, for example, bases his analysis of the discourse of performance on his reading of playtexts because, in his view, text is "the sole constant element in what goes on in the name of theatre" (1989, 4). Even this central premise can be questioned in that the playtext may be cut or modified by director and actors during the rehearsal process, and other modifications can occur during performance due to lapses in memory by an actor or to the way in which an actor's interpretation of meaning may lead to minute but significant changes in syntax or word order. If the text is a translation it may be substantially rewritten during the rehearsal process but still be credited in the program as the text that was the point of departure for the work. More problematical still is Issacharoff's insistence on the written text as "the place of inscription of virtual performance," for this leads him to underestimate the role of actors and directors in the creation of meaning and to oversimplify a very complex relationship. Which aspects of performance are inscribed in the text, how are they so inscribed, and how constraining are these indications in actual practice?

Jean Alter, too, has claimed that, although the text is only a small part of the theatrical whole, nothing else is available in a sufficiently reliable form to the analyst:

> a theory which postulates the unity of the entire theatrical process from text to performance (within a specific cultural framework) cannot justifiably draw its illustrations from all the significant steps in that process, simply because not all are available or acceptable as evidence. (Whiteside and Issacharoff 1987, 42–56)

It is certainly true that performance analysts have not yet standardized or institutionalized any method of notating or documenting performance or the work processes that lead to performance, but, if attempts to do this can be dismissed as "personal statements which must be taken on faith" (Alter), what can be said for the critic's reading of the "virtual performance" within a text? Such analyses, however subtle and intelligent they may be, reveal more about the critic's skill as a reader—or as virtual *metteur en scène*—than they do about theatre practice, and they belong to the literary economy: texts about texts, circulating amongst readers of texts.

In order to study the dynamic functioning of space in performance, it seems to me essential to deal with actual performances and with the work practices of actual theatre practitioners and spectators. The conceptual framework for this study is, therefore, neither "building-centered" nor "text-centered" but "performance-centered." It draws on experience of theatre buildings and on historical accounts of theatre-going as well as on the ideas of spatial function to be derived from analysis of playtexts, but central to the corpus of material upon which it is based are specific theatrical performances and rehearsal processes I have observed and documented. The attempt to write a performance-centered study, however, raises many methodological questions of which the most important is probably the one to which I have already alluded: can one go beyond the anecdotal, can the results of performance analysis be communicated adequately to people who have not seen the performance in question, to what extent can performance become "acceptable evidence" in Jean Alter's phrase? This is indeed the *punctum dolens* for theatre studies and for performance studies more generally. Given that theatrical performance is totally ephemeral and unrepeatable and that it can be neither recorded nor notated, how can it be talked about in any way other than the anecdotal, the partial, and in what Alter would call "personal statements"? Yet if the attempt is not made, if analyses and theories continue to be based on virtual rather than real performance, then surely the discipline loses its raison d'être, and the gulf between theatre practice and academic theorizing about theatre will remain as wide as ever it has been.

This study of space in performance is based on the experience of over ten years of observing and documenting rehearsal process and recording and analyzing the subsequent performances. All the work observed has been carried out by professional actors, directors, and designers in Sydney, although on occasions my comments about a given production may be supplemented by references to other productions of that play that I have seen in Sydney or on visits to London or Paris or that have been described by other performance analysts. The local nature of the corpus on which my theorizing is based should not be seen as somehow constraining the relevance of my observations. An important feature of theatre is that it is always local and must be local.[4] Other dramatic media such as television can reach a national audience numbered in the millions, a film can reach a massive international audience, but a theatrical production speaks to an audience numbered in thousands at the most, frequently in hundreds. The audience for film is diffused not merely geographically but temporally as well, for a film can be shown over and over again, many years after it was made. The theatre audience is located in a particular place and also in a particular time, as Janelle Reinelt has pointed out most perceptively:

> performance events which have their most potent incarnation in a particular venue, for a particular community of spectators . . . are quite changed when moved to other, more available sites—international festivals, or touring locations in the metropolitan centers of famous cities. (1995, 127)

It is this double quality of being both local and located that is theatre's strength in these days of mass media manipulation, even though it is also the reason that theatre receives far less funding than other dramatic media such as film and television.

My premise is that carefully documented, empirical studies of specific performances, not elevated to some universal status, which is in any case what happens when critics speak of the virtual or potential performance they see somehow inscribed in written texts, but acknowledged as local, contingent, and partial (in the sense in which James Clifford uses the term in *Writing Culture* [Clifford and Marcus 1986, 1–26]), are a valid basis for theoretical generalizations. They are indeed the only valid basis for people who wish to deal seriously with performance itself instead of the virtual performance "contained" in the playtext, invisible to the eyes of the profane, as Copeau claimed, but accessible to the initiates (1974, 268–69). Patrice Pavis (1996a), in his recent study of performance analysis, draws extensively on filmed versions of theatre in his analysis of theatrical function, on the grounds that the availability of the film will enable readers to verify his analyses, whereas live performance falls into the domain of the unverifiable. This, too, seems to me to be a risky strategy in that it leads to a constant slippage between the theatrical performance and the filmic devices (shot composition, editing choices, camera angle, etc.) through which it is being filtered.

Eugène Ionesco remarked frequently that, in writing about his own private, personal world of experience, he found he was writing for everyone: "Several times I have said that it is in our fundamental solitude that we rediscover ourselves and that the more I am alone, the more I am in communion with others" ([1962] 1964, 81). I would argue that the same is true of the theatre process more broadly and that careful accounts and analyses of specific performances and rehearsal processes will resonate with experiences of analysts and practitioners in many other places. This is not just because the productions I describe form part of an international canon of works, nor because certain concepts have dominated actor training throughout the Western world, nor because of the homogenizing effect on local practice of the festival circuit, but because, as Ionesco said of his own writing, "it is perhaps only through subjectivity that we become objective" (1964, 29). In opting for the specific and the local, performance studies is moving into the methodological terrain of ethnography, and, as the object of study shifts from text and virtual performance to actual performance, from the sheltered world of university theatre to theatrical production in the commercial domain, so new tasks and skills are demanded of the analyst, and new relationships must be forged between academics and theatre practitioners.

It is notoriously difficult for outsiders to gain access to rehearsals in the professional theatre and even more difficult to get permission to document or record the production process. It has also proved difficult to get permission to record performance in both the commercial and subsidized theatres (small experimental theatre groups have been by far the most open-minded insofar as recording performance is concerned, but they, too, are frequently reluctant to admit observers to the rehearsal process). The Centre for Performance Studies in the University of Sydney has for a number of years been developing collaborative arrangements between theatre practitioners and academic researchers whereby the university provides access to rehearsal space (difficult to find and very expensive to rent in the city), and in return theatre practitioners allow their work processes to be observed and documented (McAuley 1994, 183–94). Most of the productions on which I have drawn to illustrate my theoretical findings in this study have emerged from these collaborative arrangements. On some occasions the rehearsals have led to a full production with a public season (Corneille's *The Theatrical Illusion*, Racine's *Britannicus*, and Strindberg's *Miss Julie*), on others theatre artists have been funded to engage in workshop explorations around a given theatre text (Genet's *The Maids*, Molière's *Dom Juan*, Ibsen's *A Doll's House*, Chekhov's *The Three Sisters*, Pinter's *Old Times*, and Racine's *Phèdre*). The names of the artists engaged in these productions are listed in the appendix, but I would like to take the opportunity here to thank them all for their generosity in opening up their work practices to scrutiny and for sharing their knowledge and insights into their art.

Actors have often commented on how much they value the opportunity to engage in the exploratory activities required in these workshops, exploration being too often regarded as a luxury even in the subsidized theatre. It may be claimed that such workshops do not represent "normal" practice (however that might be defined), and it is certainly true that the levels of tension and focus are different in the businesslike rehearsal geared to getting a production up in six weeks, but the risks and energies in play in a workshop, especially one that is being observed and documented, are also intense. My experience as spectator and analyst in these different work processes is, however, that, whether it is a full rehearsal or an experimental workshop, there is an energy and inventiveness and a kind of dangerous edge to the work that is all too often absent in the theatre itself. Over the years that I have been privileged to watch the creative process leading to performance I have become more and more fascinated with this kind of openness as contrasted to the closure of performance, with the wealth of new possibilities revealed in even the most familiar texts, with the power of the raw moment that is often never recaptured in subsequent performances.

The emphasis on text-based theatre in this study is a recognition of its historical importance in Western culture and its place in theatre practice even in the twentieth century. It should not, however, be taken as the expression of a value judgment about the classics, the Western canon, or about modernist versus postmodern performance, nor does it indicate a failure to recognize the tensions in play in the debates between proponents of performance, group or self-devised work, intercultural performance, and the Eurocentered, text-based theatre tradition. Indeed, given the location of my study in Sydney, it would be difficult to avoid recognizing these tensions for in the theatre culture of Sydney the divisions have been particularly sharp and the rhetoric fairly brutal. Wayne Harrison, artistic director of the Sydney Theatre Company, in a public lecture in 1995, claimed that the theatre was the site of a civil war between the mainstream, text-based work for which his company is known and community theatre, and in a conference held at the Centre for Performance Studies the year before on the "Limits of Performance" there seemed to be consensus between performance practitioners for the extraordinary proposition that genuine creativity was to be found only in self- or group-devised work, while the actor in text-based theatre was a mere technician. Janelle Reinelt has remarked that the distinction between theatre and performance, which is such a dominant feature of practice and theory in the United States seems not be recognized by people whose experience derives largely from the well-funded theatres of Continental Europe (1995, 125–26). Such people are often surprised to discover the extent to which text-based theatre practice, and all that it involves, is contested in other theatre cultures, even when, as is the case with Australia, these have their roots in European culture.

It should perhaps be stressed once again that the rehearsal and performance practices observed are those of professional theatre practitioners, and, although the work has often been located at a university, the study is not concerned with university theatre. It is important to make this point because the practices in both British university departments of theatre studies and in the American system, in which actor training takes place largely at universities, have led to a situation in which it is frequently unclear what kind of performance practices underpin the theorizing that is subsequently published (trained actors, untrained students,

or student actors, paid or unpaid, production undertaken as part of a
teaching program or in response to some other artistic or social imperative) nor what was the academic theorist's role in these practices. One of
the things that theatre studies can usefully learn from ethnography is the
need to make very clear the status and role of the observer in the phenomena under analysis and whose practice is being observed and theorized.

When people speak of ethnography or anthropology in relation to
theatre, they usually do so in the context of intercultural performance or
studies of performance traditions from other cultures. Anthropological
thinking has been used to brilliant effect by Richard Schechner (1985) in
his attempt to enlarge the scope of theatre studies as an academic discipline in the United States, and Jean-Marie Pradier (1996) is currently
developing the notion of "ethnoscénologie" to refer to the study of
"organised human performance behaviours and practices" as they occur
in different cultures. My experience as a "participant observer" in
rehearsals for performance within the specific cultural community in
which I live suggests, however, that ethnographic method is equally
valuable in facilitating discussion of "own" as well as "other" culture.

Theatre is a complex phenomenon, involving many weeks preparation by a large number of artists and artisans, working in different
media, each performance is unique and unrepeatable, differing in minor
and sometimes major ways from its predecessor, the audience is different each time and, in its manner of response, has a subtle impact on the
performers. Theatre criticism, like other forms of art criticism, has traditionally been concerned with the single performance (the critic's experience of the production), conceptualized as product or object. The fact
that theatre does not really produce an object, that each performance is
only one possible combination of the variables that that particular production has conjured, and that any text can be staged in countless different ways has always rendered this kind of critical practice highly problematic. Under the influence of postmodern theory it has become
possible to acknowledge that the processual nature of theatre and the
dynamic role of the spectator in the construction of meaning are not factors peculiar to theatre but are shared by many other modes of artistic
expression. This has emboldened theatre specialists to affirm the realities
they have known all along but have had difficulty expressing in terms of
dominant paradigms that excluded such knowledge.

The theatre consists of a number of processes, none of which ever produces an object or anything with a fixed existence or form: the rehearsal process brings together a number of people and materials, choices are made, and the performance is constructed, but the performance exists only in its relation to the spectators and, as already indicated, it changes in subtle and not so subtle ways over the course of its daily repetition. The fact that we use an organic metaphor, *season*, to refer to the life of the production, is an indication in itself of the growth and change that take place. The spectators' response, both collectively during the actual performance and individually in the days and weeks that follow, forms yet another process, or set of processes, that has only just begun to receive critical attention.[5]

In the theatre nothing exists in isolation: the actor is always situated in relation to other actors, to the stage itself, and to the audience; if an actor looks at someone or something, both the person or thing looked at and the person looking are seen by the spectators; the actor's construction of character does not take place in isolation either but always in relation to the ideas, attitudes, and corporeal realities of the other actors as they work to construct their characters and the material form of their performance; the actor's work exists in relation, too, to the director and designer and the ideas and materials they bring into the process.

Being an event rather than an object, performance is radically unstable in the meanings it generates and in the activities it engages. It is evident that the critical theory needed to deal adequately with this complex phenomenon is also complex. Semiotics has been extremely useful in facilitating the careful description of performance, seen as a montage of signs and as a structure existing in space and time, but semiotics alone tends to reify the performance, to see it as object rather than dynamic process. Phenomenology, with its insistence on the receiver as well as the emitter in any transaction and its notion of "lived experience," has also been extremely valuable in providing vocabulary, analytical concepts, and theoretical sanction for intuitively felt reactions. I have already mentioned that the situation of the academic observer in the rehearsal room seems to me to have much in common with that of the ethnographer in the field, and debates in ethnography concerning reflexivity and reflectivity, and in particular the critique by feminist anthropologists of the classic ethnographic approach, have pointed up ethical and methodological problems in the analysis of rehearsal and performance process (McAuley 1998). The theoretical framework and the methods utilized in this study derive, therefore, from semiotics, phenomenology, ethnography, and sociology, but it is not for all that a semiotic, phenomenological, ethnographic, or sociological study, and indeed specialists in any of these disciplines may refuse to acknowledge the paternity I allege. Performance studies is an emerging discipline, and it is still evolving appropriate methodologies; the multifaceted approach adopted here is a response to the complexity of the performance phenomena that are being explored.

The Terminological Minefield

Given the centrality of space in the performance experience, it is perhaps somewhat surprising to find that critics do not have a precise, widely shared vocabulary to enable them to name and to talk about the multiple dimensions of the way space functions in performance. By contrast, a concept such as character has been well theorized through all its complex and problematic development, and the distinction between actor and character is clearly established and appreciated. The distinction between stage, set, and the fictional place(s) represented thereon is, however, far less clearly established. There is no term, comparable to *character*, for the fictional place, nor are there terms that will enable us to distinguish neatly between the fictional places represented onstage, those that are evoked through the offstage connection to the onstage and those that are referred to in the dialogue and which form part of the dramatic geography of the play (e.g., Milan and Naples in *The Tempest* or Troy and Athens in *Andromaque*).

Even more surprisingly, practitioners who must deal with this complex domain on a daily basis in rehearsal do not seem to have evolved much in the way of precise and commonly understood terminology either. The result is that any critic, theorist, or practitioner who wishes to refer to some aspect of spatial function, and to distinguish it from some other, must invent his or her own terminological system. This has led to a plethora of terms used to designate overlapping notions (e.g., *stage space, scenic space,* and *scenographic space*) and to particular terms being used rather confusingly to refer to quite different things.[6]

It seems desirable, therefore, to begin this study of the function of space in theatrical performance with a review of some of the categories and definitions that emerge from recent theoretical and critical work on the semiotics of theatre space. This review has a second objective: to

establish the concepts and terminology that will be used throughout the
book and, in so doing, to propose a workable taxonomy of spatial function. The goal, as in any other taxonomy, is not the naming of parts as an
end in itself but to provide an analytical tool and to convey an understanding and appreciation of the relations involved.

The writings of Anne Ubersfeld (1977, 1981) are the obligatory starting point for any theoretical reflection on the function of space in theatre.
She has made a major contribution to performance theory in her insistence on the centrality of space in theatrical communication and, even
more important, her perception of the way the space of performance
mediates the playtext and the sociopolitical, sociocultural, context of
both text and performance. She was the first to propose an extended, systematic theory of spatial function, and her taxonomy is based on five
terms: stage space (*espace scénique*), scenic place (*lieu scénique*), theatrical
space (*espace théâtral*), theatre space (*lieu théâtral*), and dramatic space
(*espace dramatique*).[7] The stage space is a straightforward notion, the stage
itself, glossed as "the playing area," but the "scenic place," as she con-
ceives it, is more complex. It is both the fictional place where the action is
occurring (the Forest of Arden, Nero's palace in Rome, etc.) and "the
topological . . . transposition of the major features of the social space
experienced by a particular group within a given society" (Ubersfeld
1977, 154). This definition draws attention to one of Ubersfeld's major
insights, namely the way the theatrical presentation of place necessarily
incorporates a sociopolitical commentary.

The stage in itself, even when set with an elaborate decor, conveys
only a limited meaning, and it does not present a fixed set of meanings
even within a given production, but it is by its nature a most compelling
invitation to semiosis, as Peter Handke pointed out when he referred to
it as "Bedeutungsraum"—a space for meaning making (Passow 1981,
237–54). Following Ubersfeld's perception that the physicality of theatre
anchors theatrical semiosis in relation to a given sociopolitical reality, it
can be affirmed that the spatial organization of the fictional world is
always to be perceived in terms of ideology (the playwright's, the production's, the spectator's own).

In the second pair of concepts, theatre space and theatrical space
(*lieu théâtral* and *espace théâtral*, respectively), Ubersfeld is again referring
on the one hand to a physical space and on the other to an abstraction
derived from the physical. Theatrical space is a general notion that refers
to the whole complex function of space in the theatre and therefore

brings together all the categories and distinctions she has made; it is virtually synonymous with theatre itself, so important is the spatial function in her view: "we can define theatre as a particular mode of spatial organization" (1981, 53).

The term *theatre space* is more specific: it refers to the place of performance, seen both as the theatre building itself, situated within the urban context, and the characteristically divided space this building encloses. Other French writers, such as Denis Bablet, also use the term *lieu théâtral* in basically this sense (Bablet 1972, 107–25).[8] In Ubersfeld's definition she again emphasizes the sociological dimension: the "lieu théâtral" is that which "brings together actors and spectators in a relationship which depends essentially on both the physical form of the auditorium and the form of social organization" (1977, 142).

The final notion in Ubersfeld's system, dramatic space, and her many practical suggestions for analyzing this in text and performance, are perhaps her most important contribution to performance theory. Dramatic space is made up of both textual and performance signs; it is accessible to the reader of the playtext and, differently manifested, to the spectator experiencing the space as constructed by the given production. It is an abstraction, posited on the on-off dichotomy and the dialectic between present and absent that theatre necessarily manifests. Dramatic space is more than fictional place, even in the expanded sociological sense that she gives to the scenic place, for it involves the dramatic geography of the action as a whole and is indeed a means of conceptualizing the whole action or narrative content of the play. She sees this as, in essence, a conflict between spaces, the invasion and occupation of one space by a usurping force, the exclusion of the rightful occupant of a space and his fight to reinstate himself, the attempt to bring another into the hero's space, etc. Dramatic space is always "multiple, divided, built upon oppositions" (1981, 58).

Steen Jansen is equally insistent on the function of the spatial system of the playtext in the construction of meaning, and he, like Ubersfeld, introduces an abstract notion to account for the way this operates. Rather confusingly, in view of Ubersfeld's terminology he calls this the stage space (*espace scénique*), and, even more confusingly, it seems to elide aspects of both her dramatic space and her scenic place. In a study illustrated by analysis of different editions of *Six Characters in Search of an Author* (Schmid and Van Kesteren 1984, 254–79) he posits the stage space as an abstraction, constructed by the reader of the playtext, which functions similarly to the narration in prose narrative, to establish the perspective within which the reader can view the fictional world presented and can assess its relationship to his or her own real world. It is the stage space that enables the reader to make sense of all the spaces presented onstage (in his terms these constitute the scenic place, or *lieu scénique*), evoked via the offstage (surrounding space, or *espace environnant*) or referred to in the dialogue (referred space, or *espace référé*), and it is a vital part of the play's system of meaning.

Both Ubersfeld and Jansen are attempting in very interesting ways to come to terms with the central fact of theatrical semiosis, the complex interplay between the physical and the fictional, and the meanings that emerge from that interplay. Jansen has also touched on another crucial aspect in the distinction he makes between *scenic place, surrounding space,* and *referred space.* Anyone who has attempted a detailed performance analysis will have discovered that there is a need for precision in naming the different types of fictionality at work in the theatre: fictional place is presented/represented physically onstage; it is presented in a close, often contiguous relationship to the onstage by the offstage, often using doors and windows to articulate both connection and separation; and it is evoked verbally, often also in ways that involve the physical disposition of the onstage. A messenger from somewhere else must come "on" via a particular access point, which will have acquired its own resonance, and this will color his or her message; the character must be placed somewhere when speaking, and this, too, will situate the "elsewhere" referred to in terms of the "here and now."

Etienne Souriau proposed the terms *stage microcosm* (*microcosme scénique*) and *theatrical macrocosm* (*macrocosme théâtral*) to refer to the fictional world created onstage and the larger fictional world, "the universe of the play" (1950, 22). Hanna Scolnicov and Michael Issacharoff have also both addressed this aspect of theatrical function but conceptualize it somewhat differently and propose different terms to account for it.

Hanna Scolnicov makes a distinction between *theatre space* and *theatrical space.* For her the term *theatre space* refers to the place of performance, and within this theatre space each production creates its own theatrical space, a concept that includes both physical and metaphorical dimensions: it is the space utilized by the performers (the stage proper, or the aisles and balconies or other parts of the auditorium) and the spaces defined "through word, movement and gesture, and with the aid of props, scenery, lighting and acoustic effects" (Redmond 1987, 11–12). This notion thus includes both Ubersfeld's *stage space* and her *scenic place* and even aspects of her *dramatic space*, and it seems to me that too much has been packed into this single term for analytical comfort. Dividing the notion in two, with the rather awkwardly named "theatrical space within" and "theatrical space without" goes some way to meet the difficulty, but the distinction that is being made between seen and unseen theatrical space, onstage and offstage places, does not really address the crux of the matter—namely, that by cramming into one category the physical reality of the stage and offstage and the imaginary, fictional places that are being created on and with them, Scolnicov's terms do not facilitate discussion of the relation between the two that needs to be addressed.

Scolnicov's illustrative analyses provide convincing evidence for her contention (which Ubersfeld and Jansen would certainly endorse) that "the articulation of theatrical space is, at its best, an expression of the playwright's philosophical stance" (Redmond 1987, 15), but the slippage between physical and fictional in her definition of theatrical space becomes problematic here. The "within" and "without" categories distinguish between what she calls "perceived space" and "conceived space" (14). I would suggest, however, that, while the offstage can perhaps be claimed as conceived space, the onstage is always both perceived and conceived, stage space and scenic place in Ubersfeld's terms. In fact, we need also to distinguish between the offstage spaces that are contiguous with the onstage in some way, indicated by doors, windows, or even simply located spatially in relation to the onstage by the actors' gestures and direction of gaze and those that form part of the wider domain of the play's dramatic geography but are not grounded in any way in the physical arrangement of stage, set, or performance. It is only the latter that can properly be called conceived space, the other offstage places being as much a combination of conceived and perceived as the onstage, even though the emphasis varies.

Michael Issacharoff uses the terms *mimetic* and *diegetic* to refer to the shown space as opposed to the recounted, and he also speaks of the "scenic" and "extra-scenic" spaces (1989, 55–56), but in neither of these pairs does he distinguish between the offstage space that is physically placed in relation to the on and other unsituated places. He claims that "mimetic space does not require mediation; in contrast, diegetic space is mediated by verbal signs (the dialogue) communicated verbally and not visually." Both these assertions are open to question: first, because the mimetic space is necessarily mediated by the actors' bodies and by the uses they make of stage and set; and, second, because the diegetic space, while certainly mediated through verbal reference, can be and often is mediated by the onstage space and the actors' use of it.

Issacharoff is concerned essentially with what he, like Ubersfeld, calls dramatic space and defines as "the study of space as a semiotic system in a given playscript"; although he acknowledges that two other systems are in operation (the architectural, or theatre, space and the scenographic, or stage, space), he hardly considers them in his study. His analyses treat what he has called mimetic space as though it were simply a category of dramatic space, and he ignores the way his own category of scenographic space always functions in practice to situate, contextualize, and make meanings with the verbal. In fact, his architectural, scenographic, and dramatic spatial systems need the addition of a fourth, which might be called "performance space" to account for the input of actors and the particular mise en scène. Issacharoff justifies his concentration on the dramatic by arguing that no methodology yet exists for the study of plays in a particular mise en scène (1989, 57); the problem with his approach is that it appears to write performance out of the theory altogether.

Patrice Pavis considers that the attempt to separate and define all the categories of spatial function in theatre is doomed to failure, but he nevertheless goes into considerable detail in his *Dictionnaire du théâtre* (1980), listing six types of theatre space and another two under the heading of "Place." The usefulness of this taxonomy is, however, somewhat vitiated by its failure to distinguish clearly between the categories it establishes. For example, *scenographic space* (terms defined in the dictionary are named in English, German, and Spanish, and this is the English term proposed by Pavis for *espace scénographique*) is used to refer to the divided space shared by spectators and performers, but this space is also glossed as *espace théâtral* (not translated), and it is not made clear how either term relates to his "theatrical space" (*lieu théâtral*), defined as the place of performance. Similarly it is unclear whether the "stage space" (*espace scénique*), defined as "the real space of the stage on which the actors perform" (146), is to be distinguished from the "playing area" (*lieu scénique*) or treated as a synonym.

The taxonomy distinguishes between "stage space" (*espace scénique*) and "ludic or gestural space" (*espace ludique ou gestuel*), defined as "the space created by the gestural activities of the actors," as Pavis rightly considers that separate categories are needed to account for the architectural space of the stage and its decor and the use made of this space by the bodily presence of the actors. His *espace dramatique* (translated rather confusingly as both "dramatic space" and "space represented") is a complex notion, for it is at once "the space referred to by the text" (Issacharoff's *diegetic space*) and "a space constructed by the spectator to make a framework for the action and the characters" (cf. Jansen's *stage space*) and even "the spatialisation of dramatic structure" (Pavis 1980, 146–47). This notion thus elides two of Ubersfeld's categories, "scenic place" and "dramatic space," and, as with Scolnicov's *theatrical space*, so much is packed into the one term that its analytical potency is impaired. In practice, of course, the fictional, the physical reality of the stage and the dramatic or metaphoric levels do constantly interweave, which is what produces the characteristic theatrical experience, but it is preferable to conceptualize the interweaving elements separately and to distinguish them by name, so that they can be used in analysis to show how particular effects are achieved.

This brief summary of terms and concepts culled from recent critical writing has perhaps been too brief to do justice to the thinking of each individual quoted. It does, however, illustrate my point about the overlapping notions, blurred distinctions, and lack of precise, shared terminology. It does also make very clear that the areas of maximum attention (and, interestingly, the most conceptual diversity and terminological inventiveness) are the onstage/offstage dialectic and the complex relationship between the physical or material reality and the fictional, illusory world created in and by it. All the commentators cited have addressed these two related issues in some way, and their emphasis vindicates my assertion that this is the very heart of theatrical semiosis. Some of the terminological and conceptual confusion that has been noted is doubtless due to the fact that performance theory of this sort is a relatively new academic pursuit, but it is also true to say that the slipperiness of the concepts and the theoretical problems they pose are evidence of the subtlety of the processes of theatrical semiosis. The spatial categories proposed here demonstrate yet again the complex nature of an art form made up of multiple, interlocking forms of expression and systems of meaning.

A Taxonomy of Spatial Function

In proposing a general taxonomy of spatial function, one is caught between mutually exclusive imperatives. The temptation is to allow categories to proliferate with numerous subcategories and sub-subcategories in an attempt to account for every nuance and every application. The countertendency, springing from an equally laudable desire to highlight the functional structure underpinning this endless variety, is to simplify rigorously; the danger here is that important distinctions are submerged and one is left wanting to problematize every category.

In attempting to conceptualize, define, and name the aspects of spatial function needed for meaningful discussion of theatrical semiosis and to explore how these aspects relate to one another, I have become very much aware that any taxonomy is necessarily the extrapolation of a theoretical understanding of the phenomenon in question. The extent to which the set of terms that follows is useful or usable by others depends in part upon the degree of consensus about the theory of performance and communication that emerges from it and also upon the accessibility of the terminology. Here the taxonomer has a choice between using familiar terms that, however, come with their potentially confusing cultural, historical, ideological baggage or coining new terms that may more unambiguously express a desired meaning but which would involve considerable mental adjustment for anyone wishing to adopt the system. Accessibility has been chosen here, with all its attendant risks of confusion, but the familiar terms like *stage space, theatre space,* and *performance space* have been defined in ways that take into account their traditional use and specify its boundaries here.

A taxonomy of spatial functions in theatrical performance needs to address five major areas, and they have been set out in diagrammatic form in figure 1. First, the social reality of the theatre experience: the first spatial fact is the theatre building itself, whether this be a purpose built edifice used exclusively for theatrical performance or a building originally designed for some other purpose that has been adapted for theatre or a multipurpose cultural center that includes a theatre (or, as is commonly the case today, several rather different theatres). The building, as it exists within or outside the urban space, in relation to other buildings and the activities associated with them, the connotations of its past history, its architectural design, and the kind of access it invites or denies, are all part of the experience of theatre for both practitioners and specta-

I. The Social Reality
    Theatre Space
        Audience Space

                        Performance Space
        Practitioner Space
        Rehearsal Space

II. The Physical/Fictional Relationship
    Stage Space
    Presentational Space
    Fictional Place

III. Location and Fiction
    Onstage Fictional Place
    Offstage Fictional Place
        Unlocalized in relation to Performance Space
        Localized in relation to Performance Space
        Contiguous/Remote Spectrum
        Audience Off

IV. Textual Space

V. Thematic Space

Fig. 1. Taxonomy of spatial function in the theatre

tors, and affect the way performance is experienced and interpreted. This can be called the *theatre space.*

The theatre space is divided; it is a place of employment for some, a place of entertainment and cultural enrichment for others. The two groups have their designated areas within the space that is, in traditional theatres, quite rigidly demarcated and conceptualized in terms of front and back ("front of house" and "backstage"). For the spectators theatre is a social event, their reception of the performance is part of a social experience, the areas within the theatre space to which they have access, which can be called *audience space,* facilitate (or discourage) types of social behavior and social interaction. The point of access to the building, the foyers, stairways, corridors, bars and restaurants, the box office, and of course the auditorium are all parts of this space, and the way we experience them has an unavoidable impact upon the meanings we take away with us. The activities that prevail here—socializing and watching the socializing of others, consuming food and drink (often alcoholic), the commercial transactions to secure access to the performance—are as much a part of the theatre experience as the central activity of watching the play and may even be the dominant memory retained afterward.

The theatre workers (excluding the "front of house staff," whose designation clearly sets them apart spatially from the other practitioners) inhabit a different domain. Their access to the building is normally by a different door, differently signaled to the outside world, frequently on a different street. What I will call *practitioner space* includes the stage door access, the whole backstage area with its dressing rooms, its hierarchy of comfort and discomfort, green room, corridors and stairways, and the stage itself.

While the stage, as seen from the auditorium, is central to the iconographic record of theatre activity throughout history, the backstage has tended to be documented only in architect's plans and normally only where the operation of stage machinery is an important part of the theatre experience. Apart from the stage and its machinery, the practitioner space is significantly the least documented, least analyzed, least theorized area of theatre space. It does, however, offer a wealth of insight into the social organization of performance, the esteem or lack of it accorded to theatre practitioners by society, and the experience of the performers, which must necessarily have an effect upon their relations with the spectator.

It will be noticed that I have so far put stage and auditorium into two different categories, practitioner space and audience space respectively, but there is a third domain within the theatre space, the place constituted by the coming together of the other two. Overriding yet subsuming the division, the divided yet nevertheless unitary space in which the two constitutive groups (performers and spectators) meet and work together to create the performance experience, is the privileged domain that I shall call the *performance space*.

Some forms of performance, like busking and street theatre, have a performance space but no theatre space; so my earlier statement that the theatre building is the first spatial fact of theatre needs now to be revised to acknowledge that it is, rather, the performance space that is fundamental to, even constitutive of, theatre. It is the performance space that is, in reality, the first spatial fact, and the theatre space, though commonly present throughout history, should perhaps be seen as an optional extra. Hollis Huston refers to what preceded any theatre building as "the simple stage": "the stage that appears around the street performer, a stage that depends not on apparatus and technicians, but on the player herself and her ability to charm" (1992, 11). Some theatre groups who work outside the traditional theatre spaces offered by their society will nevertheless select a rudimentary theatre space (a natural amphitheatre in the country, the galleries and stairways of a shopping mall) that will provide the basic features they need to establish an appropriate performance space. Others go further and renounce any semblance of a theatre space.

There is one more important physical space, one that the audience never sees directly yet one that can nevertheless have a major impact upon the spatial relations and behaviors they do see: I refer to the *rehearsal space*. Some companies have their own rehearsal rooms, some may even rehearse in the theatre, others have to rehearse in halls and studios all over town; Copeau was very keen on rehearsing outdoors in the country, at least in the early stages of the work process. The physical features of the rehearsal space, even the most apparently neutral space, can be picked up and used by the actors in their creative process, as will be shown in more detail in the next chapter.

Michael Issacharoff says that text precedes performance and that, therefore, "it is language that creates and focuses space in the theatre, or at least any functional stage space" (1989, 57), but it can be argued that the theatre space and the performance space are just as much preconditions to the eventual performance and that the organization of the stage space, which is such a dominant factor in theatrical communication, is the result of a complex weave of dynamically interrelating elements: text, performance space, the bodily space of the actors, and even features of the rehearsal space. Not enough is known about the processes involved to state so categorically that language is the primary factor, and rehearsal space has been included in this taxonomy in recognition of the complexity of the spatial genesis of the performance.

The second major category in the taxonomy of spatial features concerns what I began by calling the physical reality/fictional place duality. The second spatial fact in the theatre, the heartland of theatrical semiosis, as has already been asserted, is the constant dual presence of the physical reality of the performance space and the fictional world or worlds created. The space the spectator is watching during the performance (at least in modern theatre, where the auditorium is darkened and attention is centered on the performers) is always both stage and somewhere else. The "somewhere else" may be indicated by an elaborately realistic set or by the words and bodily behavior of the actors or by a hundred other means, but, however convincing the fictional world may be, the stage itself is always also present at some level of our consciousness. In reverse the stage always "fictionalizes" to some extent whatever is presented on it.[9]

As has been amply demonstrated in the review of spatial terminology, there have been many perceptive and thought provoking attempts to theorize this duality: Issacharoff's mimetic and diegetic spaces, Scolnicov's perceived and conceived space, and Ubersfeld's stage space and scenic place are all valid and useful ways of conceptualizing the same basic duality, and, while they point up our lack of a shared analytical vocabulary, the differences of emphasis and choice of term reveal the complexity of the spatial function in question.

These theorists and others typically propose two terms, differently conceptualized and designated, but the difficulty in accounting adequately for the complex functioning of the physical/fictional relationship in any of these ways suggests that we need more than two terms. It is not simply that the physical space of the stage presents or represents a fictional place but, as Ubersfeld indicates in her definition of the scenic place, that the spatial organization of the stage and the bodily presence/behavior of the actors constitute a commentary on the nature of the place. In Ubersfeld's view this commentary is always of a sociopolitical, sociocultural kind, the expression of the social space experienced by a particular group within a given society. I think that we can add to this very perceptive insight that the spatial organization always also includes more or less overt commentary on the very activity by which the ideas are being communicated.[10]

In Gale Edwards's production of *A Doll's House* in Sydney the floorboards around the edges of Nora's drawing room were being violently wrenched up by what appeared to be frozen ice floes. The drawing room (fictional place) was presented onstage, but the strongest message was the threatened nature of the space, the precariousness of the human relations housed within it; the drawing room plus ice floes constitutes something more than a fictional place. The rather two dimensional, cardboard cut-out effect, which was the result of the way the design was actually manifested in the scenic space of the Belvoir Theatre, was interpreted variously by spectators I spoke to as either an indication of a low production budget or of a deliberate theatricality. This is an example of the way the spatial organization also incorporates commentary on the means of production.

As this example demonstrates, we need a minimum of three terms to account for the relationship between physical space and fictional place as it operates in the theatre.[11] At the most basic level there is the physical space of the stage, extended by the performers in any given production by temporary or permanent incursions into the auditorium. This can be called the *stage space.* In any particular theatre the stage space will have its own physical characteristics, width, depth, its degree of separation from or integration with the auditorium, the number and position of its exits, the nature of the back wall or other division between on- and off stage. While some of these features can be modified by the set or usage made of the space, the basic architectural features of the building provide a physical grounding for the performance that is a crucial part of its meaning. The stage space can be single or multiple (if parts of the auditorium are used or, as in Ariane Mnouchkine's *1789,* e.g., in which the action took place on different platforms situated around the edges of a rectangular viewing place, which itself became stage space on occasion).

There is, second, the physical use made of this stage space in any given performance. This can be called *presentational space.* The physical organization of the stage extends far beyond the scenery and decor (which is why I resisted the temptation to follow Ubersfeld and others and use a term like *scenic,* or *scenographic, space);* in many productions there is little or no scenery, yet the mere physical presence of actors on a bare stage transforms it into presentational space. The notion must be seen to include the actual physical occupation of the stage space by the actors as well as the set (if any), its furniture and props, the spatial demarcation established by the lighting, the number, nature and position of the exits, and the way the offstage areas are signaled physically. Presentational space, as defined here, is still part of the physical reality; it is "perceived space" in Scolnicov's phrase, but it partially elides two of Pavis's categories: stage space and gestural space. The physical presence of the actors, their comings and goings, movements and proxemic groupings, their bodily behavior within the space are the crucial elements of the presentational space.

The third necessary term is *fictional place.* This refers to the place or places presented, represented or evoked onstage and off. Fictional place is "conceived space" whether it is on or off (Nora's drawing room is not, in fact, a drawing room). We need a number of subcategories here, but one general observation applies to all. The idea contained in fictional place is broader than the locus dramatis of the action (although it includes that, and we can retain the traditional term when we need to refer specifically to the narrower concept). Fictional place as opposed to locus dramatis has to be conceived in Ubersfeld's sense of *scenic place*, as already and necessarily incorporating a commentary on itself and on the means that produce it.

The notion of fictional place is so complex and so fundamental to both drama and theatre,[12] and its functioning has been so richly varied over the centuries, that the subcategories needed to account for it can be seen as constituting the third major area of the taxonomy. The section has been given the overall title "Location and Fiction" in order to high-light the fact that the fictional place functions according to its location in relation to the physical reality of the performance space. Stanley Long-man's illuminating article, "Fixed, Floating and Fluid Stages" (Redmond 1987, 151–60) amply demonstrates the importance of this factor as he is able to use it to establish a typology of dramaturgical styles, genres, and even historical periods.

There is, first, the onstage/offstage distinction. We have the onstage fictional place, which can be physically represented or presented through the actor (the chair on the table is a mountain because the actor is climbing it), or it can be simply spoken. William Shakespeare's "acoustic scenery" is of course preeminent in this regard: the simplicity and functional directness of a line like Roderigo's "Here is her father's house, I'll call aloud" (*Othello*, act 1) is unmatched even by the cinema's flexibility in spatial presentation.

In some plays the presentational space gives us a single fictional place; in others multiple places are presented, either alternating or suc-ceeding one another or simultaneously present in different parts of the stage space. The single, multiple, alternate, successive, and simultaneous options do not require separate categories, as they are not different in kind or function but are simply aesthetic possibilities offered by the onstage fictional place category. The critical factor for the taxonomy is not the number of places nor even the method by which they are sug-gested but their anchorage in relation to the physical space.

The second category is the *offstage physical place*, and here it does seem that we need a number of subcategories, for the function of the fictional place does change, depending on its location in relation to presentational space, stage space, and even audience space. Tim Fitzpatrick uses the terms *localized* and *unlocalized* to refer to the parts of the fictional world not shown onstage and suggests that there is a spectrum of possibilities concerning the extent to which this localization is specified (1989a, 60–62). The playtext may insist on a degree of localization—for example, the two doors in Genet's *The Maids*, one leading to the kitchen, the maids' domain, the other to the outside world; the text's specific placing of the kitchen can be contrasted to the less specific location of the maids' bedroom (the actual arrangement of the room is unflatteringly described in relation to Madame's luxury, but its location in relation to the rest of the fictional place is not specified).

Adapting Fitzpatrick's terms, the *unlocalized off*, includes those places that are part of the dramatic geography of the action (Moscow in *The Three Sisters*, Athens and Troy in *Andromaque*, etc.) but which are not placed physically in relation to the onstage, the contiguous offstage, or to the audience space. In a given production, of course, such places may be physically situated in relation to the onstage in some way: in *The Maids* Solange can, by a gesture or a look, place the maids' bedroom in an attic above Madame's room, in a basement below it, or somewhere beyond the kitchen.

Within the category of the *localized off* there are those places that are contiguous with those onstage, immediately accessed through a door or stairway or partially glimpsed through a window. There are others more or less distant from the onstage fictional place or places, which can be brought into them or clearly associated with them via a particular entrance, an object, a gesture, or even simply a look. They may even be inscribed within the presentational space by means of video or film. The range of possibilities is immense, as we are dealing here with one of the major resources of the Western theatre tradition, but for the purposes of this taxonomy all that is needed is to indicate the spectrum.

The case of offstage fictional places that are located in relation to the audience space does perhaps need to be mentioned separately, as their function is somewhat different from that of the other localized places. The localization can be written into the playtext—for example, Didi surveying the audience in *Waiting for Godot* and saying, ". . . that bog" (Beckett 1956, 15), or it can be a directorial decision: in the 1984 production of *The Seagull* by Antoine Vitez the lake that is so admired by the characters seemed to be situated either in or behind the audience. What I am calling the *audience off* is a highly potent device in that it necessarily leads the audience to identify the designated place with itself, but it is also strongly alienating of the fictional world. The power of the metatheatrical and ideological impact of such spatial use justifies a separate subcategory.

Now comes the vexed question of the text. While it is evident that the verbal is at work in all the spatial functions listed earlier, it is necessary to acknowledge the role of the text in a more direct way. The playtext contains a wealth of spatial reference, in both *didascalia* and *dialogue,* and a good deal of any play's meaning revolves around the system of space it presents. The notion of textual space is not used here in the sense that Pavis gives it (1980, 151–52), the material presence of the verbal, but more simply as recognition of the spatial structures contained in the playtext and their importance in the genesis of the performance: geographical and other place names, reference to objects, descriptions of place and space, verbs of movement and other indications of proxemic relationship, even prepositional phrases, are all part of this spatial system.

The fact that textual space has been listed as a separate category does not mean that it functions independently. Certainly, playtexts can be read and their spatial content analyzed, but textual space is made really meaningful only in performance. The playtext contains the potential for many spatializations, and that of course entails many different meanings. It is the practitioners who must select, discard, play with, the potentiality and create the staging that will articulate the meaning the play has for them. The important thing to stress here is the interactive function of the text at every stage of the meaning-making process.

The fifth and final category is concerned with the thematic level of spatial function. Whether one is working exclusively with the play as written text or with the play in performance, the way the space is conceived and organized, the kinds of space that are shown and/or evoked, the values and events associated with them, and the relationship between them are always of fundamental importance in the meaning conveyed. Ubersfeld's concept of dramatic space and Jansen's stage space are significant attempts to theorize this thematic function.

Descriptive and critical analyses of performance, accounts of rehearsal process, attempts to reconstruct historical performance, all provide convincing evidence of the centrality of the spatial function in the construction of meaning.[13] Even more interesting in this context, perhaps, is the evidence emerging from a number of recent critical analyses of the extent to which spatial organization has been written into the play-text (see, e.g., Barthes 1963; Ubersfeld 1964; Pavis 1986; Garner 1994; Chaudhuri 1995; Scolnicov and Holland 1989). Whether the starting point is a particular production or the study of a single playtext or the whole oeuvre of a given playwright, the analyses cited demonstrate that the structures of spatial use, and the articulation of fictional place and dramatic event are fundamental to the thematic concerns of playwright and production. If we can understand the spatial system, we can unravel the philosophical and ideological content of play and production.

The term used in this taxonomy is *thematic space* in order to make clear its importance in the construction of meaning, its globalizing func-tion, and the way it incorporates both text and performance. Although listed as a separate category, it must be seen as bringing together all the spatial signs and all the spatial functions from the other categories: meaning emerges only when all these functions are seen structurally as parts of the whole.

This breakdown of the spatial function and the categories distinguished within each of the major sections should make it possible to speak with some precision about the factors involved and perhaps also to perceive with more clarity how shifts in the use of certain aspects of the spatial function characterize a particular period, genre, or writer. The way the taxonomy has ordered these functions into categories and grouped them together in sections is in part a response to the spectator's order of spa-tial experience, but it is in part a mere presentational device.

Listing the categories of spatial function, as in figure 1, is certainly misleading, even though convenient in terms of exposition. It does, as has already been remarked in connection with both textual space and thematic space, give a false impression of separation between categories that in fact have to be conceptualized as dynamically interactive, and it might also convey a notion of hierarchy (but should one be reading in descending or ascending order of importance?). The two dimensions of the printed page are notoriously inadequate as a means of illustrating the complexities of theatrical semiosis, and figure 2 is an attempt to mod-ify the impression of linearity given in figure 1 by displaying the func-tions as a series of untidy, irregular shapes, enclosing and constructing one another.

The social reality of the theatre space, the relationship between the physical and the fictional that is central to the theatre experience, the

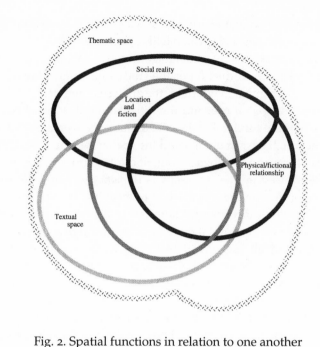

Fig. 2. Spatial functions in relation to one another

modes of interplay derived from the central relationship, are all functions of one another; textual space is critical in the construction of the
physical/fictional and in the placing of the fictional within the physical,
but it is not exhausted by, nor does it exclusively control, these functions.
Thematic space is here visualized as constructed by and emerging from
all the other categories of spatial function.

In any particular performance analysis the terms and definitions
given in the taxonomy will be useful, and all need to be considered in the
early stages of the analysis, even those like *practitioner space* and *rehearsal
space* that are normally left out of account. This is not to say that a performance cannot be understood without access to the materiality of its
production process: that is clearly nonsense, as millions of satisfied spectators have demonstrated over theatre's long history. It is equally undeniable that the practitioners themselves, with their intimate knowledge
of the production's genesis and their appreciation of all its complex
detail, see more in each performance and know more as a result of it than

the first-time spectator. The analyst needs strategies to approximate and refine upon this kind of inside knowledge.

Theatrical semiosis depends upon a combination or complex weave of interacting sign systems and forms of expression, and even within the category of spatial function there are numerous sign systems, codes, etc., at work, and they are experienced by different spectators in different ways. So what has been painstakingly teased out into separately named categories has to be recombined in any attempt to account for the way spectators make meaning.

The spectator in the theatre does not receive information in a purely linear way; while some systems are functioning in a linear manner (notably the narrative), others are perceived as a simultaneity. The problem in performance analysis is precisely the simultaneity and the range of possibilities of combination and selection that are available to the spectator at any given moment. More work of an empirical sort is needed before it will be possible to theorize with confidence about how spectators read performance. It can, however, be posited as a working hypothesis that they do combine elements of the performance into units of some sort and, further, that the performance provides a good deal of guidance about how to do this. This question will be explored further in chapter 4, but first it is necessary to examine in more detail the physical reality of the theatre building (chap. 2) and the human occupation and exploitation of the spaces it encloses (chap. 3).

2

The Physical Space

The architect's point of view is usually the most ignored and
the least understood of all, but I personally put it in the first
place, on the same level as that of the poet because, as I see it,
the one merges with the other.
     —Jacques Copeau, *Une Rénovation
          dramatique est-elle possible?*

Theatre is a complex activity, and throughout its long history it has
tended to develop specially constructed venues in order to provide
appropriate spaces for the performers and, equally important, spaces
from which the spectators can both see and hear. Indeed, it is the spectator function that is foregrounded in the name *theatre*, a word derived
from the Greek *theatron*, which means literally "a place for seeing" (Liddell and Scott 1889). In Bharata's account of the origins of theatre the
need for a building became apparent at the first performance, when the
enemies of the gods, angered at their portrayal in the play, disrupted the
proceedings by terrorizing the actors, thus making them unable to speak,
move, or remember their lines. Brahma's solution was a theatre building,
and, while his instructions to the architect of the gods, Visvakarma, are a
little vague—"Build carefully a playhouse of the best type" (Bharata-
Muni 1967, 11)—the context makes the function clear: to protect the performance from disruption and to provide a space for concentration and
focus on the part of the performers and the spectators.

Interestingly enough, it was precisely this function of the traditional
theatre building that Peter Brook found he most regretted after his years
of experimentation in found spaces of all sorts. As he put it in 1970, in his
introduction to a special issue of *Architecture d'Aujourd'hui* devoted to
the performance space: "The hardest thing is to find a space for concentration which permits every gesture to carry its full weight of meaning"
(1970, n.p.).

Since the mythical origins of theatre, recounted in Bharata's treatise, wherever human societies have developed theatre as a mode of expression, they have also constructed buildings to house it, or they have adapted existing buildings or naturally occurring spaces for this purpose. In some cultures theatre buildings serve exclusively for theatre; in others (especially those in which performances took place infrequently) they may have been used on some occasions for more general civic purposes;[1] in others theatre required a temporary adaptation of another public or semipublic space (marketplace, church, the courtyard of an inn, or the hall of an aristocratic residence). In some places the temporary appropriation became more permanent, and the original use of the building was displaced by the theatre (e.g., the theatres built in indoor tennis courts in seventeenth-century France); in others permanent theatre buildings retained features of the found spaces that had earlier been used (e.g., Elizabethan theatres, with their echoes of the temporary structures erected in inn courtyards). At some periods theatres have been extremely elaborate, luxurious edifices, statements of princely power or civic pride; at others they have been constructed so that they form part of the streetscape, distinguishable from other commercial buildings only by billboards and other conventional signaling devices. Marvin Carlson has claimed that "the theatre is in fact one of the most persistant architectural objects in the history of western culture" (1989, 6), and it is somewhat ironic that the most ephemeral of art forms should leave behind such obvious and durable traces of its presence.

Theatre buildings incorporate within themselves indications of the practices they are designed to house: the arrangement of the auditorium and the nature of the other social spaces in the building reveal a great deal about the theatregoing experience from the spectators' point of view; the decoration of these spaces and the way the theatre is signaled as such in the urban space provide insight into the ways in which theatregoing has been conceptualized in that society; the arrangement of the practitioners' space, particularly the dressing rooms and rehearsal space, the facilities provided, and the amount of space allocated provide information about the work practices involved; the nature of the stage and the fragile boundaries between stage and auditorium, and between stage and offstage, reveal a great deal about the processes of representation involved. Theatre artists are frequently obliged to work in buildings designed for earlier periods, and this can cause problems if there is too great a distance between the practice of theatre as predicated by the building and the practices deemed appropriate to the present by the artists (and spectators) involved. The theatre building is, however, also a very potent means of transmitting practical knowledge and performance traditions, for, as Edward Casey puts it, "a building condenses a culture in one place" (1993, 32). The link with tradition and practice provided by the theatre building is particularly important in an art form in which so little is written down and which is to all intents and purposes a part of oral culture.

Antoine Vitez was very aware of the constraints imposed by the theatre building itself when he spoke in an interview in 1978 of the distinction between the theatre as edifice and the theatre as shelter:

> At the end of the day there are only two types of theatre: the shelter and the edifice. In a theatre-shelter you can construct whatever kind of spaces you like, while a theatre-edifice imposes from the outset a certain kind of mise en scène . . . The edifice says "I am a theatre," while the shelter points up the transitory nature of all the codes of representation. (1991, 90)

Vitez had worked extensively in both types of theatre, and indeed a couple of years after the interview he accepted appointment to the Théâtre National Populaire, housed in that most monumental of edifices, the Palais de Chaillot. He claimed in 1978 that he had no particular predilection for either form of theatre, insisting that both have their history and both make their own demands: "It all depends each time on what you hope to produce there."

Ariane Mnouchkine, on the other hand, has always expressed a strong preference for a theatre space that provides shelter with minimal formal constraints, and she defines this as the umbrella function: "My vision of the ideal space is ultimately an umbrella, the lightest, most discreet, most flexible umbrella possible" (qtd. in Boucris 1993, 253). She has refused all offers to direct prestigious national theatres and has remained faithful to the Cartoucherie, the eighteenth-century munitions factory that she obtained in 1970 as a rehearsal space and transformed into a new kind of performance space when she could find no suitable theatre in Paris for *1789*. While the Cartoucherie has become in its own way a theatre edifice and the productions of the Théâtre du Soleil correspondingly "heavy" in terms of equipment and resources, it nevertheless retains a certain flexibility, and, compared with the Sydney Opera House or the Palais de Chaillot, it is still more a theatre shelter than a theatre edifice.[2]

Whether theatrical performances occur in consecrated theatre buildings or in "found" spaces adapted for the purpose (as was the case in many countries in the 1960s and 1970s), whether they are heavy or light in their exploitation of technology and machinery, and whatever notions of belief or disbelief prevail among the spectators, theatre is an activity that is in some way separate from daily life. The subject of this chapter is the theatre building itself, the functions it fulfills, notably in marking the separation of the theatrical from the everyday, in "framing" the activity in certain specific ways, in transforming actions from "unmarked" to "marked" (in the sense that sociolinguists speak of markedness), and in eliciting certain behaviors from people.

The idea of the frame comes from the work of behavioral sociologists, in particular Erving Goffman, who was interested in particular in the way members of a given social group "know what it is that is going on" at any particular time:

> I assume that definitions of a situation are built up in accordance with principles of organisation which govern events—at least social ones—and our subjective involvement in them; frame is the word I use to refer to such of these basic elements as I am able to identify. (1974, 11)

He speaks of "primary frameworks" that define the situation and enable us to make sense of what is occurring; his term *lamination* refers to the fact that in many social situations multiple frames may be operating simultaneously (frames within frames), and he introduces the concept of "keying" (on the analogy of musical key) to indicate the dynamic way in which behaviors that are already meaningful in terms of some primary framework can be "transformed into something patterned on this activity but seen by the participants to be something quite else" (e.g., make-believe, contests, ceremonials). Problems can arise in society if people fail to recognize the frame or if the keyed activities spill over into another frame. Theatre in Western society has traditionally been very strongly keyed and framed, but in certain forms of sport, for example, the framing seems to be more problematic: supporters of rival teams may perpetrate real violence on each other or take the aggression of the sporting contest (socially keyed as separate from "real" life, to be played out in terms of rules and agreed-upon actions) into the buses and trains taking them back to their homes.

The behavior of actors onstage is marked; spectators know that it is to be interpreted differently from apparently identical behaviors occurring in other places. Spectators in the theatre both believe and disbelieve, they play a game in which they permit themselves to believe to a certain extent what is occurring, they can even be moved to tears by this, but at the same time they know that it is not real, or, rather, that it is both not real (a fiction) and real (the actors are really present, "in the flesh," the common phrase insisting on the materiality of physical presence). Octave Mannoni uses Freud's concept of *Verneinung* (negation)[3] to describe the spectator's relationship to theatrical performance (1969, 9–33, 161–83). Just as negation permits a person to both admit and deny a fact, to admit to some level of consciousness a fact that the conscious mind refuses to acknowledge, so in the theatre we can know that something is real and not real at the same time. Spectators see the duel in which Hamlet is killed, they know that the swords are real and the bodies are real, they even know that Hamlet is dead, and they know at the same time that no one is dead.

The physical presence of performers and spectators makes theatrical *Verneinung* very different from the normal working of fiction: there is a difference between the double awareness of the reality/nonreality of Hamlet's death, for example, and the unambiguous nonreality of a recounted death, even when this death is recounted onstage (as is traditionally the case in classical and neoclassical drama). When Théramène tells of the death of Hippolyte in Racine's *Phèdre*, this death, unlike the death of Hamlet, has become pure story, albeit couched in some of the most vivid poetry Racine ever wrote; it is the telling itself that becomes the event that does and does not occur; it is the father's grief as he listens to the story that is and is not present to the spectators.

Anne Ubersfeld and others have drawn attention to the role of the performance space itself in triggering this function and permitting it to work without spilling over into the spectators' social reality:

> Denegation is the psychic operation that permits the spectator to see the physical reality of what is happening on stage, to accept it as reality while knowing (or forgetting only for brief instants) that this reality has no consequences outside the confines of the stage space. (1996, 23)

When the actor on stage says, "I love you" or "I hate you," "Will you marry me?" or "I'm going to kill you," no crime has been threatened, no contract entered into, because the stage itself functions as a frame that in Michael Issacharoff's formulation "disengages all speech acts" (1989, 9).

Postmodern performance practices have challenged this framing, insisting that what is happening during the performance is real, not sim-

ulated, but even in such performances there is an unspoken understanding between performers and spectators about what may be permitted to
occur; the performance is still framed as performance. Actions may be
real, but I think the current understanding in most places would be that
these actions should not have damaging consequences for either performers or spectators: no one should get injured, for example, and, if a
spectator's belongings are taken and used during the performance, they
should be returned undamaged at the end, spectators' clothes should not
be damaged, etc. The unspoken understanding in some places may be
different, and there have certainly been major changes over the years in
the nature of activities spectators are willing to watch (e.g., the inflicting
of real pain by one person on him- or herself or on another person or
even on an animal), but, if the performance goes beyond what is acceptable to the spectators at that time and place, there will be anger, com-
plaints, and possibly legal repercussions. In this connection, too, the
place of performance itself provides a primary framework: spectators
who are intrigued by a certain kind of performance go to places where it
is practiced and thereby enter into a tacit contract with the performers
not to be outraged by what happens.

The space is, of course, not an empty container but an active agent;
it shapes what goes on within it, emits signals about it to the community
at large, and is itself affected. The frame constituted by a particular
building or venue is not something fixed and immutable but a dynamic
and continually evolving social entity. As Henri Lefebvre puts it so pertinently:

> Vis-à-vis lived experience, space is neither a mere "frame," after the fash-
> ion of the frame of a painting, nor a form or container of a virtually neutral
> kind, designed simply to receive whatever is poured into it. Space is social
> morphology: it is to lived experience what form itself is to the living
> organism, and just as intimately bound up with function and structure.
> (1991, 93–94)

The theatre building or designated place of performance provides a context of interpretation for spectators and performers alike. Due to the
kinds of performance put on, a venue gains a certain reputation within a
cultural community; it attracts a certain kind of spectator, repels others.
Over a period of time the type of activity may change: for example, the
Aldwych Theatre in London was so closely associated with farce in the
1920s that it gave its name to a genre—the "Aldwych Farces"—but in the

1960s and 1970s, while it was the London base for the Royal Shakespeare Company, it became the primary venue for intelligent productions of the classics and of interesting new plays. Returning to London after an absence of several years in 1984 and knowing that the Royal Shakespeare Company had moved to the Barbican, I nevertheless found myself still checking the newspapers each week to see what was on at the Aldwych and being somewhat dismayed at the bland, commercial fare being offered. This personal anecdote illustrates both the way a given venue can come to seem causally connected to a particular kind of performance and the time lag involved before members of a cultural community recognize that change has occurred.

If the principal function of the primary framework constituted by the theatre building is to signal to all concerned that, once inside, we are in the realm of "denegation," an equally important one is to set in motion the spectators' work of meaning making. Everything that occurs onstage is perceived as potentially meaningful by spectators, and, even if nothing is happening, that too will be interpreted as meaningful. Manfred Wekwerth has described an experiment in which an actor with a neutral expression stood on the stage and did nothing, but spectators nevertheless experienced this in a variety of ways and interpreted what they saw to be occurring. He used this experiment to conclude that "the primary player in the theatre . . . is not the actor but rather the spectator" (1972, 46–48), but I would say, rather, that it reveals the power of the theatrical frame. What the actor thought was nothing was perceived as something because the spectators were ready to perceive meaning. The fact of coming to a theatre, sitting in an auditorium and watching other people, especially other people framed by the stage, is a powerful stimulus to semiosis.

The fact that theatre is such a heavily marked activity, taking place in specified venues, the onset of the performance elaborately signaled via numerous other conventions (curtains, lights, the traditional "trois coups" in French theatres) invites speculation that this is precisely because people have needed to mark the separation between it and everyday life, perhaps because the contaminating effect of mimesis has been feared. Within the theatre there are usually a number of thresholds that the spectator must traverse: the purchase of a ticket, verification of this by uniformed staff in foyer, further verification by ushers in the auditorium who indicate the seat allocated. At this stage of the theatre experience the fictional world has usually not yet been activated, although the set may be visible, but the spectator has been progressively further and further removed from the world outside, permitted to move further and further into the world within.

Ariane Mnouchkine's productions are famous for the elaboration of the threshold stage: as seats are not numbered, spectators must come an hour before the show if they want to be well placed; having marked their chosen seats, they then wander around the large hall, possibly eating a meal, looking at the visual display (always relevant to the production) or browsing among the books and photocopies of newspaper reviews laid out on shelves around the space. The time serves as a buffer zone in which one can slow down, distance oneself from the stresses of the real world, and be gently inserted into both the world of the performers (who are visible in their dressing room space under the scaffolding on which the audience seating is built) and into the fictional world of the play (the dressing room space is usually vibrant with this world), the set is fully visible onstage, and the musicians are preparing their instruments. In *Les Atrides* something even more striking occurred. For this production a deep trench had been dug in the floor of the main hall (the performance space in my terminology), and spectators had to cross over this on little walkways; looking down into the trench, one saw a host of half-buried figures, warriors, and horses, reminiscent of an archaeological excavation. The distance in space and time between Aeschylus, Euripides, and the present was made manifest, the silent figures in their serried ranks, half-exposed, half-swallowed up in the earth, were an invitation to reflect on the ancient provenance of the plays we were about to see and on the miracle of their survival and continued relevance to the present.

Not many directors pay as much attention to the spectators' transition from outside to inside as Ariane Mnouchkine, but the onset of the performance is normally marked in very definite ways, for this is where the denegation begins. In older-style theatres there may be a curtain; there may be some musical cue or simply the dimming of lights in the audience space and the raising of lights in the practitioner space. In some French theatres, as has already been mentioned, the tradition of the stage manager hammering out the *trois coups* is still maintained, even though lighting and curtain cues may also be in use. The end of the performance is also marked in conventional ways such as the raising of the house lights and the lowering of the curtain, and there is the important ritual of the curtain call in which the actors appear as themselves rather than as the characters they have played and in which the spectators can show their appreciation.

The curtain call is important because it reveals the actors as actors and marks a formal end to the ambivalence of denegation. Some directors rehearse and plan the curtain call carefully; actors can still be in character to a certain extent, or they can play another role (e.g., the role of actor exhausted in the pursuit of his art, hanging onto the curtain for support, as I have heard it said of certain Shakespearian actors of the old school), or they can make a very definite statement about the distinction between the character and themselves (e.g., taking off a wig to reveal their own hair). If the curtain call has clearly been staged and choreographed, some spectators may feel a kind of pleasure that the performance is continuing; if it goes on too long or is too obviously staged, this pleasure may turn to irritation or a vague disquiet: it is as though the performers are refusing to relinquish their hold on the audience, will not release them back into real life. In a production of Sartre's *Huis clos* at the Seymour Centre in Sydney in 1979, the director (Igor Persan) instructed the actors to remain onstage, in character at the end of the play, and to remain there until the last spectator had left the space. This left the spectators feeling distinctly uneasy; there was no clear end point to the play, no moment at which one could clap and thereby return the experience to a neat category of "theatrical performance," no way of knowing when one could/should leave. Each person had to make the decision for him- or herself, and the actors told me that on one occasion it took two hours before everyone had gone. In fact, the play had become a happening, the focus shifting from the dramatic fiction to each spectator's own actual experience, the decision to stay or go.

In order to structure this reflection on the functions fulfilled by the physical place of performance, I shall follow the spatial categories established in the preceding chapter and consider in turn the building itself as it exists within or outside the urban space, then the audience space within and immediately outside this building, then practitioner space within the building, rehearsal space wherever it may be situated and its relation to performance, and finally the presentational space.

The Theatre Building

Edward Casey, in his phenomenological study of place, explores what he calls "a series of paired pre-positionings" (notably outside/inside, alongside/around and between/with) in order "to grasp more fully how the lived body dwells in architectural settings" (1993, 122), and they have proved a very helpful basis for examining the lived reality of the theatre building.

The building, as Carlson has pointed out, is an enduring feature of the urban environment in Western culture, and it necessarily exists in relation to other buildings and is "placed" in relation to center and periphery. As cities grow and develop, locations that were once peripheral may become central, and vice versa: Shakespeare's Globe Theatre on the south bank of the Thames was once outside the city limits, but the south bank—location of the National Theatre, the National Film Theatre, and the Museum of the Moving Image—is now not only a cultural center but would be perceived by most Londoners to be near the center of town; similarly the boulevards that in the nineteenth century circled the outer limits of Paris (location of theatres still in use today, such as the Porte Saint Martin and the Théâtre Antoine) are now near the center and have been replaced, as it were, by a further ring of outlying theatres in working-class suburbs such as Bobigny, Créteil, Ivry, and Nanterre. In Sydney the theatres are mostly located in or around what is known as the Central Business District, but the demographic center of the town is now at least twenty miles to the west, where there are very few theatres. Locating a theatre in a working-class area does not mean that it will attract a working-class audience, as numerous experiences have shown (Joan Littlewood at Stratford East, the theatres in the Parisian *banlieue rouge* just mentioned), but the location nevertheless makes some kind of statement about who is expected or encouraged to participate and who might feel discouraged from attempting to do so.

The surrounding buildings and the activities associated with them (part of Casey's "with") add a further dimension to the framing function performed by the building. It is no accident that the Palais Garnier, the extravagant and luxurious opera house built in Paris for Napoléon III and named significantly in honor of its architect, is located in the vicinity of the stock exchange, the head offices of banks, and the big department stores. This is visibly the "big money" end of town, and, though foreign students may sit on the steps in front of the building, few can afford the price of a ticket with a decent view of the stage. The concentration of theatres in London's West End is located in close proximity to Soho. The fact that the glamour and activity of a street like Shaftesbury Avenue backs immediately onto a more dangerous and raffish area, renowned in the past for its striptease joints and prostitutes, seems to say something about the ambivalent position of theatre in England. The location of the theatre building necessarily makes some statement about the way theatre is perceived by society more generally and by its practitioners (whether or not they have any real choice about where they practice): is it part of high culture in association with art galleries and concert halls in a modern arts complex, is it a commercial product to be marketed like any other in association with other commercial activities, or an outpost of culture in the deadly environment of freeways and concrete apartment blocks inhabited by the working class in many cities, is it part of leisure culture or tourist culture or (a theatre on a university campus) the world of education?

In big cities today it is likely that there will be several centers, and there may be groups of theatres situated in different places, in a *with* relationship with very different activities and subgroups within the overall urban population. It is also possible that a given theatre may exist, in a sense, in opposition to its environment, either because the inhabitants are hostile to it (at the Belvoir Street Theatre in Sydney there were for many years numerous notices warning patrons to make no noise when leaving the theatre) or because they are simply not interested. The exterior surrounds of some theatres are used by the urban population for their own purposes (the steps in front of the Palais Garnier are a popular meeting place for tourists, the surfaces in front of the Palais de Chaillot or the arts center at Créteil are places of predilection for skateboarders and rollerbladers, who attract audiences for their own feats of skill and daring, the Sydney Opera House is a major tourist attraction and its forecourt is usually thronged with crowds of people who have little or no interest in what goes on inside the building). This kind of appropriation of the buildings has more to do with their appearance, their location, and the nature of their surrounds than the fact that they are theatres, but it does reveal something about the divided nature of urban populations and theatre's typically uncomfortable stance, desiring communion and finding that its appeal is to a very limited social group.

Throughout its history theatre practitioners have frequently made use of already existing buildings, converting them for their own purposes. From the churches and marketplaces of medieval Europe to the indoor tennis courts of the Renaissance and the factories, warehouses, markets, and abattoirs of the twentieth century postwar move away from existing theatre buildings, the theatre has a long tradition of appropriation and adaptation. In these circumstances, too, the connotations of

the building's earlier use may spill over to color in subtle ways the theatre activity. The architects of the conversion may wish to disguise to the
maximum the building's previous use, or they may exploit this. The
Wharf Theatre in Sydney, home to the Sydney Theatre Company, is situated on a disused finger wharf on the harbor. There is a reminder of this
past existence and the heavy manual labor that occurred there in the
rough wooden floor of the pier that now constitutes the long indoor
walkway patrons must negotiate before they reach the bar, restaurant,
and the theatre itself. The connotations of the place go further: the theatre seems to be located on the very edge of the continent, and the precariousness of its situation and the constant presence of water on all
sides is a reminder of the importance of the sea for all the people who
have worked on that wharf, the link with home for early settlers, their
yearning for "over there" and their ambivalence toward the Australian
landmass. The decoration of this long walkway, framed posters of earlier
productions, speaks mainly of the theatre itself, but, as the walls are
pierced by large windows looking out over the harbor, there is a
strangely mixed message: a celebration of the achievements of this particular theatre and of the (mainly European) culture it represents and a
continuing reminder of the fragility of its implantation here.

An important function of the location of the theatre building,
whether this is used exclusively for theatre or is the site of other activities, whether it has been built specifically as a theatre or has been converted from some prior purpose is to determine in part at least the audience for the performances put on within its walls. The nature of the
performances is obviously the major determinant of who will come to a
particular theatre, but the venue is also a potent factor. It is obvious that
theatres in far distant suburbs, or in areas that are deserted after dark or
that do not have easily accessible public transport or readily available
parking will deter all but the most committed, but location seems to exercise a power of exclusion that goes well beyond these easily explained
factors. In recent years I have met people who will not go to a theatre
located on a university campus because the university is an alien world
to them, others who feel uncomfortable attending an avant-garde theatre
because it is located at the end of a narrow passage between two buildings, and others who go frequently to the cinema but have never been to
the theatre because they are intimidated by the sense that theatre is a
domain that belongs exclusively to initiates.

This latter point raises the question of the immediate environs of the theatre, Casey's categories of "alongside and around," for before going into the theatre we experience it from the outside. Some theatres, notably those Marvin Carlson (1989) would describe as "monumental," demand respect: if the entrance is at the top of a flight of steps, the spectators must ascend and, in so doing, are separated from the rest of the city but also offer themselves as spectacle to those who are simply passing by. A theatre like the Atelier in Montmartre, set at one end of a little tree-lined square, is immediately inviting due to the human dimensions of the relationship between the building and its surroundings. Coming out after the show into the lighted space under the trees one is tempted to linger and chat.

By contrast, the Barbican Theatre in London seems to have no exterior, and I found my first experience of this theatre very alienating: approaching from the tube station, surrounded by what seemed a wilderness of anonymous modern buildings, I was following the yellow indicators on the pavement, my eyes on the ground, when I suddenly found that I was inside the building. I was already in the foyer and had entered the theatre without realizing it. Some theatres, like the Sydney Opera House, for example, are known primarily for their exteriors, which may pose its own problems for the artists whose work occurs inside, but theatres like the Barbican or the Theatre Royal in Sydney, which are so embedded in their surroundings that they deny spectators the opportunity to experience them from the outside, are highly problematic. The idea of an interior without an exterior is peculiarly unnerving, for users of buildings need to be able to relate the inside to the outside, perhaps especially in the case of theatres that are normally so inwardly focused.

Discussing Paladio's Palazzo Chiericati in Vicenza, Edward Casey reflects at length on the portico which he describes as "an interspace . . . an interstitial structure [that] does not importune the visitor to go either in or out" (1993, 126). Theatres presumably want to importune, or at least encourage, visitors to enter, but some modern buildings make it very difficult even to find the entrance. Approaching the resplendent arts centers in certain Australian state capitals on foot rather than by car may involve the unwary spectator in a lengthy trudge around the base of a monolithic structure that appears to have emergency exits but no entrance doors at all. The approach by car is usually much simpler, the dimensions of the buildings less daunting, but, if the parking lot is underground, the experience is often one of entering a lift in the parking lot and emerging from

Fig. 3. The Théâtre de l'Atelier in Montmartre. (Photography by the author.)

it into the theatre foyer. The laudable aim of protecting car drivers from the dangers of the night and from inclement weather may have the further consequence of diminishing their contact with the physical reality of the place and thus, I would argue, in some undefinable way diminishing the overall experience.

The major function of any building, theatre, or simple dwelling place, is to mark the distinction between inside and outside, the third of Casey's "pre-positionings." As I have indicated in my remarks concern-

Fig. 4. The square in front of the Atelier, where children play by day and theatre patrons stroll at night. (Photography by the author.)

ing some modern monumental theatre architecture, it can be difficult for the individual user to negotiate the articulation between inside and outside (and this, of course, contributes to the sense many people have of being excluded from what goes on in such places). The experience of the theatregoer is one of penetration further and further into the building until one reaches the point beyond which one cannot go, the point that Iain Mackintosh does not hesitate to designate a "magical area," the place where "the worlds of audience and actor interconnect" (1993, 144).

Privileged (wealthy) theatregoers can approach this more closely: the most expensive seats in most theatres are those closest to the stage; others may be substantially removed either vertically (in upper galleries) or horizontally (placed at the back of the auditorium)—but the theatre building is one that emphasizes this sense of inward progression. A theatre such as the Palais Garnier dramatizes the progression every step of the way for the spectator with mirrors, monumental staircases, and galleries, the Wharf Theatre too provides spectators with a lengthy progression, but here the experience is not so much one of penetration to the heart of the building as skirting along its side (perhaps part of the sense of being on the edge that I have already mentioned). In the Palais Garnier the experience is so overwhelming that one may lose the sense of purposeful progress toward the center, but in smaller and simpler theatres the center is soon reached and the experience of inwardness and separation from the outside correspondingly lessened.

Theatre is an art form that plays intensively with notions of inside and outside, particularly in relation to the onstage/offstage relationship and its use in presenting fictional world(s), as will be discussed in the final section of this chapter, but the theatre building itself, in its relation to its surroundings, is also part of this interplay. There are theatres that blend with their environment, others that may dominate it, and yet others that seem to have become lost within it, each mark the distinction between inside and outside in different ways, each provide a different experience of crossing the threshold for the theatregoer, require a different kind of physical and mental effort.

For Jacques Copeau, in the epigraph to this chapter, the architect's contribution to the theatre experience is as crucial as that of the poet. While Artaud dreamt of a radically different kind of theatre, he shares with Copeau the perception that, in the theatre, language and space are essentially interdependent. Copeau acknowledges that his understanding of the importance of the building and the spatial organization was not that of most of his contemporaries, and Iain Mackintosh, writing fifty years later, confirms that nothing much has changed in terms of audience perception of the important role played by architecture in the theatre experience:

> Many mistake decoration for architecture. Others put the architecture, along with the ease of getting a drink at the bar, of parking or of buying a ticket, as a necessary adjunct to the evening, not central to the event. (1993, 1)

It seems to me that, while spectators might not put into words their knowledge, they do nevertheless know in their bodies which theatres make them feel comfortable, which ones feel exciting, which are soporific or alienating. We know and experience places through our bodies, as Edward Casey argues: "My lived body is the locatory agent of lived places, the subtender of sites, the *genius loci* of all that has come to be called 'space' in the west" (1993, 105). In the architectural design of theatre buildings it is therefore especially the relation of scale between the human body and the building itself that is of crucial importance to the performance experience. This will be discussed in more detail in the following sections devoted to audience space and practitioner space within the building, but, even in terms of the exterior of the building and notably in the way the articulation between outside and inside is managed, the architecture itself is constraining the theatregoers' experience in very definite ways.

For Henri Lefebvre any space is socially produced; even "Nature" itself, insofar as it is "apprehended in social life by the sense organs, has been modified and therefore in a sense produced" (1991, 67). This means that space is always in a relation to what he calls power, and the analysis of space involves consideration "(of the) dialectical relationship between demand and command, along with its attendant questions: 'Who?', 'For whom?', 'By whose agency?', 'Why and how?' " (116). Whether power is represented by the church, king, town councils, or the government funding agencies of the late twentieth century, theatre is always in a rather ambivalent relation to it in that the activity theatres represent is both desired and feared by power, both supported and heavily policed and controlled. The building itself is one way in which control is exercised: a massively monumental theatre dominating the surrounding urban space may make a strong statement about glamour, affluence, the desirability of access, and so on, but to the individual theatregoer the experience of climbing a huge flight of steps or of entering the building through a massive doorway may be rather a reminder of the individual's lack of power. As Edward Casey puts it: "the disparity in scale between openings and bodies reminds us of the body's comparatively diminutive proportions" (1993, 124). A theatre that is disapproved of by power, one that is censored or denied funding (the contemporary equivalent of censorship) will be obliged to find cheap accommodation, probably in an area of town where other forbidden activities take place, and the discomfort of the space will exercise a certain deterrent effect on spectators.

The theatre at St. Quentin en Yvelines, a new town on the outer edge of the Paris region, occupies one whole side of the civic center and seems on the surface to be a very generous gesture on the part of the institutions that fund it and a statement of confidence about the place of theatre in the cultural life of the community (see fig. 5). I found the very monumentality of the building vaguely unsettling, however, when I attended performances (the windows and doors along the front of the building must be over thirty feet high, and, although the door that people actually use to gain access to the building is normal height, it is placed off to one side, which rather gives one the impression of using the tradesman's entrance). The doors within the theatre are also extremely high, and I was reminded of Henri Lefebvre's observation that "verticality and great height have ever been the spatial expression of potentially violent power" even when this may be masked beneath "signs and surfaces which claim to express collective will and collective thought" (1991, 98, 143). The oppressive experience of entering the theatre seemed to me to be directly related to disparities in scale of the sort to which Edward Casey refers.

Audience Space

Theatre is an art form that is critically dependent on the expressive capacities of the human body, and the theatres that "work" best for actors and spectators are ones that are sensitive to the physical dimensions of the body. Simon Callow has written of the difficulty he had performing in the vast old Manchester Opera House:

> Trying to get through to the gallery was like standing at the bottom of a mountain and trying to reach someone at the top. At the beginning of each performance you opened your ribs and didn't let them down till the end. By the time we got back to London, both of my sides were covered in bruises. (1985, 60)

The disparity between the carrying power of the human voice and the architectural reality was thus, painfully, inscribed upon the actor's body. The move to increase the size of theatres has usually come from architects with grandiose visual ideas and from profit-hungry managements and has usually been resisted by actors, who want spectators to be able to see the detail of their facial expression and to hear the subtleties of their vocal delivery.

Fig. 5. The municipal theatre at St. Quentin (entrance on the left). (Photography by the author.)

Spectators, too, have objected to increases in size that fail to respect the bodily basis of the actor's art. Iain Mackintosh quotes an observant response from a disgruntled spectator to Henry Holland's new Drury Lane in 1794:

> I adjourned to Drury Lane Playhouse where I enjoyed the highly wrought exhibition of Mrs. Siddons's performance as Katherine in Henry VIII although lost and sent to waste in this wide wide theatre where close observation cannot be maintained—nor quick applause received! Restore me, ye overruling powers of the drama to the warm close observant seats of Old Drury where I may comfortably criticise and enjoy the flights of fancy. These now are past. The nice discriminations of the actors' feelings are now all lost in the vast void of the new theatre of Drury Lane. (1993, 35)

The "overruling powers" have rarely heeded actors or spectators like John Byng, and yet the decisions they make, and the buildings that are produced as a result weigh heavily on the experience of the spectator and on the kind of performance that then comes to dominate the repertoire. Big stages lead inevitably to big shows, with the emphasis on extravagant visual display, and, while sometimes it is the big shows that create a demand for big theatres (as is happening at present in Sydney, e.g., under the pressure of what might be called the Cameron Mackintosh phenomenon), it is usually the building itself that, having been built, needs to be filled. Strindberg, trying to develop a new kind of drama, knew that he needed a new kind of theatre space: his Intimate Theatre required proximity, both between the actors on the stage, and between the stage and the auditorium. Indeed, twenty years before the Intimate Theatre, in the preface he wrote to *Miss Julie*, in 1888, he had already stressed this point:

> if, first and foremost, we could have a small stage and small house, then perhaps a new dramatic art might arise, and theatre once more become a place of entertainment for educated people. (1955, 73)

If the actor is reduced to a distant blur for most spectators, even if one can hear every word (usually the case in modern theatres tuned acoustically for the spoken voice), the venue will nevertheless be unsuitable for a large part of the dramatic repertoire.

Adolphe Appia, the forefather of modern scenographic design, often quoted a phrase attributed to Protagorus: "man is the measure of all things," as it summed up for him all that was wrong with the elaborately pictorial scenic art of his day and pointed the way toward a solution. Man was, of course, literally the measure of things before the metric scale imposed its abstract standard: in earlier times measurement was based literally on the human body: the "brazza" (length from elbow to fingertip), the hand span, the inch, the foot, and the pace, so the relative proportions of building and body were continually present in the minds of the builders and architects. Appia's major insights concerned the relationship of the actor to the scenic space, but the wisdom of Protagorus has to be applied to the theatre building more generally, for the spectators, too, are physically present in the performance space, and it is through their bodies that they experience the performance. The arrangement of the auditorium itself, the nature of the frontier zone where presentational space and audience space meet, and the other social spaces in the building all need to be examined in terms of the experiences they constrain and what they reveal about theatre as an activity in a given society.

The auditorium can be divided vertically into tiers as in the eighteenth- and nineteenth-century proscenium arch theatres, derived from

Italian renaissance designs, or seats can be arranged in a single raked block, as pioneered by Wagner in his Festspielhaus in Bayreuth, which seems to have been the preferred style among architects in the post–World War II period. The advantage of the vertical division is that it brings more spectators closer to the stage; the disadvantage of this style of auditorium is that the sightlines are usually very bad. In the Palais Garnier, for example, there are twenty-one hundred seats, but only fifteen hundred of them have an adequate view of the stage, and many fewer have a really good view. Harald Zielske claims that in a U-shaped auditorium divided into tiers of boxes (the traditional Continental auditorium) only about one-fifth of the spectators can see and hear well (Arnott et al. 1977, 23–44). The advantage of the single tier is that the sightlines are dramatically improved, and every seat commands an uninterrupted view of the stage, but, on the other hand, a great many spectators are a long way back, and they can see little detail of facial expression. Many opera goers in Paris, when given the choice between the new theatre at the Bastille and the Palais Garnier, seem perversely to prefer the latter,[4] which suggests that there are compensations in the traditional auditorium that modern architects have failed to recognize.

In the traditional italianate theatre there is a lateral division in addition to the vertical tiers: seats in the lower galleries and at the back of the stalls are arranged in boxes, separated by low partitions. In the nineteenth century when the boxes were rented for the season, the audience was thus made up of personal or family groups as well as the undifferentiated public seating, and the boxes made possible a range of greater or lesser seclusion within a nevertheless public place. Visitors could enter a box during the intervals through its back door or stroll along the passageway in front of the boxes, stopping to converse with occupants; ladies could sit discreetly toward the back or indulge in more active socializing by sitting at the front. This combination of public and semiprivate spaces and the amount of movement around the auditorium presupposed by the arrangement of boxes and promenade space facilitated a range of different activities, different levels of attention to the play. In a single-tier auditorium there may be a central aisle, or sometimes two, which provide for a degree of lateral division, but in many modern theatres there is no central aisle, and the audience is seated in long rows accessed from either side. This certainly reduces the mobility of the spectators, and, if it is combined, as at the Barbican, with a door at the end of each row, the lateral division of the audience can be so strong that there seems to be a loss of focus from the stage. Each door exerts its own attraction for its row of spectators, and energy seems in a strange way to be leached off rather than being directed toward the stage.

In a horseshoe-shaped auditorium, even when modified for today's audiences, spectators are very much aware of other spectators, and the show is by no means exclusively on the stage. Privileged spectators sat on the stage itself in seventeenth-century France and, although the lighting was such that they would not have been clearly visible to many spectators (Marvin Carlson makes the very pertinent point that the auditorium was better lit than the stage at this period [1989, 140]), their presence had the potential to attract attention away from the actors. In Continental theatres the royal box was normally situated at the center of the first circle, thus ensuring that the king enjoyed an optimum view of the perspective stage picture, but it also ensured that large numbers of spectators placed at the sides of the auditorium, where they had a very partial view of the stage, had an excellent view of the king or other royal personages. The English tradition placed the king and queen in proscenium boxes where they could enjoy close proximity to the actors performing on the wide forestage and, of course, also be seen to be doing so by their loyal subjects. The thrust stage favored by Tyrone Guthrie and the traverse arrangement that was popular in the 1970s can be seen, in a sense, as a democratic continuation of this much older tradition in which the audience is part of the show, providing in these cases not a rival show, an opportunity to stare at the rich and powerful, but a reminder to the spectators of their own presence, of their importance in the total performance event.

The central premise of Henri Lefebvre's seminal work is that "(Social) space is a (social) product," and he makes a number of further claims that are highly pertinent to this discussion of the social space of theatre:

> that the space thus produced also serves as a tool of thought and of action; that in addition to being a means of production it is also a means of control, and hence of domination, of power; yet that, as such, it escapes in part from those who would make use of it. (1991, 26)

Spectators' ability to move around in the auditorium and the nature of the social interaction that can take place are to a considerable extent controlled by architectural design, and conventions such as darkening the auditorium ensure that spectators' attention is fixed on the stage. Indeed, some actors get very irritated if there is evidence of anything other than rapt attention on the part of spectators, and the problems incurred by students taking notes for subsequent performance analysis (hardly evidence of lack of attention) indicate that audience behavior is strongly policed even in our ostensibly laissez-faire societies.

Old-style theatres segregate the audience in vertical levels according to ticket price, and the design of the building makes it very clear who is welcome in which part of the building, the degree of comfort they can expect, and how much of the stage they will be able to see. The architects were thus the agents of a highly stratified society; Charles Garnier, for example, could refer unashamedly to the stairs leading to the upper galleries in his opera house as "la division du corps social." The control exercised by architects today may be differently directed, but it is no less powerful than in Garnier's time, as is evident in a wonderfully revealing phrase attributed to Victor Glasstone (architect of the Barbican Theatre): "The absence of aisles in the stalls will obviate the horror of actors fooling about in them—a dated practice . . . that should be forbidden" (Bergan 1990, 34). It is, of course, not just in the older theatres that audience (and actor) behavior is constrained by the space, and alternative theatre spaces can be equally, perhaps even more, constraining. Spectators may be obliged to stand up for the duration of the show, they may be required to move from site to site during the performance, they may be jammed uncomfortably close together on benches, they may be sitting on the floor. Many of these practices are in fact attempts to find alternatives to the traditional organization of the audience space and are part of a critique of the dominant bourgeois theatre that strongly marked the theatre in the 1970s. They are corroborating evidence for Lefebvre's claim that socially produced space escapes in part those who would make use of it. The irony is that, in the cause of liberating spectators from the constraints imposed by the traditional theatre spaces, equally powerful constraints are imposed.

Emerging from many recent discussions of theatre space is the vital and somewhat mysterious question of the way the arrangement of auditorium and presentational space facilitate (or impede) the flows of energy between the two. This factor, it seems, is the crucial one determining whether or not a given space will "work," whether or not spectators and actors will feel that the theatre experience is enhanced by the space, or whether, as for Simon Callow in Manchester, the space is a problem to be overcome. The first important fact to note is that the energy must flow both ways and not simply from actor to audience. The perceptive John Byng knew in 1794 that it was as important for Mrs. Siddons to receive his "quick applause" as for him to be able to "closely observe" her; John Gielgud speaks in his memoirs of the power of the Old Vic Theatre "to transform a collection of human beings into that curious, vibrant instrument for an actor—an audience" (qtd. in Bergan 1990, 96). From Gielgud's perspective the audience is an instrument upon which the actor plays, the vibrancy of its response vital to the actor's playing, and his comment is all the more interesting in that he recognizes the importance of the space itself in facilitating the flow of energy from the audience to the actor on the stage.

There are spaces that enhance and others that stifle response. Lenelis Kruse and Carl Graumann point out in a psychological study of theatre that, if psychologists treated the subjects in an experiment in the way that spectators in many theatres are treated (no exit possible during the experiment, rigidly fixed seating, firmly forward looking, the space darkened to focus attention on a single lit space, a similar reduction of sound among the subjects to focus on the sound emanating from the lit space), then this would be "to eliminate or at least maintain at a low level, undesired individual emotion" (Arnott et al. 1977, 149–57).

Psychologists make a connection between what they term the "information rate" of a building or environment and the psychological arousal levels among inhabitants or users (Arnott et al. 1977, 158–80). If the information rate is low, the building will be perceived as bland, even boring, and the inhabitants will be understimulated, even depressed. It was for this reason that hospitals began in the 1960s to introduce a little color into their stark white rooms, and schools began to hang pictures along their utilitarian corridors (Sommer 1969). Yet so many modern theatres, built with great optimism at this time, and the older theatres that were confidently modernized in the same period have a low information rate (dark-painted walls in the auditorium so as not to attract attention away from the stage, a large amount of empty space above the heads of spectators in the single tier auditorium, dark upholstery on the seats, removal of the divisions into boxes, and imposition of uniformity of seating), and it has only been with hindsight that the connection between the information rate of the audience space and the passivity of spectators has been postulated.

It can be suggested that the lack of mobility of modern audiences, the lack of communication between members of the social subgroups constituting the audience, now removed from their boxes and placed in long rows facing the stage, the low information rate of the audience space generally, and the ease with which the spectacle can be seen and heard all contribute to lower the energy levels in the auditorium, to create a kind of inertia where there was once dynamism. Iain Mackintosh concludes his study of theatre architecture with a convincing hypothesis: "almost all successful theatres might be analysable in terms of fields of energy" (1993, 168).

Audience space, as I have defined it, includes, in addition to the auditorium, all the other social areas in the theatre building, notably the stairways and corridors leading from the outside world into the auditorium, already evoked, the cloakrooms, bars, and restaurants, and the box office, site of the preliminary financial transaction that opens up the otherwise forbidden space of the interior. In these spaces, as in the auditorium, the nature and quantity of the decoration contribute to the information rate of the building and thus to the spectator's predisposition to arousal by the performance. At the Comédie Française there are busts of famous dramatic authors (the most recent being Tristan Bernard, who died in 1949) lining the corridor that leads to the pleasant salon in which spectators congregate in the intervals, there is a large statue of Voltaire at one end of this salon , busts of the "holy trinity" (Corneille, Racine, and Molière) over the massive fireplace at the other end, and above all there is the actual chair used by Molière in *Le Malade imaginaire*, protected now in a glass case and placed somewhat incongruously under a large television screen on which latecomers must view the performance until they are permitted to enter the auditorium. All of this provides an environment for cultured spectators that is redolent of the past; it stresses the role of the writer (theatre thus seems to exist to serve the written word), but it also provides (in Molière's chair) a tangible reference to the unbroken tradition connecting present to past and to the physicality of theatre.

Access to the auditorium can be very direct, and one can feel that the world outside is in close proximity, or the auditorium may have to be approached by multiple stairways and corridors. In a theatre like Sidetrack in the working-class Sydney suburb of Marrickville, when the jet planes roar overhead, the actors' voices are momentarily obliterated, and spectators are reminded of the fragility of the wooden walls and corrugated iron roof, of the precariousness of the separation between inside and outside and perhaps, by extension, of the vulnerability of the human body in the face of modern technology. The contrast with a palatial theatre like the Palais Garnier in Paris could not be more absolute: once inside the latter, spectators still have a considerable way to walk before reaching the auditorium, let alone finding their seats. As one proceeds further and further into this theatre, the world outside begins to seem very far away; even more bizarre, the exotic smoking rooms, the corridors and salons with their mirrors and chandeliers, are so elaborate and enthralling in themselves that one can even be tempted to linger there rather than going into the auditorium. Visitors flock to the building every day simply to wander around these public areas (the auditorium is often closed for rehearsals), and the performances must be compelling indeed to rival with the impact of the building itself.

In London the West End theatres frequently segregate their spectators even more radically than the seating arrangements in tiers that has already been mentioned. In these theatres there are often different entrances, situated on different streets for the different levels of seats. Thus, in the Aldwych, for example, spectators in the cheaper seats enter the theatre from a side street to find themselves confronted immediately by a stairwell. They must then climb a couple of flights of uncarpeted stairs, the walls unrelieved by any decoration, before finally entering their part of the auditorium (upper circle or gallery).

The connection between going to the theatre and the consumption of food and drink is long-standing, and there are fascinating differences in the customs and conventions that prevail in different places in this respect. In the 1940s and 1950s matinee audiences in London's West End theatres could have a tray of tea and cakes brought to their seats in the interval, and, while this quaint custom has been discontinued, it is very common for alcoholic drinks to be sold at interval, and the bar is a common feature of the audience space in most theatres. In Sydney many theatres contain a restaurant, and, although this is not so in Paris, where cafés and bistros are to be found on every street corner, it is increasingly the case in suburban theatres and in the modern arts complexes. This is, in part, a response by theatre managements to the difficulties modern audiences have in getting a meal after work if they are going to the theatre, but it seems to me that more is involved here than the good business sense of modern theatre managers. The effect is to signal very clearly that theatre is part of the leisure industry, and what is being sold is a good night out; this impacts in subtle (and not so subtle) ways upon the choice of productions. Interestingly enough, it still does not seem to be accepted behavior to eat during a theatre performance, in contrast to the cinema, where the consumption of popcorn and Coca-Cola has become de rigueur in many parts of the world.

The phenomenon of the megamusical has brought merchandising to the theatre, and so in a number of theatre foyers space has had to be found for a shop where souvenirs of the performance can be sold. In subsidized theatres, too, as in many museums and galleries, it is increasingly common to find a gift and souvenir shop; for example, the Comédie Française and the Palais Garnier have shops that sell books and videos of their own productions as well as a range of tasteful and expensive souvenirs. This commercial activity around the theatre underscores the commercial basis for the theatre itself and is to an extent in conflict with the idea of theatre as art. In the suburban theatres around Paris and in regional arts centers there is often a bookshop in the theatre foyer. These may sell playscripts and books associated with the current productions, or they may stock a more broadly based performing arts collection, but in either case they function to signal the inscription of the theatre in a wider cultural project. Here it seems that the concern is less the commercial exploitation of theatre than the provision of a cultural resource to an area otherwise bereft of such benefits.

These observations concerning the audience space would be incomplete without some reference to the box office, or the site of financial transaction. Usually situated very near to the main entrance, sometimes in the foyer, sometimes in an interstitial space between outside and inside, separated from the foyer by doors through which one can obtain tantalizing glimpses of the domain within, it is in most Western theatres clearly part of the audience space. Indeed, it is frequently the first space to be negotiated by the spectator, for without a ticket one will not be permitted to enter any further into the building. The status of the box office changes, however, depending on the nature of the theatre space. The busker's open guitar case on the ground in front of him is situated in practitioner space (spectators may approach it to put coins in it but would be unlikely to touch it or place themselves between it and the performer); a street performance at which a hat is taken round for contributions resituates the financial transaction both spatially and temporally in relation to the performance. The location of the box office gives some indication of the predominant relationship between spectator and theatre or event (paying customer, member of a club, worshiper at a shrine, etc.), and of course this will be further elaborated by the nature of the transaction and the amount of stress associated with it (from the length of the queues to the friendliness or otherwise of the box office staff).

Theatre practice over the centuries has tended to accentuate the distance between the financial transaction and experience of the performance. To Corneille in 1636, seeking an image at the end of *L'Illusion comique* to indicate to the spectators that what they have just been watching is a play within the play, the obvious choice was a scene in which the characters (thus revealed as actors) are counting and sharing out the box office takings. Rex Cramphorn, in his production of the play in 1978, replaced this scene with one in which the characters come on to take a curtain call, because he thought that for contemporary audiences Corneille's image would be meaningless or confusing, so far removed have most actors become from the financial transactions associated with the performance event. In contemporary theatre practice the spectators themselves are also distanced, in that the purchase of a ticket precedes entry into the performance space, occurs in a liminal space, may indeed in these days of telephone bookings and credit card payments take place in the virtual space of electronic technology. It is as though the theatre needs to separate itself from the contaminating effect of the financial transaction, as though we need to get that over with elsewhere so that we can commune with art or perhaps so that the illusion of the fictional world will not be destroyed by any reminders of the fact that this is play and we are paying for our pleasure. Indeed, it seems that the distance is accentuated the more the performances in question are a purely money-making activity, but the location of the box office at the front of the theatre is a continuing physical reminder of the financial realities.

Practitioner Space

It is difficult to write about this area of the overall theatre space as it has never been systematically documented in the past and is, still to this day, regarded as private by practitioners. In edifice theatres such as the Comédie Française, the Palais Garnier, and the Sydney Opera House in which visitors pay to go on guided tours of the building, they are rarely taken to see the actors' dressing rooms, and visitors are usually not permitted to walk on the stage either. Theatres may be public places, listed by Vitruvius and others as "utilitarian public buildings," but they contain certain areas that are extremely private.

Practitioner space, as I have defined it, includes the actors' point of entry to the theatre building, usually quite separate from the public entrances, possibly on another street, the dressing rooms, green room, or other social space provided for the artists, and the areas around, under, and above the stage that the spectators never see; one of the major features of all these places is that they are private, inaccessible to the public. The stage itself is, of course, the heart of the practitioner space, and, although this is seen by the public, and indeed seen intensively, it is nevertheless still utterly separate from the audience space. Simon Callow delights in the separation of public from private:

> The division between the auditorium, with its velvet and gilt, or even its mauve and grey concrete, and the functional stage, with its ropes and wires, its steep black brick walls, its little purple lights and tables full of props, wheels and weights, staircases leading down into the bowels of the building, and ladders leading up to the giddy flies, remains a potent phenomenon: the romance of work, the juju of craft—and all secret. Our kingdom. (1985, 181–82)

Backstage is the world of work, of craft, it belongs to those who have the skill to make it work, and it seems that their power to do this is in part dependent on keeping the working reality of the theatre carefully hidden from the eyes of the profane.

One exception to this in the contemporary theatre seems to be the lighting, for not only are batteries of lights hung on the front of galleries and boxes in even the most illusionistic theatres, but the lighting operator is often visibly situated in the auditorium with all his or her associated high-tech equipment. The intrusive presence of modern theatre lights can be somewhat disconcerting in a carefully restored eighteenth- or nineteenth-century theatre such as the Comédie Française or the Deutsches Theater, though much less so in the functionalist theatre buildings of the 1960s onward. Revealing the source of the lights was part of Brecht's attempt to demystify the theatre, to show that the performance was the result of work, not magic, and his practice has been so influential that the lighting grid has come to form an accepted part of the decor in modern theatres. So much so, indeed, that it is often hardly noticed by the spectators.

In the early days of professional theatre the separation of spectator and actor, backstage and front of house, was by no means as complete as it has since become. In France privileged spectators sat on the stage itself, and, as Rotrou shows in his play *Saint Genest,* written in 1647, some were in the habit of going backstage even during the performance: there is a scene in the play-within-the-play in which Genest, the manager of the troupe, complains to the emperor for whom he is performing about the behavior of members of the court who have invaded the backstage area during the first interval and are importuning the actresses.

The need for privacy and seclusion during both performance and the work process leading up to it can be justified on many grounds, but it must be acknowledged that this privacy also serves to hide the sordid nature of the working conditions provided for actors and production staff. Anthony Hopkins, in the foreword he wrote for Ronald Bergan's beautifully illustrated historical account of *The Great Theatres of London,* makes the very pertinent point that "sometimes there is too great a contrast between the glamour and luxury of the front of house and the cramped squalor back stage" (1990, 6), but he does not give any information about which theatres he has in mind in this connection. Nor does Bergan discuss the backstage arrangements in any of the theatres he describes, and there are no photographs of "cramped squalor" to offset the elegance of auditorium and foyer recorded in his book. It is as though there is a tacit agreement among everyone concerned to ignore the fact that the conditions in which actors work are frequently shabby, even dirty, drafty, and unacceptably spartan.

In some theatres there are only two dressing rooms, one for men and one for women. At Belvoir Street, where this is the case, privacy is even further reduced by the fact that one of these rooms can be accessed only through the other. As these dressing rooms are on a floor below the stage, actors must negotiate a steep and narrow staircase every time they come from the dressing room. While such lack of privacy can be stressful, it can also provide a sense of community, and the energy that this generates can be palpable in the subsequent performances. The communal dressing room at the Sydney Theatre Company's Wharf Theatre ("six rows of dressing tables, three tables per row, with only a flimsy curtain as a concession to modesty") is singled out by Paul Goddard as one of the major attractions for actors of working in that theatre:

> over the years, this communal set up has proven to be a fertile ground for play where the cast, who might not have seen very much of each other during rehearsal, can really come together . . . Watching some of the more senior members of the profession backstage has been one the most enduring joys of working in Wharf 1. (Qtd. in Spinks and Baird 1995, 86)

At a theatre like the Comédie Française, where actors form part of a permanent ensemble, members of the troupe each have their own dressing room, which they furnish with their own belongings, but this is hardly possible when actors are moving in and out of theatres every few weeks.

Fig. 6. An example of "cramped squalor." The stage door
entrance in a Parisian theatre that shall remain nameless. (Photography by the author.)

Simon Callow has described how important the dressing room is to an actor, how during a long run it takes on more and more the quality of a home from home, and how actors need to personalize the space in some way:

> You lay out your make-up in front of the mirror, you hang your towel up and pin a couple of cards to the wall. In these little ways, it begins to be *your* dressing room. By the end of the run, you'll need a pantechnicon van to haul away the accumulated interior decorations. (1985, 183)

Allocation of dressing rooms (who gets a private room, who must share with one or two others, who is in the communal room, who has the dressing rooms with convenient access to the stage, who has four flights of stairs to negotiate, who has the luxury of a private shower or bathroom) is clearly a very delicate matter and potentially a source of friction. The celebrity status of the actor and the size of the role in the play are the major factors taken into account, so it is evident that, even in such a functional matter as provision of dressing rooms, complex questions of self-esteem and morale are involved.

The stage door is the physical manifestation of the demarcation between the world at large and the "secret kingdom" of the theatre practitioners, between public and private, between outside and inside. Any door is, as Gaston Bachelard argues in his *Poetics of Space*, an incitement to dream, and, depending on whether the door is open or closed, the dreams fall into two distinct categories (1957, 200). A stage door is, however, never wide open, nor is it locked and bolted; it is, as Bachelard might say, "a door of hesitation," and it is a particularly potent force in that the separation that it marks is so absolute. It remains resolutely closed and may even be guarded by an official doorkeeper, and when it does open it is only for a moment. Spectators gathered in the darkness outside hoping for a glimpse of a favorite actor after the play (or is it that they are confusing actor and character, and are there because they are reluctant to quit the fictional world created onstage, desiring [in vain] to bring the fiction of the play into contact with their own reality?), "stage door johnnies" in top hats, carrying flowers and bottles of champagne and bribing the doorkeeper to let them in, the "star" leaving the theatre, mobbed by autograph hunters, these are all images in our collective imaginary, sedulously cultivated by Hollywood.

The reality is frequently rather bleak: unmarked doors, suggestive of warehouse or factory rather than theatre, basement entrances in

Fig. 7. The factory-style stage door at the Théâtre Mogador.
(Photography by the author.)

anonymous courtyards, armored doors in back streets, doors opened
only to those possessing the security code, doors guarded by uniformed
doorkeepers. At the Sydney Opera House the artists' entrance has been
demystified to the extent that it is situated between a scenery bay and the
souvenir shop, adjacent to a major public entrance. There is no sign indicating that this is the artists' entrance, but there is no secrecy either. It
consists of a glassed-in booth in which the doorkeepers sit, visible to any
passersby, checking people's credentials and signing them in before

admitting them. Once admitted, there is a flight of stairs leading directly into the canteen, usually crowded, and then corridors leading to offices and dressing rooms. The dominant impression is of public service efficiency, a large institution that provides clean, functional working conditions but no romance. Access to the backstage at the Comédie Française through the administration entrance, upstairs through the little Foyer La Grange (where press conferences are sometimes held), is controlled by the actors in that the door handle can be activated only from their side of the door. Anyone privileged to be invited as far as the Foyer La Grange must then sit and wait until the door opens. This is indeed a door that is highly charged with psychic power, in Bachelard's terms. It is evident why Strindberg should choose a stage door as the object that haunts the dreams of the Officer in *A Dream Play*. The stage door at the Mogador is controlled by an intercom and consists of a smaller door cut into the huge metal gate through which scenery is delivered. The impression is of a factory entrance, and this is confirmed when one is admitted and finds oneself in a long concrete driveway, the blank walls of neighboring buildings on either side.

Social space for the practitioners in their domain is rarely provided except in big theatres. Even when such space is made available it is usually rudimentary (a few armchairs, a coffee table, and possibly a drink vending machine) and will be resumed by the management if the production in question needs an additional room for quick costume changes or if there are a large number of performers. In big theatres there may be a canteen (more or less institutional in atmosphere), a bar, or even a comfortable communal sitting room (the one at the Comédie Française is hung with numerous fine portraits of famous actors of the past and must contribute to the sense actors in this company surely have of being valued, of belonging to a highly privileged elite).

This last point raises the broader question of the nature of the frame that the physical reality of the theatre building provides for the practitioners. What does this framing tell them about the activity they are engaged in and about the way this activity is valued in society? It is evident that theatres vary considerably in the degree of comfort and in the facilities provided for the people who work there, but the key factor that seems common to all the types of theatre building I have explored is the sense of separation between the workaday world of production and the glamour/leisure framing of the spectator's experience. The practitioner's experience is framed as fundamentally utilitarian. To come into a theatre through the stage door is to be struck by two things: the complexity and power of the "machine" of the stage and the unadorned, often bleak nature of the areas occupied by the theatre workers. It may be that it is the power and complexity that constitute the dominant frame, which is borne out in Simon Callow's joyful assumption of ownership, but the spartan conditions, the squalor noted by Anthony Hopkins, provide a further underlying message that the actor's profession is not very highly regarded by society at large. The strong demarcation between audience space and practitioner space, experienced from the audience side, serves to constitute the practitioners' domain as one of mystery and romance. Experienced from the practitioners' side, it serves rather to construct the spectators as a potentially dangerous force: so disruptive that they must be kept on the other side of the barricade formed by the stage door, imposing by their presence in the auditorium a rigid discipline of silence and invisibility on the stage crew and constituting a "wall of death" when viewed from too close.[5]

Rehearsal Space

There is a further, often ignored, aspect of practitioner space that needs to be considered: the rooms used for rehearsal. These are never seen by the public as the rehearsals are very much part of the hidden domain of theatre production, but they can have a significant impact on the final production. Some theatre buildings include rehearsal space, the dimensions of which more or less match those of the stage, and these rooms may at times be rented out to other companies, rehearsing with a view to performance in completely different venues. Companies that occupy their own theatre may be able to rehearse for several weeks onstage and in the actual decor, but most groups are obliged to rent rehearsal space wherever they can find it.

In an established theatre like the Deutsches Theater, for example, plays are rehearsed in the decor on stage for several weeks, and the company also owns rehearsal space in a building near the theatre. Plays in the season's repertoire alternate each night, and new productions are brought into the repertoire progressively. Each night after the performance, the stage crew strike one set and erect another for the next morning's rehearsal; the rehearsal must finish at 1:00 P.M. so that the set for the evening's performance can be put in place and checked. Such luxury would be unimaginable in most places, and, even in relatively well-financed theatres such as the Sydney Theatre Company, no play can be rehearsed onstage for more than a couple of days, and most of this time is taken up with technical rehearsals. Companies that do not have regular access to a particular theatre must rent rehearsal space, and the spaces available for rental may bear little relation to the actual stage that will be used.

The nature of the rehearsal space, its level of comfort or discomfort, cleanliness, warmth, and the facilities provided, are a further dimension of the physical framing of the practitioners' experience that has just been discussed in relation to the backstage space in the theatre. The location of the rehearsal space in the city, ease of access by public transport, and security after dark are other features that can weigh heavily on the people obliged to work there, and it must be acknowledged that actors frequently put up with physical conditions that would provoke strike action in other workplaces. The fact that in a city like Sydney suitable rehearsal space is difficult to find and expensive to rent is a significant factor in determining not only the quality but also the quantity of theatre produced there. It also determines to a certain extent what sort of theatre is produced: young, experimental, and avant-garde theatre groups can rarely afford the development and rehearsal time they need, and so the law of the market functions as effectively as state censorship in determining whose voice may be heard in the theatre. As Lefebvre argues "space is a means of control and hence of domination, of power" (1991, 26), and one of the major forms of control is determining who shall have access to what space.

Over the last ten years I have observed and documented a number of rehearsal processes and have become fascinated by the way spatial features of the rehearsal room, which may not be part of the set design, are utilized by the actors, even to the extent of becoming a significant part of the spatialization of the action. In one project actors were working on the scene in *Phèdre* in which Phèdre, thinking that her husband is dead, confesses to Hippolyte that she loves him. They were exploring the performance implications of a number of different English translations of this scene, and the work was being done in a space made available by the University of Sydney: a large rectangular room with high windows on two sides, which had originally been built (a hundred years ago) as a school. There were no props, apart from Hippolyte's sword, and no furniture. The floor was covered with very shabby linoleum that bore the

marks of many earlier projects, and on the part of the floor the actors
were using there was a large circle, about three meters in diameter,
scratched deep into the lino. As the actors (John Howard and Gillian
Jones) worked at the scene in Robert Lowell's translation, the characters
began to take shape as a coldly hostile Hippolytus and a passionate,
physically active Phaedra. John Howard stood with his arms folded at
the center of the space, and Gillian Jones circled around him, more and
more frenetically, occasionally coming in closer to try and touch him. It
was not apparent to me or, I think, to anyone else watching the development of the scene, that the circle on the floor had anything to do with the
circular movement of the actress or with the highly accentuated notion of
center/periphery that emerged from the blocking, and this was never
discussed between the actors and the director.

Some days into the project, however, when the actors had begun to
work on another translation of the scene (Tony Harrison's *Phaedra Bri-
tannica*, set in colonial India), a decision was made to lay some hardboard
sheets over the unsightly lino. Harrison's translation inspired the actors
to develop two very different characters: a morally upright, physically
inhibited Governor's Wife (Phèdre) and a diffident, unassertive Thomas
(Hippolyte). When the work began, the old floor was still in place, and
the first attempts at blocking situated Thomas at one side of the space,
with the Memsahib occupying the center, and it seemed to me that,
though the relative positions of the characters were reversed and the
bodily tensions were very different, the actors were still working with
the idea of center and periphery. When they arrived for the second session of work the new flooring was in place and, by chance, the boards
had been laid so that four rectangular sheets came together at the center
of what had become the presentational space, thus forming a faintly visible cross on the floor. During the course of this session a blocking was
developed based on the notion of distance, and I was intrigued to notice
that the two actors positioned themselves always in relation to the horizontal and vertical axes formed by the cracks between the sheets of hardboard. Once again, the discussion between actors and director was more
concerned with character and motivation, and yet the physical realization of the ideas discussed made active use of the lines on the floor. The
circularity of the Lowell version had become so well entrenched in the
actors' body memory that it was not affected by the removal of the circle
on the floor, but the introduction of the cross marking horizontal and
vertical axes at a moment when the blocking of the scene was quite

unformed was clearly of critical importance, even though it is unlikely that the participants were consciously aware of this.

In another project the set had been designed before the actors began their work, a very common procedure in contemporary theatre practice. On this occasion actors were working on the same scene from Genet's *The Maids* in two different presentational spaces, one a proscenium arch stage, set with a realistic bedroom, as described in the stage directions, the other an open stage covered with a white cloth that also ran up the back wall, furnished with only two objects: the white dress, hanging up against the back wall; and the poisoned tea, contained in a huge teapot placed on a high stand diagonally opposite the dress. Elaine Hudson and Robyn Gurney had begun by preparing the scene in the realistic space, rehearsing in the set, but, when they were scheduled to begin work on the stylized version they could not get access to the theatre and had to use a rehearsal room elsewhere in the building. There were no windows in the small rectangular room they were obliged to use and no furniture apart from a few stacking chairs, although the floor was clean and polished. The overwhelming feeling was one of enclosure. The actors looked around the space, clearly feeling at something of a loss about how to proceed. They then sat on the floor in the middle of the room and decided to reread the whole scene. As they read and reread, they gradually began to physicalize the action of the scene, locating this exclusively in terms of their two bodies and the floor they were sitting on. The next day, working in the set dominated by the strong verticals of the dress hanging on the back wall and the high stand with the teapot, they nevertheless remained sitting, lying, crouched, or crawling on the floor. Furthermore, a very strong sense of imprisonment emerged from their performance, notwithstanding the open stage surrounded on three sides by spectators, and it was as though they had brought the oppressive enclosure of the rehearsal space into the theatre with them.

It is well-known that the moment of transferring work from rehearsal space to stage is often fraught with tension and a sense that what had been found in the one space has been lost in the transfer. This occurs even when the set design has been known from the beginning, when the dimensions have been scrupulously respected throughout, and when the actual props have been used in rehearsal. Movements and gestures that were clear and compelling in the rehearsal room seem somehow diminished, and intensive work is needed to discover anew how such moves can be made compelling on the stage. All this is evidence of

actors' extreme sensitivity to spatial factors, to their own bodily experience of place, and of the complexity of the process by which a performance takes shape. The rehearsal space is never a neutral container and,
however bleak and empty it may seem to the observer, it is likely to
imprint aspects of its own reality on both the fictional world that is being
created and even on the physical reality of the set that will ultimately
replace the mock-up so carefully indicated within its confines by means
of gaffer tape on the floor and bits and pieces of furniture.

Presentational Space

A theatre building, as has often been remarked, is centripetal, and it is
the stage that is at the center, seeming to exert a magnetic force on everyone entering the building, whether it is approached from the auditorium
or from the practitioners' domain. In the terminology I have adopted the
stage is both stage space and presentational space (a notion that includes
the scenographic arrangement of the stage in any particular performance
and its occupation by the actors), and it possesses a rather ambivalent
status in that it is both very definitely practitioner space and yet in a certain way is also part of the audience space. No modern spectator would
willingly go onto the stage during the performance, and, if spectators
have to cross the stage before or even after the show in order to get to or
from their seats, they do so hastily and with a definite sense of trans-
gression, of being "out of place." Yet the stage is the focus of spectators'
attention throughout the performance and before and a space that is so
intensively watched becomes part of the watchers' physical and psychic
reality. The spectators possess the stage by virtue of their intensive
watching, but, of course, this possession is dependent upon the stage
being revealed to them, and the theatre is an art form in which the
process of revelation has been exploited in every conceivable way.

　　Gaston Bachelard devotes a whole chapter of his *Poétique de l'espace*
to cupboards, drawers, chests, and caskets because for him these con-
tainers are "veritable organs of the secret psychological life" (1957, 83),
and the complex dialectic between inside and outside, hidden and
revealed, given and withheld, that such objects perpetuate in our domestic lives is for him a source of endless fascination. It seems to me that any
stage (not just the illusionistic box stage, although this is obviously a
prime example) has a psychic function that is analogous to Bachelard's

casket and that the theatre is constantly playing with the possibilities of revelation, with the relationship between the shown and the not-shown, the shown and the partially shown.

The way the interface between auditorium and stage is marked is highly significant. Spectators, having crossed the threshold from the public space outside the theatre to the theatre itself and traversed all the intervening interior thresholds to be admitted to the auditorium, may find that the stage is already open and accessible (or partially accessible, depending on lighting levels) to their gaze, or it may be closed off with a curtain. The performance proper begins when the curtain opens, and it ends when the curtain closes, and it may be temporarily interrupted for brief periods by the same means. Even though this revealing and hiding function has been taken over by lighting in much modern theatre practice, the function itself is so fundamental to the theatre experience that the curtain (the material object that represents the function) figures as an emblem of theatre, even to people who must rarely go to the theatre: for example, on TV game shows when teams must mime the titles of books, films, or plays, the sign that the title in question is that of a play is a gesture indicating a curtain opening.

The stage curtain, closed at the beginning of the performance, constitutes the stage as object, and it is something to be experienced from the outside, an object in the spectators' world. The curtain itself may be more or less gorgeous, more or less an object of contemplation in itself, or it may be a purely functional screen, serving in the most basic way to block temporarily the spectators' access to what is behind. The magnificence of the curtain may invite the spectator to pause, to contemplate it for itself (a statement about the glamour and excitement of the theatre experience); it may carry some significant design (e.g., the dove on Copeau's Vieux Colombier curtain that has been incorporated into the design of the renovated façade of the building, or John Olsen's "curtain of the sun" for the Sydney Opera House), it may speak of the age of the theatre and past tradition (the dusty grandeur of faded red velvet in many older theatres).

Whether the curtain is magnificent or purely functional, and whatever the further connotations of its design, its psychic function is the same: to provoke a sense of anticipation, to indicate that, although we have penetrated thus far, there is yet another threshold before us. The curtained stage is Bachelard's closed casket, something to be experienced from the outside, an object in the world, but one that nevertheless suggests tantalizingly that there is an interior, that something will be revealed. As soon as the curtain opens and the world within is revealed, the inversion of exterior and interior occurs, the spectator enters the world of denegation, the world outside recedes, loses its power temporarily in face of the superior power of attraction of the performance. The performance is, however, marked as performance, and its power is fragile: the least technical hitch or untoward occurrence can destroy it, and the reactions of irritation or mockery that these can trigger in the spectators is evidence of the profound level of the psychic forces in play.

In the move out of traditional theatres into found spaces in the 1960s and 1970s, and in the remodeling of old theatres that occurred at the same period, the front curtain was often abandoned along with the proscenium arch and the whole emphasis on illusionistic staging. The dialectic of the hidden and the revealed is, however, so fundamental to theatre that, even in the most literal of task-based performance, it tends to reassert itself. In the work of the Sydney Front, for example, while the group's aesthetic eschewed acting in favor of doing, a major recurring trope in all their shows was the dynamics of revelation. The most radical instance of this occurred in *The Pornography of Performance* (1989), in which the spectators entered the performance space to find a number of large cylindrical tubes standing at intervals around the space. The tubes were perforated with holes at strategic positions, and spectators were encouraged to put their hands into the holes; when they did so, what they found were the naked bodies of the performers, each one standing inside his or her tube. The performers were anonymous, hidden, but utterly vulnerable in that they were naked and had their arms above their heads, offering and yet at the same time withholding their bodies from the spectators.

Lighting is the principal means utilized in contemporary theatre to set the hiding/revealing dialectic in motion, and the infinitely varied effects achievable with modern lighting technology have brought the lighting designer to the fore as one of the key creative figures in the contemporary theatre. The stage can be a black hole, or it can be readily visible to the spectators as they come into the auditorium: elements of the set can be dimly present if the stage is only partially lit, clues to what might follow, a source of reverie and anticipation to each spectator. Until the set is occupied by the performers, however, it exists in a kind of lambent state, an incitement to dream rather than an active element in a complex total artwork. The course of the performance can be interrupted by blackouts, either marking the ends of major segments of performance after which the exterior reality is allowed to reassert itself (and the spectators may even be encouraged to leave the auditorium) or, more mysteriously, maintaining the spectator in the dramatic fiction but nevertheless interrupting this, marking a temporal or spatial hiatus in the fiction without interrupting the performance. In some modern productions in which lighting levels are kept very low throughout (Giorgio Strehler's production of *L'Illusion comique* at the Odéon in Paris in 1984 was an early and brilliant example of this kind of lighting, which has since become something of a fashion) there is a sense of partial revelation only, of a vast domain that is suggested but withheld; one glimpses rather than sees.

The physical reality of the stage is a given of the theatre building, and, although it can be altered in appearance by the set, it is for the practitioners a major factor in determining many aspects of the performance. These same physical features also serve to condition in subtle and often unrecognized ways the spectators' response. Spectators may blame the production for what is in reality a feature of the building, and, conversely, practitioners may blame the building when what is at fault is their failure to take into account its unavoidable physical features. John Howard's comments on performing in the Wharf Theatre provide insight into the extent to which actors must adjust and tune the different components of their performance to compensate for specific qualities of the building:

> Because the audience is sitting above they feel like they're further away from you than you do from them when you're performing. If actors are not careful, they don't speak loudly enough to be heard by the back rows. The audience can feel slightly excluded. A lot of the sound goes up into the lighting rig where the structure absorbs it. Your vocal energy has to be as clear as in other, larger spaces, but you have the chance to be a bit more subtle in terms of gesture and facial expression. (Qtd. in Spinks and Baird 1995, 89)

The dimensions of the stage in relation to the bodies of the performers, and in relation to the auditorium, the width of the stage opening (relatively narrow in relation to a fan- or horseshoe-shaped auditorium or virtually as wide as the auditorium, as is the case in many modern theatres), the depth of the stage, the nature of the interface with the audience (from the traditional end stage to the many varieties that have been explored during the course of this century: open, thrust, traverse, in the round, etc.), the degree of separation from the audience (if there is a forestage, the actors can approach the spectators more closely, an orchestra pit creates a strongly marked separation, a proscenium arch tends to enclose the actors in their separate space, a simple platform offers them to the spectators' gaze whether or not there are steps or ramps facilitating physical access between the two spaces), whether the stage is flat or raked, and how steeply raked, the amount of space at the sides and the back of the stage, the number and position of doors to the stage, and where they lead in the practitioner space are all extremely important features that impact upon the nature of the performances that will "work" in the space, the nature of the acting required, and the degree of physical stress on the practitioners.

Any stage is an instrument: some are very complex in what they can offer and what they demand, others are much simpler, but all require the creative input of a number of artists and artisans, skilled in different but related techniques, and all these practitioners need to learn to play the instrument that is the stage, just as a musician needs to learn to play his instrument. Knowledge of a particular form of stage can be lost, especially where so little craft knowledge is written down, for in an oral culture like that of the theatre it takes only a couple of generations for knowledge to be lost. In the contemporary theatre, in which actors are usually hired for the given production only, in which there are very few ensemble companies occupying their own theatre, in which directors and designers tend increasingly to be freelance, and the most prestigious travel from city to city, even country to country, rarely staying in any one theatre for more than a single production, and in which theatres are constantly being demolished, rebuilt, or remodeled, it is difficult for any group to gain an intimate knowledge of a particular instrument.

It can take years for actors, directors, and designers to learn how to use a certain theatre and even longer before that theatre becomes really necessary to them in artistic terms. The Drama Theatre at the Sydney Opera House is a case in point: an extremely wide proscenium opening and a relatively shallow stage transformed any dramatic exchange into a tennis match for spectators near the front, while for those near the back the experience was sometimes akin to that of watching a cinemascope film on television. It has taken twenty years for designers to find ways to use this stage so that it enhances rather than detracts from the dramas presented on it. Introduction of new stage machinery, such as a revolve, can also take time to become more than a gimmick and for artists to find an inner necessity in the use of such equipment. Other theatres, ostensibly highly desirable in terms of performance potential, are ignored for years (such as the old style proscenium arch theatres in Paris during the

1970s or the delightful thrust stage, so beloved of Tyrone Guthrie, in the York Theatre at the Seymour Centre in Sydney that has rarely been well used in the twenty-five years of its existence).

The presentational space is made up of both the architectural features of the stage as it exists in any given theatre or performance venue and the organization of this space for the production in question. At certain periods over the long history of theatre in the West, visual spectacle has become dominant in the theatre experience (court masques and "spectacles à machines" in seventeenth-century England and France, the late-nineteenth-century theatre in which shipwrecks, storms, fires, and all manner of spectacular scenic effects were incorporated into the drama on the slimmest of pretexts), and it seems that we are again moving toward a theatre in which the visual component is dominant. The designer has become a major force in contemporary theatre, and, although the director still has the overall artistic control of the production, the quasi-authorial function that has been evolving over the course of the century since directors first emerged as a creative agent in their own right, is more and more seen to be exercised by a creative team. The members usually include the director, the designer, and, working in close collaboration with the latter, the costume and lighting designers. The task is not simply to provide magnificent spectacle and scenic effects as in earlier periods of visual excess (although this may also be a requirement) but to convey in a striking visual manner what the production is about, hence the need for a shared vision and artistic compatibility. For Matthias Langhoff the decor is the creative development of the "idea" contained in a performance project, "its transformation into a working, material form" (1996, 9). It is the word *working* in this description that seems to me to best articulate the desired quality: however elaborate the decor, however magnificent the scenic effects (and in the contemporary theatre these can be lavish indeed), their function is a dynamic or active one, and they are not conceived as a mere pictorial backdrop to, or container for, the dramatic action.

A well-known designer, speaking to students about his work on some recent and highly successful musical productions in Australia and Britain, referred to the "creative people" in the production; when pressed to elaborate, he specified these as the director, the designer, and the composer, and he explicitly excluded performers from this group. It is clear that contemporary theatre practice, especially in the larger subsidized companies, endorses this view of the creative process insofar as the design is commissioned and largely complete before the play has been fully cast and certainly before the actors have done any work together. Antony Sher provides valuable insights into the problems this practice poses for the actor, and indeed for the production as a whole, in his diary account of the production of *Richard III:*

> I now feel encumbered by the monster image. But we are being pressurised to make up our minds—the wardrobe staff can't begin to make my costumes until the exact measurements of the deformity are settled. This seems to be putting the cart before the horse. Ideally, I would like several weeks working just on the text, then a couple of weeks experimenting with shapes and movements, and only then should we decide what he's going to look like. Of course that's impossible with the theatre system in this country. For instance Bill D's set designs had to be in by February. And however exciting they might look, they closed all other options long before rehearsals—and the real exploration of the play—had even started. (1985, 160)

For the actors the "real exploration" of the play is what occurs in the rehearsal room, yet for a successful designer working in big-budget productions the actors are not even included among the "creative people": the tension between these two perceptions of the theatre process is evident, and, as the history of theatre shows, the expressive power of the art form is always reduced if one of its constituent voices becomes too loud, another suppressed.

One of Peter Brook's insights, gained after years of experience, is that the set is much more a function of the theatre building than of the play: "The principle of the decor is determined by the theatre building rather than by the play" (1970, n.p.), and so he argues it is folly to take a play *and* its decor on tour. It is the building itself, the architectural features of the presentational space in their relationship with the audience space, that demands a certain kind of decor, a certain kind of staging, while the play can accommodate itself to numerous styles of decor or even none at all. In Brook's opinion, then, it seems that the "play," and perhaps even a given production of it, exists in a way that is independent of any particular presentational space.

A completely different view of the function of the decor is that of André Antoine, who designed his own sets and saw this as part of the director's role. For Antoine, elaborating the theory and practice of naturalism in the theatre and at the same time inventing the role of the director, the primary function of the set was to create in as much detail as possible the fictional world of the dramatic action. For any given scene, or fictional place, he liked first to work out the disposition of all the rooms or places around and beyond it, the design had to situate the room *in* the house, the house *in* the city, then he would decide on the arrangement of all the elements in the room, even those that would not be seen, and only when the design of the *locus dramatis* as a whole was complete would the question of the position of the audience be considered. The angle of vision from which the audience would view the fictional place, determined by the removal of the famous "fourth wall," was considered only after the fictional place had taken on as full and as detailed an existence as possible (Antoine 1903, 596–612).

It is interesting to discover that David Williamson, writing *Don's Party* in 1972, used a very similar method, not simply to create a vivid sense of place but also in order to structure the dramatic action of his play (which occurs at a party held on the night of a general election):

> But how to get it on stage? A party? Everyone on stage all the time. Couldn't be done. Could it? I drew a map of the layout of a typical suburban house of the time, made cardboard tabs with each character's name on and kept moving them as the party progressed so I would know who was where and who, therefore, was likely to collide and create the next disruption. (1997, n.p.)

The action of the play thus emerged from the spatial organization of the fictional place, and the sequence of events was determined by the "collisions" this spatial organization permitted.

A third perspective on the function of decor and the place of the design process is provided by accounts of Caspar Neher's work with Brecht and the insights that Brecht derived from this long collaboration. For both of them the "set needs to spring from the rehearsal of groupings, so in effect it must be a fellow-actor" (Willett 1986, 98), and Neher began always with the action, drawing dozens of sketches of nodal points in the action, which were then used by the actors and Brecht as a starting point for the blocking when they began to rehearse. He would be present in the rehearsal room, watching the actors as they discovered the logistics of the physical action, incorporating details from this work into his final set designs. As Egon Monk recalled, Neher would never begin to sketch the space or even talk about it "until he knew what was supposed to *take place* in it" (106), and the first sketches were moments of action (e.g., an open window with a woman leaning out, a door with a man leaping through, but no indication of where the window or door were situated). The set was thus not a backdrop or a container for the action or a representation of the fictional place but, rather, an integral part of the action, a "fellow-actor," as Brecht observed.

The power of the presentational space to constrain or inflect the meanings emerging from the actors' work or to encapsulate and, as it were, body forth these meanings is well illustrated in the two productions of *Britannicus* that Rex Cramphorn directed in 1980 and 1982, in Sydney and Melbourne, respectively. The two productions used essentially the same text, translated by Cramphorn himself, they sprang from essentially the same directorial conception of the play, and yet they were markedly different in atmosphere and in the meanings they conveyed. In Sydney the presentational space was a square, flat surface surrounded on three sides by steeply raked seating; in Melbourne the performance space was too shallow to allow for a similar arrangement, the stage was a raised platform of an irregular hexagonal shape, and it included two long ramps projecting through the audience space, effectively dividing this into three sections.

The Sydney set (see fig. 8) consisted of a painted floorcloth, a back wall with a tall central door decorated with a Roman eagle and gilt laurel wreath, and opposite the door a stone bench. Behind the bench, in the audience space, there was a drum kit and music stand for the percussionist who accompanied the whole performance. The design on the floorcloth was reminiscent of a Roman mosaic pavement, and it included a pattern of sun rays overlaid by strongly marked geometric lines, marking major vertical and horizontal axes as well as diagonals leading from the central door to exits situated at the corners of the space (conceptualized in the dramatic geography of the piece as leading to the interior of the palace on the left and to the city beyond on the right). In the Melbourne set there was also a central door, placed between two obliquely angled walls (see fig. 9), with a small bench diametrically opposite the door, and here the whole set (door, bench, walls, and floor) was painted black. A complicated pattern of lines, marked by silver tape, accentuated the main focal points of the set (door, bench, walls, the two ramps leading into the audience space) and the relationship between these points. In the Sydney set the lines on the floorcloth led unequivocally to the central door, adorned with its symbol of imperial power, while those in the Melbourne set created a kind of web or maze. Actors leaving the stage by

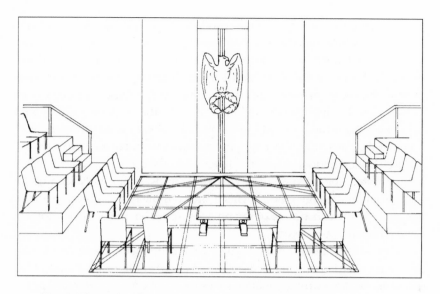

Fig. 8. Floor plan for Cramphorn's Sydney production of *Britannicus*

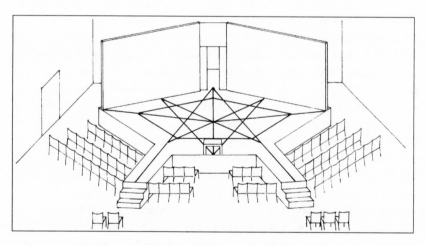

Fig. 9. Floor plan for Melbourne production of *Britannicus*

the diagonal exits in the Sydney production passed between the high banks of seating and left the performance space by doors in the side walls; in Melbourne actors leaving the stage by the two ramps walked through the audience space and sat on chairs against the back wall, behind the spectators, until their next entrance. The reason for this is that actors would either have had to circle around the sides of the audience and exit behind the back wall of the presentational space (thus suggesting that they were all proceeding in some way to and from Nero's room) or use the single door out to the foyer from the audience space (which would defeat the purpose of having two ramps, supposedly leading to two different offstage places). This is an example of a decision made in response to the constraints of the physical space having a crucial impact on the meaning conveyed.

The actors' moves in the Sydney production were plotted in terms of the geometric lines marked on the floor, with the result that certain positions became strongly loaded in terms of notions of power and powerlessness. The door (leading to the emperor's domain) was the place of maximum power, the diagonals leading away from it were places of weakness, the central vertical line, running from door to bench, the central horizontal line (particularly the mid point), and the horizontal line running across in front of the door were all positions of relative strength. Major speeches were delivered from nodal points in the design, and one of the effects of this spatial discipline was that the emotional and sexual conflicts involved were always seen in relation to the political power game.

In Melbourne the complex pattern of lines on the floor had emerged from the actors' movements in the space, and they marked the most frequently used pathways, but in performance there was no sense that these pathways constrained or controlled the characters' movements. The black walls and floor created a sense of interiority, and the space beyond the back door, also painted black, seemed to represent a further dimension of interiority. This was Nero's personal space far more than the seat of political power, and the web of lines on the floor were a kind of emblematic representation of the complexity and murky depths of the human forces in play. The set was painted with gloss paint that created a somewhat self-reflective surface under the strong stage lighting and created a subtle impression of narcissistic self-absorption that contributed to the depoliticization of this production compared to the Sydney one. It seemed to me at the time that the Sydney production presented a powerful statement about the limits of political power, about the moral and spiritual forces that can override political power. The Melbourne production, by contrast, with its emphasis on the twin images of the labyrinth and narcissistic self-reflection, seemed less concerned with political power than with the monstrous human reality that fuels the power conflict and with the vulnerability of the personal space.

The unsettling presence of the offstage actors in the audience space functioned as an image of the disruption their characters represent to Nero's control over Rome, but it also functioned as a strong counter-attraction to the backstage space beyond the door in the back wall. Thus, while the power of this space was somewhat diminished, it remained intangible and mysterious, in contrast to the vaguely troubling presence of the actors behind our chairs.

Whatever the reasons for the shift in ideology between the two productions, some of which have been illuminated in the interviews with actors recorded by Mark Minchinton in his analysis of Rex Cramphorn's work (1996), it is evident that spatial factors are extremely important in the overall result. The different spaces constrained the actors in different ways, created different viewing conditions for the spectators, and were instrumental in producing very different sets of meanings.

In Edward Casey's phenomenological study of place he devotes several pages to discussing the opposition between here and there, what he calls the "primary placial dyad" through which we experience the world and indeed through which we experience being. Being necessarily involves being-here, and being-here is intimately bound up with the body, for, as he says:

> it is by my body—my lived body—that I am here. My lived body is the vehicle of the here, its carrier or bearer (Träger), as Husserl called it.
>
> My here depends on my body: if I am sitting at my desk, then my here is the desk, if I go to the fridge to get a drink then the fridge, or perhaps the kitchen, is my here:
>
> . . . the fate of the here is tied entirely and exclusively to that of the body. If there are experiences in which my body does not figure, then these experiences will lack a here, or will possess only a quasi or pseudo here. (1993, 51)

The examples he gives of such quasi-here states include mystical and trance experiences and states induced by illness or physical damage to the brain. He does not mention the theatre, but it seems to me that in the theatre the spectator is regularly in a state of being only partly here and that the theatre experience involves both a here and a pseudo-here for the spectators and, in different ways, for the actors as well. Indeed, the theatre has chosen this very phenomenological terrain for its playground, which is rendered possible only by the very materiality of the here constituted by both the actors' and the spectators' bodily presence.

In the theatre it is not simply a question of imagining or dreaming of an "elsewhere," a "not-here," for the not-here is here, the elsewhere is materially present, on the stage and in the bodily behaviors of the actors, and, if it has further dimensions of existence in the imagined places beyond the stage, they too are continually perceived in relation to the materiality of the stage (i.e., the here of both spectators and actors). But, however powerfully we may experience the elsewhere, it never completely displaces the real here in which our experience is grounded, for we know that we are in a theatre. Our psychic state, as spectators in the theatre, involves a continual movement from here to not-here and back again. The spectator is continually tossed from awareness of his own being at one moment to awareness of the being of the actor at the next (more or less dominant depending, e.g., on factors such as the celebrity status of the individual, the danger involved in the performance, or even something like nudity) to the here of the theatre space, and the (multiple) here of the fictional place(s).

As all analysts of space point out, it is at the outer edges of a given space and particularly at the interface between two spaces, at the border zones that the analysis becomes most interesting. This is certainly the case in the theatre, where the interface between stage and auditorium, practitioner and audience space, has been dramatized and elaborated through numerous conventions over the theatre's long history. The other interface, the one between stage and offstage, is even more fraught with meaning, especially when considered in its relation to the stage-auditorium interface.

If the stage is like Bachelard's casket, opened when the lights go up or the curtain is raised, then what is revealed is another casket, for there is always another closure beyond, however this may be manifested in material terms, whatever its relationship to audience space and to the world outside the theatre. The principal quality of the presentational space, whatever form of theatre is involved, is that it is in a relationship both to the spectators (closed off, revealed, closed off again) and to a (normally) hidden area of practitioner activity. The most constant element of the presentational space is a back wall of some kind, a closure that might be a simple curtain or an elaborately built structure and which functions both to focus the spectators' attention on the actor and to mark the limits of the stage, the interface with the offstage. It is the creation of a division between on and off, inside and outside, that permits the interplay of seen and unseen, revealed and hidden, and it is this interplay that has proved such a powerfully expressive tool in terms of the fictional worlds constructed through the performance. The fictional world onstage is connected to a further fictional domain via the off stage, and, as suggested in chapter 1, the modalities of the connection relate to the physical reality of the stage and its offstage.

For Bachelard, as we have seen, the very word *door* is an incitement to dream, and in the theatre the door, or material means providing access from the offstage to the onstage, is especially charged with symbolic significance. Whether there are real doors, leading to *skena* or tiring house, or whether there are multiple access points as in a traditional wings and border setting, whether the doors are part of the fictional world, as in one of Antoine's naturalistic sets, or whether the only door is the one the spectators have used to enter the performance space, the nature of the door articulates the relationship between the here and the beyond. Bachelard claimed that the door opens up two different dream spaces depending on whether it is open or closed, on whether we are opening it or closing it, whether we are door openers or door closers, on whether we perceive ourselves to be inside or outside in relation to the door, and he goes on to observe with great acuity:

> If one were to give an account of all the doors one has closed and opened, of all the doors one would like to re-open, one would have to tell the story of one's entire life. (1957, 201)

Perhaps one can also recount the history of Western theatre by telling the story of the doors that link the on to the off, of the outside/inside relationships that are thus created, of the position of the characters and of the spectators vis-à-vis these interiors and exteriors.

In the Greek theatre the door(s) in the *skena* were understood to lead into the interior of house or palace, and the presentational space provided for both a fictional exterior to this interior place and a public space (occupied by the chorus) that could be related more or less explicitly to the fictional. In Shakespeare's theatre the doors in the tiring house wall (and whether there were two or three is still a matter for conjecture between scholars) were conceptualized as leading to both exterior and interior places, and it has been argued that the constant shifts in fictional location (onstage and off), the relationship between the fictional places located offstage and those represented onstage, were articulated through a highly sophisticated system of use of the stage doors (Fitzpatrick 1997, 207–30). In the typical wings and border settings that dominated the seventeenth and eighteenth centuries there were no doors, and the relationship between off and on is correspondingly diluted, the spaces between the wings providing a kind of multiple access. Actors, of course, aware of the physical value of the door to mark their entrances and exits, used the proscenium doors and fought with managers and proponents of the new perspective sets to be able to continue to do so. With nineteenth-century naturalism came the solidity of the box set and real doors, able to be slammed, as Cocteau desired in *Les Parents terribles*. The off could now figure as either outdoors in relation to the on, or it could provide a further level of interiority (cupboard, bedroom, or other private space— thereby giving rise to countless possibilities of comic misunderstanding), but, increasingly, the fictional place of the action came to be conceptualized as indoors, with all that this entails in terms of narrative focus. In the 1970s and 1980s the movement away from traditional theatre buildings and their stage machinery was part of a more general questioning of the fictional status of the stage and an obsessive preoccupation with the present reality of the performance itself. It is significant that contemporary performance practice so frequently resorts to the use of light and blackout to reveal the actors already in situ, rather than letting them physically enter the space. The focus is thus on the here (the performance on the stage) rather than on the articulation of here and there. As performers' interest in narrative and fiction has declined, so too has their imaginative exploitation of the on/off relationship.

These comments, even though they have been too brief to do justice to the complexities involved, are nevertheless sufficient to demonstrate the connection between the materiality or otherwise of the doors, their placement in the presentational space, and the dynamic role they can play in the dramatic action. The material object opens up much larger questions of theatrical aesthetics and the ideology of performance, for the connection between the onstage and the off is the means of bringing into focus the reality status of the one in relation to the other and, indeed, the relationship of the dramatic fiction to the society in which it is being performed. The theatre space can be seen to be mapped onto the real space of the city (either literally, as in Athens, where exits along either *eisodos* were conceptualized as leading in an analogous manner either to the city of the dramatic fiction or to places outside this city (Scolnicov and Holland 1989, 45–62) or, more metaphorically, as in the medieval towns where the pageant wagons brought the incidents and stories of the Scriptures into the familiar environment of everyday life), or to be radically separated from it (as in escapist entertainment of many varieties).

In this chapter the focus has been on the physical space of the theatre building and the stage, but we now need to consider the dynamic function of the actor in energizing this material reality, for it is the work of the actor/performer that transforms it from mere bricks and mortar, wood and polystyrene, into a highly expressive instrument.

3

Energized Space: Moving Bodies

A space of time that is filled always filled with moving . . .
  —Gertrude Stein, *Lectures in America*

Man thinks with his whole body.
  —Marcel Jousse, *L'Anthropologie du geste*

The theatre building and the spaces it encloses have a powerful bearing on the meanings created by the performance, as has been demonstrated in the previous chapter, but in themselves they communicate only in limited and relatively simple ways. The stage, even when set and lit ready for the performance, will keep the spectators' attention for a very short time if no actors are present, for in the theatre it is the presence of the actors that makes the space meaningful. It is through the body and the person of the actor that all the contributing systems of meaning (visual, vocal, spatial, fictional) are activated, and the actor/performer is without doubt the most important agent in all the signifying processes involved in the performance event.

Grotowski had realized this when he was developing his notion of "poor theatre" in the 1960s: stripping away the accretions of commercial exploitation in order to rediscover theatre as an art form, he found he was left with the embodied reality of the actor, "we consider the personal and scenic technique of the actor as the core of theatre art" (1969, 15). Jacques Copeau had discovered the same thing fifty years earlier, when fighting his own battle against commercialism and the excesses of the first generation of "star" directors. In order for the theatre to be revitalized, he wanted a bare stage and what he called "real actors," for he had realized that theatre was at its most potent when staging and decoration were reduced to the minimum and the actors had to draw on the full extent of their bodily and emotional resources:

> The more the stage is kept bare, the more powerful the effects that can be created there through the action. The more austere and rigid the stage, the

more freedom there will be for the imagination to play . . . On a bare stage the actor is obliged to create everything, to draw everything from his own being. (1974, 220)

Theatre is an art form that draws on a large number of signifying systems, and, as Tadeusz Kowzan found when he attempted to categorize them, the majority are dependent on the bodily reality of the actor (1975, 206). Eight of the thirteen systems Kowzan saw as making up the "language" of theatre are produced directly by the actor (words, diction, facial expression, gesture, movement, makeup, hairstyle, costume). The remaining five systems that, according to Kowzan, constitute the overall sign system of theatre (props, set, lighting, music, and sound effects) are in his view external to the actor, but it can equally be argued that they, too, function primarily in relation to the actor. Objects on the stage tend to merge into the background, and they become meaningful only when handled, looked at, or referred to. It is through the agency of the actor that objects are brought to the attention of the audience, and it is the actor who creates the mobility[1] that is characteristic of the theatrical function of the object: the actor can, with a gesture or an act, transform a walking stick into a machine gun, a bundle of rags into a baby, a chair on a table into a mountain. The set conveys a limited amount of information in the absence of the actor, as has just been stated, but becomes a powerfully expressive instrument when occupied and activated by actors. Stage lighting, too, functions largely in relation to the human presence, revealing, masking, situating it, and enhancing mood and atmosphere suggested by other means. In a film the music may seem to emanate from some discursive space separate from the dramatic fiction and to constitute a narrative voice in itself, but in live performance music tends to be either produced by performers who are visible in the presentational space or to exist within the dramatic fiction (e.g., when a character switches on a radio or record player). Furthermore, in much contemporary performance the sound operator is visible in the presentational space, sound equipment may be operated by the performers, and the technical production of sound and/or music is frequently part of the performance.

The actor/performer is at the heart of theatrical semiosis, and in the theatre there is no meaning without the agency of the performers. Even in text-based theatre, in which the play is a powerful communicator in its own right, and indeed has another form of existence through the medium of print, it is only through the actor that theatrical communication occurs. Actors lend their bodies and voices to the characters they present, and delve deep into their own emotional and psychological experience to give life to the fictional beings who then live on in the imagination of the spectators. It is the actors who are present in the space, who offer themselves to the fascinated gaze of the spectators, and who undertake, night after night, the task of interacting with these spectators, subtly adjusting their performance to the particular demands of the moment.

In this chapter my concern is the actors' use of space, the ways in which their presence energizes the performance space, and the ways in which they activate space so that it functions in the meaning-making process. Gertrude Stein was not in fact referring to theatre in the phrase, quoted as epigraph to this chapter, but "a space of time filled with moving" is nevertheless a striking image for a theatrical performance, and I suggest that it is movement rather than mimesis that is the characteristic feature of theatre. Any attempt at performance analysis corroborates this, as will be demonstrated in more detail in chapter 4. Performance analysis reveals that the performers' movements are key signifiers, particularly in relation to the verbal component of performance that they articulate and construct as discourse. The actor is first and foremost a person who moves, and even when the scope for movement is radically reduced, as in Beckett's *Not I*, for example, in which all that moves is the mouth, the spectators' attention becomes so riveted to the tiny area of light and the moving lips that the experience is almost painful.

The centrality of the actor in theatrical semiosis, and the role of movement in this can be illuminated by contrast with the situation in film. In film, meaning is constantly mediated by the camera and the editing process, and the actor is simply one element, albeit a highly charismatic one, among many that the camera records. In the theatre there is no mediating camera, and it is the actor who gives meaning to the other elements. Movement is, of course, important in the cinema (known in popular parlance precisely for this feature) but in the cinema movement is controlled, even produced by camera, shot composition, shot size, and montage, whereas in the theatre it is produced only by the actor. The experience of making a film can be painful for theatre actors, used to being at the center of a collaborative work process through which the performance gradually takes shape and to a sense of responsibility for the whole work as it is performed nightly to an audience. Dusan

Makavejev, commenting on the misunderstandings he had with Simon Callow during the shooting of *Manifesto,* conveys with limpid clarity the limits of the film actor's expressive and creative function:

> In film, as soon as the camera moves closer than medium shot, the actor becomes the stage. When a tear rolls down the actor's face, the *tear* is the actor and his *facial skin* is the stage, while his face is the *background.* Anything in the film can act, the tree, the boiling milk, the fly on somebody's nose. It depends on the director's decision. (Callow 1992, 254)

That is to say that the "active" element in film is that which has been brought to the spectator's attention by the composition of the shot, the choice of shot size and the editing. For Makavejev the "actor" is simply the active element in the shot and this can be animate or inanimate; in a film it is indeed the director who ultimately controls the communicative process through his control of the camera and the montage, whereas in the theatre it is the actors who, through their dominance of the presentational space, exercise this function.

A very telling example of the way the filmic process can, in a sense, bypass the active agency of the actor to make powerful emotional meaning with that actor's performance is provided in Mikhalkov-Konchalovsky's film of *Uncle Vanya.* Near the end of the film, after the Professor and his beautiful wife have left, the focus shifts to the doctor who is also preparing to leave. The old nurse asks him if he would like a vodka and there is a medium close shot of him as he says, "Why not." Then the film cuts to Sonya, just sitting down at the table next to Vanya, picking up her pen to continue with the routine work of managing the estate. Astrov is also in the shot, looking fixedly at Sonya and the shot functions to remind the spectator of the scene the night before in which she had begged him not to drink and he had clasped her hand and vowed to stay sober. The next shot has Astrov moving toward the barometer, almost crumpling under the weight of his own thoughts. The emphasis is on the doctor in this whole sequence, the memory of the earlier scene that motivates his anguish is brought about by purely filmic means, that is, the cut to Sonya at the table.

I have seen several productions of the play in recent years but none of them has exploited the moment when the old nurse offers Astrov a vodka to throw the focus back to Sonya. In order for this to occur, and this is the difference between theatre and film being explored here, it is the actress playing Sonya who would have to do something: put down her pen with a sudden gesture, look up quickly from her writing and fix her gaze on Astrov, even make some sound to draw attention. The moment could function either to reveal Sonya's realization that Astrov had forgotten his vow, that he is preoccupied with the departure of her beautiful stepmother, and that she means nothing to him (the realization that most productions defer until his actual exit) or, as in Konchalovsky's film, to be part of Astrov's own realization that he cannot love Sonya and of the pain and hurt that he is causing.

In the theatre, however the actors may have determined the emotional content of such a scene, it is their physical actions in the space (gestures, moves, looks) that will articulate it for the audience. As the *Uncle Vanya* example makes clear, onstage it is principally movement, even something as minimal as a shift in orientation, a look or a gesture, that draws the spectators' attention and enables meaning to emerge in relation to words or other signifying systems. The physical presence of the actor onstage is in itself a powerful signifier, for not only does this energize the space and focus the attention of the spectator, but it means that any interaction is necessarily spatialized. If two actors are present onstage, they must be placed physically in relation to each other and the dynamics of their physical placement will necessarily create meaning. The words they speak will function differently and take on different meanings depending on the physical orientation of the speakers to each other, to the audience and to elements of the presentational space.

The actor onstage is a complex figure, for, as Otakar Zich pointed out in his structural theory of the actor's signifying process,[2] there are always at least three elements functioning simultaneously: there is the actor him- or herself who is physically present in the space, there is the character that the actor presents who comes into existence in the minds of the spectators through the actor's performance, and between the two there is the "stage figure," that is to say, the physical manifestation of the character or persona constructed by the actor and the other artists involved in that production (using the body of the actor, costume, makeup, gesture, etc.). The three levels of semiotic function activated by the person of the performer can be mapped onto the multilevel spatial function described in my taxonomy as stage space, presentational space and fictional place, for they are causally related. Michael Quinn has pointed out that the celebrity status of the actor can constitute a fourth term (1990, 154–61), another persona that is perhaps as fictional as the character, one that is separate from the real social being of the actor, even though it may be cultivated by the actor's publicity agents, and even though it may impact upon the real social being (as, for example, when the actor's sexuality is in conflict with the "sex symbol" role projected by the agents).

All these elements function in relation to one another and to the spectator, who is, of course, the other vital element in the communicative event. To appreciate what is going on in performance it is necessary to consider the two-way relationship that is set up between each of the terms: performer and stage figure, performer and character, performer and spectator, stage figure and spectator, character and spectator, character and stage figure. In some postmodern performance the performer/character relation has been virtually effaced while the performer/stage figure relation is dominant: an extreme case of this is the work of Orlan; in this performer's work the stage figure has imposed its imperatives on the body of the performer so totally that the performances consist of the surgical operations whereby the body of the performer is gradually transformed into the desired figure (Lovelace 1995, 13–25). Here the stage figure has invaded and permanently marked the body of the performer.

In order to facilitate discussion of the spatial function of the actor/performer, the performers' bodily action in space has been broken down into a number of categories, but this breakdown is artificial insofar as it is acknowledged that in performance a move, a gesture, and the words that accompany them are inextricably linked. This is true for the spectator perceiving them and possibly also for the actor performing them, though observation of many different rehearsal processes demonstrates that the elements are indeed separable while they are being constructed. Words and phrases are articulated through gesture and moves, and vice versa, actions are carefully elaborated, and a couple of minutes of stage action may take several hours to construct. The major categories to be discussed are as follows: the modalities of entering and exiting the presentational space; movement within that space, position and orientation; and gesture. These modes of bodily action all function in relation to speech, for in the theatre speech becomes a spatial function: whatever is said in the theatre is necessarily positioned in some way in relation to the performance space, and the position becomes part of the meaning conveyed. In some performance traditions there is a disjunction between the performers whose task is to speak and those who move or control the moving figures, in some the mapping of word to gesture is highly codified, in some the speech itself is in codified forms, in some it resembles everyday speech in the world outside the theatre, but in all of these traditions the meanings created by the words are shaped, even determined, by the spatial factors inherent in the performance reality.

Entrance/Exit

The moment of entering the presentational space is extremely important for the actor as is evident from the fact that conventions have been developed in many different performance genres to heighten or mark the moment of entrance. These may involve the material reality of the performance (the drum roll, musical flourish, and spotlight of circus or music hall) or be activated from within the fiction (the classic "But soft, the king approaches" or "Who comes here?"), but the function is similar: to draw the spectators' attention to the physical point of entrance into the space and to mark the moment in some way.

In some performance genres the moment itself can be considerably extended: in the Balinese dance form *topeng panca* each masked dancer enters from behind a curtain hung at the back of the presentational space, and for each character there is an elaborate entrance sequence during which the music becomes more and more urgent and the curtain is shaken several times to draw attention to the hidden presence of the dancer. When the curtain finally parts, the moment has become a kind of epiphany, the masked dancer is revealed in a moment of stillness in the liminal space behind the now open curtain; when the dancer enters the presentational space proper and begins to dance, the curtain closes again. In No theatre, entrances are all via the *hashigakari* (the long ramp that extends from the back of the stage at a diagonal angle and leads to the specially curtained entrance point through which all characters enter), so the audience has time to observe each character for an extended period before they set foot on the stage itself.

In Western theatre, with its traditions of realism, it has been more customary to accentuate the moment of entrance from within the dramatic fiction. This may involve the reaction of characters already present onstage, or there may be a line of dialogue of the sort quoted earlier to alert spectators to the arrival; the entrance may be accentuated by the energy level of the actor, or the number of people entering at the same time (e.g., a king with all his train). There may be a kind of double entrance, in that a minor character (servant or confidant) may come on first to announce the imminent arrival of the major character. In contemporary performance, in which the whole idea of fiction has been displaced and the focus of interest is the materiality of the performance itself, an action such as entering a particular space becomes interesting in itself: Robert Meldrum has described how he and Jenny Kemp worked for weeks on entering a room:

> Sometimes we would work in (Jenny's) terrace house. We did an enormous amount of work with one of us sitting in a little lounge-room. The point was to watch the other one enter the room. You'd sit there and the door would open, and all they had to do was come in. We'd alternate; we just did it obsessively, over and over, watching different ways of entering a room. (Minchinton 1996, 328)

Whatever the mode or purpose of the entrance, the moment is charged for the performer—actors sometimes speak of "working up" an entrance—and their physical appearance, bodily demeanor and energy level all receive particular attention at that moment.

For the spectator, also, the entrance of a character constitutes an important performance event, so much so indeed that entrances can be said to segment and therefore to structure the performance continuum. In the seventeenth-century French court entertainments, from which both opera and ballet have developed, the "entrée" was recognized as a structural unit rather similar to the act or scene in drama (a work would be described as "un ballet en 3 entrées"), and it is the entrance or exit of a character that marks the beginning of a new scene in French classical dramaturgy. The structuring function of the entrance and exit, and of movement more generally, will be discussed at length in the next chapter for it is a key factor in both production and reception of meaning in the performance event.

The importance of entrances and exits and the importance of stage architecture in providing the material basis for their occurrence is central to the long struggle waged by actors to retain the forestage and the proscenium doors in English theatres. When architects and designers introduced the new perspective scenery developed on the Continent in the seventeenth century, the actors performed on a forestage in front of it, where they could be seen and heard, while the painted wings and flats were placed behind the proscenium arch. There was, thus, a separation between actor and scenery, and entrances and exits were made through the doors on either side of the proscenium arch. As the demands of scenic spectacle became more and more compelling, architects and managers tried to remove the forestage, abolish the proscenium doors, and confine the actors within the picture frame. Actors resisted the removal of the proscenium doors for over thirty years, succeeding on several occasions, as Iain Mackintosh recounts, in having them reinstated. While the unnamed writer in the *Sunday Times* of 20 October 1822 (1993, 31) could see only the affront to scenic realism they constituted:

> Doors which oft with burnish'd panels stood,
> And golden knockers glittering in a wood,
> That served for palace, cottage, street or hall,
> Used for each place and out of place in all.

For the actors it was clearly far more important to have the possibility of making a strong entrance or exit, and it was the doors that provided that possibility.

Exits, too, are important moments in the performance for, apart from their role in structuring the performance continuum, they function very powerfully to activate the offstage as fictional place. The fictional world onstage exists in a relationship to further fictional domains and, as has been argued in chapter 2, it is the physical interface between onstage and off that actualizes the relationship. The actor is the active agent whose physical comings and goings make manifest the interface and the exit is a particularly potent moment in raising the spectators' consciousness of the "there" beyond the "here." In classical and neoclassical dramaturgy, the identity of the onstage fictional place does not change during the performance, which means that the offstage fictional places are themselves also in a stable relationship to this onstage world and this, in turn, enables the actual exit points to acquire a heavy thematic load during the course of the performance. Elizabethan dramaturgy conceptualizes time and place in a completely different way, for there the identity of the onstage fictional place is continually shifting and, with it, the identity of the "localized off."

The many spatial references in the dialogue of Shakespeare's plays, especially those clustered around entrances and exits, function as a simple, direct, and extremely economical means of indicating the fictional location of both the onstage and offstage action. Characters frequently specify where they are going when they exit, so, for example, when the Countess of Auvergne says to Talbot and his soldiers as she leads them offstage, "and think me honourèd / To feast so great a warrior in my house" (1 *Henry* VI, 2.3), it is understood that they are going into her house, that the door in the tiring house wall represents the door to the Countess's house; at the end of the very next scene, however, Richard Plantagenet says to his companions "Come let us four to dinner," and the audience now understands that the identity of the localized off has changed, and that that door leads to another house in another place.

Shakespearian and classical/neoclassical dramaturgy represent opposite ends of what may be seen as a spectrum of expressive potential regarding the representation of time and place in the theatre. Peter Holland claims that there is an "intensity of meaning generated by entrance and exit" in Sophocles, Racine, and Beckett that is unknown in Shakespeare (Scolnicov and Holland 1989, 45–62), and his perceptive analyses provide convincing evidence of the thematic charge an exit can be made to carry. The flexibility of spatial location in Shakespeare is clearly an equally powerful tool and it has only been with the development of cinema that there has been a dramatic medium able to match Shakespeare's practice in this respect. The important point for my present argument is, however, that, whether we are talking about Shakespearian flexibility or Sophoclean intensity, it is the physical reality of the performance space that makes such thematic functions possible, and it is the actor whose exits momentarily endow the offstage with fictional life.

Given this connection, it is perhaps something of a paradox that the exit is frequently a moment when the presentational can briefly take precedence over the fictional, but this seems nevertheless to be the case. An actor who has performed with great skill, or who delivers his final lines with great passion, "making an exit" as they say, may receive a round of applause, something that momentarily displaces the fictional world, draws attention to the performer rather than the character. In certain theatrical genres the act or scene may end with a rhymed couplet when the rest of the dialogue is in blank verse or prose, the couplet thus functioning as a punctuation mark, drawing attention to performance structure. John Gielgud claims in his memoirs that until well into the 1930s it was customary in London for actors to take a curtain call at the end of each act of a play and that they would do this even if their character had just been seen on his deathbed. The act may even end with a song, as in nineteenth-century French vaudeville, and here the presentational convention completely displaces the fiction until the beginning of the next act. These are the most obvious examples of the phenomenon, but it is present in some form even in naturalistic drama where the presentational is rigorously subordinated to the fictional. It seems that whenever the exit functions to locate the offstage as fictional place it functions also to activate a subliminal awareness on the part of spectator that it is no such thing.

When an actor comes into the presentational space he is entering a fictional world that is already present, created by set, objects, lighting, the action that has already occurred, etc. In the No the performer's progress along the *hashigakari* slows down the moment of insertion into the fiction and offers it up for contemplation, and even in the Western realist tradition the entrance is charged with particular energy for not only does it constitute a new event within the fiction, but it marks the moment when the performer enters into the fiction.

Like the exit, the entrance may also be an occasion for the presentational to take precedence over the fictional. The demands of realism and credibility have militated against practices such as acknowledging the first entrance of the principal actors with a round of applause but this can still happen. For instance, when Gérard Depardieu played Tartuffe in Jacques Lasalle's production of the play in 1984, his first entrance was frequently greeted with applause, doubtless as a result of his celebrity status: the film star appearing live onstage displaced the fiction. To spectators who had bought tickets primarily to see their idol in the flesh, the wait must have seemed interminable (the character does not make his first entrance until act 3), and this may also have been a factor precipitating a shift of focus from the character/stage figure/spectator relationship to the performer/stage figure/spectator or even purely to performer/spectator.

Modern lighting techniques make it possible for the performers to be discovered *in situ* rather than entering the space. While the intention here may be to prevent the mechanics of entrance and exit from contaminating the fictional, the effect in practice is to permit the presentational to assert its presence as strongly as ever: if the blackout is incomplete the spectator can become aware of silent figures taking up their positions, or see the stage hands placing or moving objects, and if the blackout is total its duration will necessarily be such that it becomes noticeable in itself (actors cannot get on- and offstage in the split second it takes in film to shift from one fictional location to another). In the rare case of a total blackout the spectators have time to become aware of their situation as spectators and may even have a moment of disquiet at finding themselves in pitch darkness, surrounded by strangers. When a film cuts from one fictional location to another there is no fissure between the two when the spectator could become aware of the film as film, although the dissolve does permit this to happen. However the junction points are handled in theatre, there is a momentary return to consciousness of the presentational on the part of the spectator. The vogue for blackout to cover shifts in fictional time and place in theatre does not prevent this, but it does prevent the actor dominating the moment of exit and entrance and it is perhaps part of the shift in creative agency in the theatre in recent years away from the actor toward the director and the designer. It is worth pointing out that it also removes some of the opportunity for active involvement on the part of the spectators and may be a contributing factor to the apparent passivity of modern audiences.

The materiality of the connection between onstage and off is an important part of the meaning-making process in theatre, for while the meaning may emerge primarily from the nature of the fictional place(s) deemed to exist offstage (at the end of *Oedipus Rex,* the important thing is not the nature of the door but the fact that beyond the door is the palace interior and in the palace is the dead body of Jocasta), it may also emerge from the way the actors in a given production utilize the material connection, and indeed from the way this has been realized by the designer. In Rex Cramphorn's production of *Britannicus* in Sydney that has already been mentioned (see chap. 2), the door to Nero's chamber was the central feature of the set. A sliding door, split down the middle and decorated with the Roman eagle and laurel wreath, was a clear symbol of political power, the place it led to was the seat of power, and the relationship of all the characters to this place of power was articulated through their use of the door.

Agrippina paced up and down outside, never actually touching the door, bemoaning the existence of the barrier between her son and herself, striking poses in front of it on her reiterated references to her forebears, her claims to power undermined by the fact that she was always outside, never inside. On entering or exiting, Nero habitually thrust the doors wide apart, evidence of his confident ownership of the space within, and when he stood in front of it the painted laurel wreath seemed to encircle his own head. John Howard (the actor playing Nero) was the only actor tall enough to create this effect, which added to the impact of his authority and exercise of power. In contrast to John Howard's aggressive manner of thrusting the doors open, when Britannicus goes through the door (on his way to the banquet of reconciliation when he will be poisoned), the actor (Robert Menzies) opened the doors only a few inches, then turned and faced Junia for a few moments with the doors framing his body almost like a coffin, then quietly slid them closed.

The only other character to be seen entering the place was Narcissus, at the end of act 4; Tony Mack, playing Narcissus, followed Nero across the threshold, then turned and looked around the stage before closing the doors. His expression of smug arrogance made clear that this was his moment of political triumph. Later, after the murder of Britannicus, Nero is prevented from following Junia by Agrippina, demanding an explanation of what has occurred; Nero feigns ignorance, but Narcissus intervenes with a blustering defense of their actions and, in this production, stood in the open doorway while he did so, making clear that he now spoke in place of the emperor. At no time until act 5 were the doors left open for longer than was necessary for the entry or exit of the characters using them, making the place beyond seem even more desirable and unattainable. In act 5, from Burrhus's violent arrival after the murder, the doors were left wide open until the end of the play. There was a sense almost of sacrilege, certainly of profound disorder associated with this gaping door that built up powerfully during Albina's account of what had just happened outside the palace. The inner space was left empty and unprotected, attention focused elsewhere, and the strong impression that was created was of a power vacuum.

Another feature of the actors' use of the door that contributed an important layer of meaning became apparent to me only when comparing the production with the same director's later production in Melbourne. In Sydney the doors were opened by the character using them, usually Nero, thus making clear that the notion of power associated with the space within was subject to the control of the individual. In Melbourne the doors seemed to open by magic, and it was furthermore a magic that worked only for Nero. Agrippina approached the door frequently but it remained resolutely closed; when Nero wanted to leave the stage it would open on his approach and it opened similarly to allow Britannicus to go to the death planned for him by Narcissus. As political power does not operate by magic but is the result of human will and human action, the effect of this method of opening the door was in some way to depoliticize both the space and the conflict around it. The local-

Fig. 10. Britannicus goes to his death. Robert Menzies framed by
the door in Rex Cramphorn's Sydney production of *Britannicus*.
(Photography by Derek Nicholson.)

ized off had become Nero's inner space, a psychological rather than a
social or political place.

I have discussed this production at length in order to illustrate how
the modalities of entering and exiting the presentational space can be
used to make meaning in the theatre. This is, obviously, only a small part
of the expressive potential of the presentational space as activated by the
performer, and movement within the space provides even richer scope
for meaning making.

Movement, Position, and Orientation

E. T. Hall was the first to point out that there were significant differences
between societies in terms of spatial behavior: what is experienced as a
comfortable social distance between speakers in one country is felt to be
too close by members of another culture, and may therefore be interpreted by them as threatening or intrusive (1959). He coined the term

proxemics to refer to the study of human beings' bodily occupation of
space, and since he first published his observations a great deal of work
has been done by sociologists, cultural anthropologists, social psychologists and others on the way people move, position themselves in relation
to other people in particular spaces, and interpret spatial behaviors.

This is all highly relevant to theatre and performance, for the way
spatial behavior in the theatre is interpreted obviously relates to spectators' understanding of such behavior outside the theatre context: some
performance traditions, such as classical ballet or kathakali, for instance,
have highly codified systems of movement that are remote from everyday behavior, but in others the performance draws on this and mimics it,
while at the same time rendering it more expressive than the everyday.
John Harrop has remarked that "for the imaginative actor, a realistic setting offers great opportunity for discovering interesting and varied
choices without destroying the illusion of reality" (1992, 88). As we have
just seen, there are many different ways to open a door, and there are
many ways to perform all the minor actions involved in everyday living.
Onstage every choice is pregnant with meaning in terms of the dramatic
situation and the character whose existence is being created from hundreds of such details.

The moving body is, of course, an object of fascination in itself, particularly the highly skilled, trained bodies of dance, sport, or martial arts,
for example, and in the contemporary theatre the emphasis is often on
the body of the performer rather than on character or dramatic fiction.
Movement can be fragmented, endlessly reiterated or used to decon-
struct other practices. The bodily presence of the performer in the presentational space exerts a powerful sense of attraction, although it can be
difficult to say exactly what this consists of. At the beginning of
Julie-Anne Long's performance in EventSpace 1992, performed in an
exhibition gallery at the Performance Space in Sydney, while the spectators were milling around waiting for the performance to begin, a woman
carrying a shopping bag came unnoticed into the large rectangular room
through the door at one end that all the other spectators had used and
began to walk across to the other end of the room. There were no particular lighting or sound effects, and yet, before she had reached the middle
of the room, the majority of the spectators knew that the performance
had begun. Reflecting on this experience afterward, it seemed to me that
there must have been some special quality of bodily tension or purpose-

fulness that triggered our attention and told us that here was a performer rather than another spectator.

Movement within the presentational space is an important theatrical signifier; it functions always to draw attention to the performer, and it is the means whereby the performance space is fully activated. Movement may be meaningful in itself, or it may function rather to construct meaningful spatial groupings (either between performers, or between performer and object or element of the set), and these, in turn, may convey ideas about character and the fictional situation. Whatever else they are doing, the performers' movements also function to structure the performance continuum (see chap. 4), and they are always compulsively watchable. This is to say that, whether or not the performance is telling a story or creating a fictional world, the performers are necessarily displaying their bodies and their movement skills for the pleasure of the spectators.

A great deal of time is spent in rehearsal in elaborating movement and gesture, in placing action in relation to the presentational space, in mapping words onto actions and vice versa. The process known to English-speaking actors as "blocking" is concerned essentially with the construction of moves and groupings and with the placing of the action, and it is fundamental to the creation of theatrical meaning. No one seems to know where the actual term comes from, nor even how long it has been in general use. The *Shorter OED* (1970) does not mention any theatrical usage in its entry under *to block* or under *blocking,* and, while the *Macquarie Dictionary* (1981) does include a reference to theatrical usage, it regards it erroneously as a matter of writing: "to write in stage directions (on a script)." The term may seem to contain within it the notion of blocks, that is, segments of dramatic action that combine like building blocks to form larger units but this is a misleading image, even though not entirely false. The analogy is perhaps the physical shaping process involved in blocking a hat or establishing the rough outline for a picture, but, whatever the origin of the word, the process involves both establishing a narrative or action sequence and finding ways of physically articulating this in terms of the stage space itself.

The scene from *Uncle Vanya* that has been discussed above is often blocked in such a way that all the attention is focused on Astrov: he and the Nurse are typically downstage center, Sonya and Vanya are sitting quietly upstage, if neither reacts when he accepts the offer of vodka, nor looks up when he drinks it, then the result will be that spectators are unlikely to make any connection between the present moment and the scene in act 2. To achieve Konchalovsky's interpretation of the moment a different blocking would be required (Astrov would have to make some move or gesture toward Sonya that would enable spectators to make the connection with the earlier scene, and then move or turn away to express his anguish), and yet another blocking would be needed if one wanted to use that moment to mark Sonya's realization that her love was hopeless (in this case it would have to be Sonya who made a move, drawing the spectators' attention away from Astrov toward herself, so that the memory of the earlier scene could be activated and his action in drinking the vodka seen through her eyes).

Some actors and even some directors affect a very disparaging attitude toward blocking, claiming that it is essentially a mundane matter of regulating the traffic flow onstage. In fact, a director who is incompetent at blocking is like an artist who is a poor draftsman: he may have wonderful ideas, be a sensitive interpreter of text, be able to inspire actors to great depths of feeling, but all of this will be dissipated if there is no physical structure to show it forth.

Keir Elam defined it as "predetermining the configurations of bodies onstage both to create visual patterns and to emblemize relationships" (1980, 65). This formulation is too pictorial, for what is involved is not merely the groupings of bodies but the movements that lead to these groupings, but at least Elam makes clear that both the presentational and thematic levels are involved. It is through the blocking that the space is activated and made meaningful, that the fictional world is mapped onto the presentational space, that the action is spatialized and thereby given specific meaning.

The absence of movement is as important as movement, and the utterly immobile body exerts its own fascination, as is made evident by the crowds of spectators who gather around street performers posing as "living statues," their faces painted white, their skill being to remain absolutely immobile for half an hour at a time. In the theatre, as elsewhere, it is in relation to stillness that movement is defined. John Harrop makes this clear when he teaches his student actors that a move onstage needs to be, as it were, framed by stillness: "When an actor has reached the end of a movement, the image he or she presents should be absolutely still and clear, like a full stop at the end of a sentence" (1992, 47). The stillness thus draws the move to the attention of the spectator, it brings it into existence as a completed entity within the flux of being, and calls for some effort either of aesthetic appreciation or interpretation on the part of the spectator.

In traditional Western theatre meaning typically emerges from the interaction of words and movement in the given space. Diction, intonation, and other paralinguistic features of the actors' delivery are obviously important factors in inflecting the meaning conveyed, but even more important is the spatial organization of the action for this can give specific meaning to the words spoken. With a different spatial organization the same words can be endowed with radically different meanings. Actors exploit possibilities arising from the position of speaker and listener(s) in the fictional world, movement or the lack of it, orientation, and the objects and elements around them in the presentational space in order to create meaning in relation to the words they speak. A few examples will illustrate this point.

Robert Lowell's translation of *Phèdre* contains very specific indications concerning action: lines such as "why does he scowl and look away" or "Is this Phaedra, fleeing, or rather dragged away/sobbing?" or "Who tore this empty scabbard from your belt?" are highly explicit and, in fact, create problems for actors. Such highly pictorial writing can make performance redundant, especially when the verse is highly energized and full of striking imagery,[3] and the actors who worked with this text in the translation project that has already been mentioned referred to it jokingly as the "radio version." In the scene in which Phaedra first confesses her guilty love to Hippolytus, the actors created a structure in which Hippolytus stood at the center of the space, his arms folded across his chest, rigid with disapproval, while Phaedra paced around frenetically. Her movements were highly stylized and nonrealistic as she circled obsessively around him, back and forth in a semicircle behind him, occasionally moving in closer, then racing on, sometimes completing a full circle around the front of him. The energy of this pacing, its total lack of realism, drew attention away from the words to the emotional power of the actress and created a sense of danger: the dominant image was a caged tigress or perhaps a predator circling its prey. In rehearsal Gillian Jones referred to this circling action as Phaedra "winding in on Hippolytus." Rather than letting the words tell the story of Theseus in the labyrinth, killing the minotaur, she created a labyrinth around Hippolytus, showing how he was entrapped in the web of his stepmother's perverse desire. In this example the violent energy of the movement became the dominant signifier, but the image created was a response to an image in the text: the labyrinth referred to in the speech was displaced and what we saw was Phaedra herself as both labyrinth and hunter.

The placing of the actors within the presentational space is another crucial signifier, as Brecht was one of the first to recognize. John Willett's account of Brecht's collaboration with Caspar Neher makes it clear that Neher did more than simply design the sets for Brecht: his preliminary sketches were not concerned with the set as such but showed key moments in the dramatic action, and the "configuration of bodies" (to repeat Elam's phrase) in these sketches served as a guide to both Brecht and the actors when they began to block the dramatic action. Neher's input into the rehearsal process was perceived as so valuable that, as Egon Monk recalls, if Neher had failed to provide a sketch of a particular moment and was not in the rehearsal room when work on that scene began, Brecht and the actors would frequently agree to defer the process until he could be present (Willett 1986, 106–15).

For a director like Brecht the grouping and position of actors vis-à-vis one another and in relation to the space itself are vital to the meaning that will be conveyed. His word for this is *Stellung*, and, as John Rouse has pointed out, the word "refers both to physical and attitudinal position" (Zarilli 1995, 233); *Stellung* is a means of revealing both the characters' attitudes and those of the actors and director toward them, and, like *Gestus*, it is ideologically loaded. While his work had little else in common with that of Brecht, Rex Cramphorn was convinced of the importance of position in the creation of meaning in the theatre. He worked intensively with the actors in his Actors Development Stream project at the Playbox Theatre in Melbourne to explore what he called "meaning through position" (Minchinton 1996), and my comments on his Sydney production of *Britannicus* have illustrated something of the wealth of meaning that he and his actors managed to convey through movement and position in the space. Cramphorn frequently used a painted floorcloth (as in *Britannicus*) or some other means of marking the floor so that the plotting of the moves and the placing of the action would become more visible to spectators. The white line marking the central vertical axis in his production of *The Theatrical Illusion* (see fig. 11) was originally there during rehearsals to guide the actors in placing themselves, but he decided to leave it there throughout the play's run as a means of assisting the spectators to perceive what he called the "emotional geometry" of the action.

Fig. 11. *The Theatrical Illusion:* the white line marking the central vertical incorporated into the set design. (Photography by Derek Nicholson.)

Objects or elements of the set can also play an important part in articulating the meaning of an action or speech and the position of the actor in relation to an object or element of the set can be crucial. A number of instances of this type of "meaning through position," noted in different productions of Genet's *The Maids*, are discussed in chapter 5. In these examples very different meanings were created for the same moment of action, using the same verbal content, and in each case it was the actors' position in relation to objects in the presentational space that enabled the meaning to be articulated. Indeed, it can be argued that this is one of the major functions of the object in modern theatre practice.

"Meaning through position," in Rex Cramphorn's phrase, was used to brilliant effect in Giorgio Strehler's production of *L'Illusion comique* at the Théâtre de l'Odéon in Paris in 1984, not in relation to objects but to the performance space itself. On two occasions Strehler brought the audience space into the fiction. The first occurs near the end of the play when Alcandre reveals to Pridament that what he has been watching is a play, that his son is not dead but an actor; Alcandre then launches into a speech in praise of theatre, which is, he says, no longer to be seen as a dishonorable activity but as providing pleasure to royalty and respectable incomes to its adepts. In Strehler's production, when Alcandre referred to the king, he turned and bowed deeply and reverently toward the royal box, still a feature of the audience space, although now reserved for the president of the republic. With that one gesture the audience of the 1980s was transported to another time; the king was in our midst. Corneille's play ends with Pridament acknowledging the respectability of theatre and announcing his decision to go to Paris to find his son in the theatre there. As the audience in Strehler's production applauded and the actors began to take their curtain calls, Pridament entered the auditorium from the back of the stalls, applauding like the rest of the audience, and, as he walked toward the stage down the central aisle, he said something like, "That's him!" or "There he is!" Clindor leapt down from the stage, and the longed-for reunion between father and son took place before our delighted eyes. Our reality as spectators in Paris in 1984 had been displaced once again, and the performance we thought we were applauding was revealed as one taking place in the Paris of the dramatic fiction.

The imaginative use of the material reality of the theatre in achieving these reframings was breathtaking, the more so because what was being reframed was not merely an aspect of the fiction onstage but the situation of the audience itself. Our reality was twice transformed into fiction, entirely appropriate in a play about the power of theatrical illusion, and demonstrating a mastery of this power worthy of the wizard Alcandre himself. Significantly, these brilliant effects were achieved by the simplest of spatial means: a look, position in relation to stage and audience and, of course, sensitivity to the historical resonance of the theatre building itself.

The placing of an actor within the presentational space can be used to make meaning in terms of the fictional world, or to "point" a line of dialogue (i.e., give it a specific meaning in terms of the dramatic action), but a particular position can also be selected on purely presentational grounds. Even in the latter case, however, the meaning of the scene will be affected. In Molière's *Dom Juan* there is a scene in which Don Juan begins to seduce a peasant girl while his servant, Sganarelle, tries to dissociate himself from such immoral behavior. The part of Sganarelle was originally played by Molière and yet he has written here a scene in which Sganarelle has very little to say. Was this to provide a little respite for himself during a demanding performance, or to give other actors in the company an opportunity to shine while he withdrew a little? In fact,

Molière often wrote major scenes for himself in which he has very little to say but in which he is able to react to what others are saying and doing, and it seems to me that the point of such scenes is precisely the scope that they provide for comic business. Modern directors (and even actors) seem often to be so obsessed with language that they do not exploit the opportunities these scenes provide and, for example, require Argan to sit through the whole boring pseudo-opera scene in *Le Malade imaginaire* without intervening or let Orgon hide under the table in *Tartuffe* and not show himself throughout the whole seduction scene.

In the two different productions of *Dom Juan* workshopped in Sydney in 1991 the actors playing Sganarelle placed themselves very differently in the presentational space during this scene. Rupert Burns sat downstage left on the very front of the stage and became an interested spectator of the scene. He expressed a degree of boredom, rummaging in his bag, finding an apple and eating it, and reacted with disgust (choking on a mouthful of apple) when his master claims to love Charlotte "sincerely and honourably." Drew Forsythe, a very experienced comic actor, positioned himself toward the middle of the space. He was carrying a large suitcase (the two men are supposed to be on a journey) and sat down on it wearily as soon as his master launched into his seduction routine. He was thus ideally placed to react to everything that happened and, at one moment, even found himself sandwiched between the enthusiastic lovers. It was thus impossible for the spectators not to refer continually to Sganarelle's reactions as the scene progressed, while in the other version, notwithstanding the varied business that Rupert Burns introduced, he remained substantially peripheral and spectators did not look at him for minutes on end.[4] The position of the actor in the space was of crucial importance to the amount of spectator attention he received and to the kind of interaction between the characters that could be developed.

Orientation of the body is another important feature of interpersonal communication and it can signify a great deal about a person's attitude to his surroundings. In the theatre orientation is always determined in relation both to the spectators and to the characters, objects and other elements of the presentational space. The major positions (full face, three-quarters face, profile, and back) determine the spatial plane that is activated, and, of course, the body is articulated so that two planes can be activated at once: the body can face one way and the head can be turned at an angle, or the body can be turned at the waist so that the legs and feet activate one spatial plane while the head and trunk bring another into play. Spectators perceive and interpret orientation both in terms of their knowledge of interpersonal behavior in society at large and in terms of the conventions prevailing in the theatre. When actors first turned their backs on the audience in the early days of naturalistic performance, spectators booed. They had not become familiar with the notion of the missing "fourth wall," and they were not sensitive to the expressive possibilities of the human back. Because theatre space is never empty, the activation of spatial planes through orientation of the performer's body is always a means of bringing people and things into a relationship, of making connections.

An excellent example of the meaning-making potential of orientation is provided by Lauren Love in her feminist critique of contemporary American mainstream theatre. She wanted to show that Gwendolyn in *The Importance of Being Earnest* is not in love with John Worthing but, rather, with the idea of being in love; in the scene in which Worthing proposes to her and Gwendolyn tells him that she knew she was destined to love him as soon as she discovered his name was Ernest, Lauren Love found that she had been placed by the director into a downstage position for this speech, at some distance from John who was slightly upstage. She found that, as "the male character took possession of the female character through his gaze," this blocking of the scene functioned to "reinforce John's position as subject and Gwendolyn's as object." In order to subvert this traditional (and patriarchal) view and make her own interpretation of the moment clear, she turned away from John and faced toward the audience.

> It seemed to me that if Gwendolyn turned to address the audience, she could resist the objectification by breaking the exchange of gazes between the male protagonist and the spectator. And so I presented the text to the audience, showing them Gwendolyn revelling in her masquerade as the Romantic Heroine. (Zarilli 1995, 284)

Lauren Love's account reveals the actor's sensitivity to the impact of position and orientation in the making of meaning in the theatre.

Gesture

In his encyclopedic survey of work on bodily communication Michael Argyle at first makes a distinction between communicative behaviors in which there is no intention to communicate (termed "nonverbal behavior") and those in which there is such an intention. It soon becomes evident that many signals contain both intentional and unintentional information, and Argyle abandons the categorization, introducing the broader term *bodily communication,* and recognizing that "the spontaneous expression of emotions is part of a wider system of communication which has evolved to facilitate social life" (1988, 4). As far as gesture is concerned, however, he maintains the criterion of intentionality: in his system gestures are "voluntary bodily actions, by hands, head or other parts of the body which are intended to communicate" (188), and they are to be distinguished from the physical expression of emotion where there is no intention to communicate, for instance, when a person's hands clench with anxiety or tremble with fear.

In the theatre it is well understood that every aspect of bodily behavior and bodily appearance is communicative, whether or not it is intended as such by the actors: the bodily tension in an actor suffering from an attack of stagefright may be seen as part of the fiction by spectators and interpreted as the character's stress or it may lead to the actor's performance being judged stiff or unconvincing; similarly, if a tall actor is performing with a number of shorter men then the relative body heights will have an impact upon the emotional interactions and power relations spectators perceive, whether or not this was intended by the director in selecting those particular actors, whether or not the actors have thought about this aspect of their performance. The frame constituted by the performance event means that everything the spectator perceives is interpreted, becomes part of the overall meaning for that spectator, and so gesture in the context of theatre must be taken to mean the voluntary and involuntary actions of any part of the performer's body that can be perceived by the spectator. This includes things that in everyday life might be seen rather as the spontaneous expression of emotion, for in the theatre it is not always possible to distinguish between actors' construction of their characters' "spontaneous" emotion and the involuntary expression of their own emotion, and it also includes the shifts in bodily orientation that might not be seen to constitute gestures in everyday life but that are part of a conventionalized system of bodily behavior on the stage.

An action that cannot be seen by the spectators by which one actor communicates with another actor (e.g., to alert him to some untoward detail) is not a gesture in these terms. If, however, the action were to be seen by some spectators then it becomes a gesture (and the spectators will be trying to make sense of it or be disturbed or amused by it). This makes clear that, in the case of theatre, a gesture is not simply something that the performer does, but it depends upon both performer and the possibility of perception by the spectator, and this in turn is dependent upon the spatial reality of the performance event.

Facial expression, like other aspects of the actor's physical appearance, is a visual signifier and is a very powerful part of the actor's bodily expressivity. It is, however, not dependent upon the spatial reality of the theatre, and that is why it is not dealt with in any detail in this chapter. Unlike film and television, in which the face is foregrounded and becomes the primary channel for emotional communication, there have been many highly successful performance traditions in which the actor's face was not clearly visible to the majority of spectators, either due to the size of the theatre, or to methods of lighting, or to the fact that masks were worn. The act of looking, on the other hand, is extremely important in terms of the actor's exploitation of space, for in the theatre a look is very much a spatial act. The person or thing looked at is present in the space together with the person looking, and a look always functions in some way to make a connection between them; it directs the spectator's attention within the space and is one of the performer's most powerful strategems in activating the whole space.

The nature of bodily expressivity, and indeed even the actual parts of the body that are deemed or permitted to be expressive, varies from culture to culture and period to period. The *Natyasastra* goes into a great deal of detail concerning gesture, which is categorized according to the part of the body that produces it (Bharata-Muni 1951). For Bharata-Muni there are six "major limbs" (head, hands, breast, sides, waist, and feet) and another six "minor limbs" (eyes, eyebrows, nose, lower lip, cheeks, and chin), and all are to be carefully trained and controlled by the performer to maximize precision and expressivity. Western actors do not possess the kind of control over all the designated limbs that is required for the performance genres that derive from the *Natyasastra*, nor are Western spectators trained to perceive the subtle differences involved: nine separate gestures are listed for the eyeballs, another nine for the eyelids, six for the nose, while a whole chapter is devoted to the hands, for which there are sixty-seven precise gestures, each associated with a specific emotion or psychological state. In the European theatre the actor's body has been exploited in different ways at different times: attention has variously focused on the upper body (eighteenth- and nineteenth-century dramatic acting), the face (modern dramatic acting), or the whole body (Callot's engravings of the commedia dell'arte suggest that the performance involved the whole body in a way that was almost like dance). Tadashi Suzuki stresses the importance of the feet, and other Asian performance traditions also exploit the connection between performer and ground more intensively than is customary in the West. Costume (or the lack of it) is another important factor in determining how much of the body can be seen, how much can be made expressive, and the extent to which the body is either naturalized or rendered strange or different.

Eli Rozik distinguishes between performative (or instrumental) and communicative gestures (1993, 8–17); the former are the gestures involved in accomplishing some act, such as lighting a cigarette or calming a crying child, the latter are intended to convey meaning to another person or animal. In normal social life these two categories are frequently blurred, in that it is possible to overlay the performative with a communicative message, either intentionally or unintentionally: one can, for example, light a cigarette aggressively, flirtatiously, etc., and, as all mothers discover, their own fatigue or distress can communicate itself to their crying child so that the calming gesture has the opposite effect. In the theatre the performative is always overlaid by the communicative, and even the gestures of the stage hands placing items of set or props between scenes convey messages about the work process involved and the aesthetic assumptions underpinning the mise en scène. In task-based performance, in which the performers are not acting but doing, the gestures are still both performative and communicative, and indeed can become compulsively watchable even though no ostensible meaning is being communicated. This has been demonstrated in much contemporary performance, but perhaps never so convincingly as in the 1996 Melbourne Festival of the Arts, where a group called Urban Dream Capsule undertook to live for the three weeks of the festival in the window of a big department store. This turned out to be one of the most successful "performances" in the festival, crowds of people gathered day and night for weeks on end to stare in fascination even when the men were simply cooking a meal, cleaning their teeth, or reading the newspaper.

When Stanislavsky talked about "physical actions," Brecht talked about "Gestus," or when Artaud called the actor "an animated hieroglyph," they were all referring to the gestural expressivity of the actor. These three practitioner/theorists have each played a seminal role in the theatre of the twentieth century, and each placed the gestural action of the performer at the center of his aesthetic. While these aesthetics differ widely from each other, and the practices they engender are equally diverse, the significant fact is that gesture is crucial to each one.

Gesture is not merely a manner of supplementing or bypassing language in communicating with others, or of involuntarily signaling one's feelings, but it is tied at a deeper level to the physiological conditions of human existence as well as being profoundly rooted in culture. Marcel Mauss (1950), developing the new discipline of ethnography in the first decades of this century, observed that a great many bodily behaviors that within one culture may seem to be natural, automatic, even innate are revealed as culturally determined when seen from a comparative perspective. He had in mind such things as the way people sleep, eat their food, swim, jump, rest, etc., and referred to them as "body techniques" rather than gestures or actions. He argued that, while they are perceived by the members of a given culture as natural, as the only way to do the thing in question, they are in fact culturally determined. It is now widely accepted that the body is enmeshed in culture from the moment of conception (the mother's activity and diet during pregnancy, techniques of childbirth, methods of handling the newborn baby, all differ from culture to culture), that the way people use their bodies at any moment of their daily life, even when asleep, is the product of their cultural "habitus" (to use the word in the way Mauss himself does), and that this habitus can vary significantly even in societies that are geographically and developmentally close. Indeed, Mauss's interest in the phenomenon was triggered by his noticing, when fighting in the trenches in the 1914–18 war, that English soldiers marched in a very different way from the French, and that neither army could readily adapt to the bodily practice of the other.

In the theatre body techniques can be as important as more overtly expressive behaviors, either in the service of ever greater psychological realism (the way a person walks, runs, sits, and stands being fundamental to that person's being) or because they enable performers to experience their own bodies and to live in the moment in a highly concentrated way. Mark Minchinton has described how impulse work, such as the Running, Walking, Standing exercise, can function to "create subtle and profound changes in the perception of time and space both for spectators and performers":

First, the performers attempt to locate their "own" individual impulses free of the need to interact or even notice the others they are sharing the space with (naturally, performers are not able to completely screen out the other performers, they must avoid running into each other, and the movement of someone running past close by must affect the performer). Second, the performers allow themselves to "become aware" of the other performers in the space and to "interact" with them, but still within the strict limitations of RWS. "Becoming aware" and "interacting" with others in the space is done through the eyes, ears, nose, sense of vibration through the floor, and through the sixth sense. (1996, 200)

For spectators at this kind of performance, the experience is less the familiar theatrical one of looking and trying to make sense of what one sees, than experiencing the present moment in all its "presentness" for oneself. Once the pressure to "make sense" (i.e., project hypotheses toward the future, review past inferences in the light of the present action) is removed, it is possible for the spectator to be fully in the present; becoming aware of the performers' movements in themselves, rather than of meaning conveyed by movement, can lead to a heightened sense of the moment on the part of the spectator and the performer, as Minchinton states.

In everyday life gesture functions very strongly in relation to speech, either to supplement it with illustration, to mark its articulations and rhythms, or to clarify its deictic content. In the theatre all these functions are operative, and may be more or less exaggerated in comparison with everyday behavior, more or less conventional, more or less recognizably "theatrical." More important, gesture is also one of the means at the actor's disposal to link speech to place, to direct words across the space to a specific listener, or to the spectator, and to create more complex meanings than is possible with words alone. It is thus through gesture as much as through the other means described in this chapter that speaking becomes a spatial act in the theatre.

A couple of examples will help to indicate something of the wealth of meaning that can be created in performance by a single gesture. The meaning clearly does not reside in the gesture alone but in the dynamic interrelationship between language, place, body, and time that it sets up and, of course, between the fictional and presentational levels that are constantly in play during any performance.

In *The Three Sisters* there is a scene in act 3 in which all three sisters are together in the bedroom shared by Olga and Irena on the night of the fire. Masha is lying on one of the beds after sending her husband home, and Irena launches into a long speech, virtually to herself, in which she complains about the emptiness of their life, and then bursts into tears. In Elisaveta Fen's translation the scene continues as follows:

> *Irena:* Oh, how dreadful it is, how dreadful, how dreadful! I can't bear it any longer, I can't, I really can't . . .
> *(Enter Olga. She starts arranging things on her bedside table.)*
> *Irena (sobs loudly):* You must turn me out of here! Turn me out; I can't stand it any more!
> *Olga (alarmed):* What is it? What is it, darling?

In a production of the play directed by Stewart Chalmers, Masha (played by Lyn Pierse) was not lying on a bed but standing upstage and, when Irena started to cry, she turned and made a half step toward her as though she were going to comfort her, then as Olga bustled in she aborted the gesture and looked rather enigmatically at Olga, then turned away as the latter assumed her normal "maternal" role in relation to Irena. This play of looks and the aborted gesture gave a vivid insight into Masha's position as the middle daughter (neither surrogate mother nor surrogate baby), the difficulty she has in establishing a full relationship with Irena given the dominant presence of Olga, and her marginalized position in the emotional economy of the family.

When the play is performed in the traditional way, with realistic set and props, Masha is normally lying on the bed at this moment and attention is focused first on Irena, and then on the interaction between Olga and Irena; in such productions it is as though Masha were not present. In this production a decision had been taken to remove all the furniture and so Masha became an active (if shadowy) presence, standing upstage, looking out toward the fire, and her presence shifted the emotional balance of this particular moment decisively. This scene is a good illustration of the way that skilled actors work with words and actions, mapping the one onto the other to create their own original meanings, and of the way that gesture can function to trigger the spectator's imagination. It is also significant in terms of my overall argument that this gesture, with all the undercurrents of meaning it set flowing, was in fact generated by the nature of the presentational space. An abstract space rather than a naturalistic bedroom threw the expressive responsibility back onto the actors and ensured that Masha's presence was a dynamic part of the scene.

Words that are ambiguous, or even puzzling, can be given a clear meaning through the use of a gesture, or, alternatively, a thematically relevant ambiguity can be suggested in a phrase in which the textual meaning seems unambiguous. A wonderful example of the former occurred in the *Phèdre* workshop that has already been referred to in this chapter. Robert Lowell's translation of *Phèdre* contains a number of images that have no equivalent in Racine's austere text and which are rather obscure. For instance, when declaring her love to Hippolytus, the queen allows herself to be confused by the physical similarity between father and son, which permits her to approach the son as though he were her husband. In French the moment is as follows:

> Que dis-je? Il n'est point mort, puisqu'il respire en vous.
> Toujours devant mes yeux je crois voir mon époux.
> Je le vois, je lui parle; et mon coeur . . . Je m'égare,
> Seigneur, ma folle ardeur malgré moi se déclare.

Lowell has translated this as follows:

> What am I saying? Theseus is not dead.
> He lives in you. He speaks, he's taller by a head,
> I see him, touch him, and my heart . . . a reef . . .
> Ah Prince, I wander. Love betrays my grief.

There is no *reef* in Racine's text, and it is not clear what the word means in this context nor where it has come from. I have already described how Gillian Jones performed this scene, pacing energetically around Hippolytus (John Howard), who stood massively unmoved at the center of the circle created by her movements. When she said, "I see him, touch him," she moved in closer (in response to Lowell's very directive text—Racine's Phèdre "speaks" but does not "touch"), almost touched his arm, but, rebuffed by his partly averted body, quickly moved away again and continued with her frenetic circling. Suddenly the image came alive for me: her movements contrasted with his rocklike immobility created the idea of waves beating on rocks, and I saw Hippolytus as the reef on which she was foundering.

The examples drawn here from *The Three Sisters* and *Phèdre* demonstrate the complexities of meaning that can be achieved in the performance of text/narrative/character-based theatre and provide insight into why this performance tradition has played the part that it has in Western culture. Performance based on a preexisting written text has been judged severely in recent years as being mere illustration or interpretation of the already written, but, in fact, the text is only one of the elements that dynamically interact during the production process to create the work, and in performance it is always the performance itself that dominates.

The title of this chapter is "Energized Space: Moving Bodies," but so far my focus has been, rather, the semiotic functions performed by the actors' bodies in the space. I have shown that the movements of the performers into, out of, and within the performance space are crucial signifiers in theatrical semiosis, but in the theatre it is not enough to speak simply about meaning, for there is always something else. The final section of the chapter, therefore, is concerned with this "something else": the energy that comes from the physical reality of the body, the live presence of performers and spectators together in the same space, which is fundamental to the theatre experience.

Energy, Presence, and the Fragility of Performance

In the last twenty-five years there has been something of a revolution in the way the body is conceptualized in Western philosophy, sociology, and even medicine; no longer demonized (or feminized) as the animal part of man, to be disciplined and controlled by the reason, or seen simply as the material container for mind or spirit, it is now increasingly perceived to be at the center of a complex web of interrelationships with every aspect of the individual's being and with the world surrounding that individual. The implications for the theory and practice of performance are profound, for the theatre more than any other art form draws on, plays with, and exploits the reality of the human body.

Notions of character, mimesis, narrative, and even representation have been subverted and displaced, and the body of the performer has come into focus as never before. Sometimes requiring extraordinary training, skill, and virtuosity (as for example in Butoh and related practices), sometimes merely engaging in what Marcel Mauss called body techniques, sometimes subjected to extreme conditions that force the spectator into a voyeuristic complicity with violence and reveal a troubling underside to the "performance contract," sometimes present but unseen by any observer, the body of the performer/artist has become both the subject and the object of contemporary performance. Actor training institutions have, somewhat belatedly, begun to recognize that these developments call for a shift in the nature of their own practices, and, as Philip Zarilli shows in his book *Acting (Re)considered*, the dominant psychological paradigm underpinning actor training in the West is gradually being modified by what he calls "a psychophysiological paradigm" (1995, 178).

The postmodern avant-garde described by Henry Sayre has, since the 1970s, been using performance in its attempt to develop an art "founded upon contingency, multiplicity and polyvocality" (1989, xii), and contemporary performance thus has a complex genealogy, deriving as much from the visual arts as from different theatre practices, such as those documented by Zarilli. While the presence of the artist's body is radical and subversive in terms of any visual arts practice, it has always been a necessary part of the theatre experience, and, significantly, it has, even in the theatre, constituted something of a scandal from the very beginning. The reality of the actor's body always subverts representation in some way and opens up the possibility for something real and uncontrolled to occur, and it is one of the major factors in what Jonah Barish (1982) has termed the "anti-theatrical prejudice" that has been a recurring feature of society's response to theatre throughout the history of Western culture. When Aristotle defended the theatre against Plato's strictures, it seems he could do so only at the expense of performance and its bodies, focusing attention on the nature and the structure of the fictional and downplaying the importance of the presentational.

During the course of this century there have been many different attempts to recuperate the performance reality, under attack from Plato onward, and to engage seriously with the human presence that is the necessary concomitant of performance. Antonin Artaud, for example, waged a relentless polemic against the cultural establishment of his day whose members, centuries after Aristotle, were still obtusely missing the wood for the trees:

> In any event, and I hasten to say so at once, a theatre that subordinates staging and material realization, that is to say everything about it that is specifically theatrical, to the text, is a theatre for idiots, fools, perverts, grammarians, grocers, anti-poets and positivists—that is to say Westerners. (1964, 50; my trans.)

The very thing that theatre possessed that other art forms did not, the very thing that made theatre so precious in the eyes of Artaud, was precisely the thing that society and even other theatre practitioners seemed to value least. Because only theatre involved the immediacy of the per-forming body, it was through theatre that Artaud felt it might be pos-sible to break through language and all other dead or empty forms and touch life itself:

> Furthermore, when we speak the word "life," it must be understood we are not referring to life as we know it from its surface of fact, but to that fragile, fluctuating centre which forms never reach. (1958, 13)

The actor for Artaud, and for many who have explored the paths he opened up, is no longer there to "hold the mirror up to nature," to trans-mit someone else's meaning, to tell someone else's story, but to be, to give, or make an offering of his or her presence. In such performance the making of meaning is subordinated to the experience of the present moment; the goal is an experience beyond meaning. Rodrigue Vil-leneuve even makes a connection between the absolute presence of the actor in this kind of theatre and the Christian notion of the "Real Pres-ence" in the consecrated host (1993, 86–95), and the connection is neither blasphemous nor inappropriate. Throughout Grotowski's work, for example, there has been a tendency away from performance as a mode of representation toward performance as a means of evoking some other dimension of experience, and, as for Artaud before him, it is the per-former himself who has the experience, not the spectator. In the work that he has been doing at Pontedera since 1986, there is no spectator apart from Grotowski himself, at the most an occasional witness (his word), and art has become a vehicle, through which the performer may pass "from a so-called coarse level—in a certain sense, one could say an 'everyday level'—to a level of energy more subtle or even toward the *higher connection*" (Richards 1995, 125).

Practitioners such as Grotowski have moved away from theatre practice insofar as this involves making performances to be shown to an audience, and for many performance art practitioners *theatre* is a pejora-tive term evoking pretense, sham, mere show. It is nevertheless true that the experience of energy, the power of the here and now, the dangerous edge of contingency, that all their work draws on have been part of the experience of theatre throughout its history. Performance practitioners today talk of "presence," "focus," and "energy"; a hundred years ago, when Kierkegaard was describing the fascination of farce and the per-formance of a particular actor at the Königstädter Theater in Berlin, he said that it was not Beckmann's ability to create character that distinguished him but his "effervescence of spirit" (1941, 67).[5] Kierkegaard referred to spirit where a contemporary theorist would doubtless refer to energy, but there is surely a profound connection between Beckmann's "effervescence," Barba's notion of the "extra-daily" (1985, 369–82), and what I experienced when the female performer walked across the floor of the gallery at the Performance Space. Whatever names are given to this and wherever it is deemed to be located, it is an important dimension of the "something more" that is always present in the theatre, and it seems to transcend differences in performance style and genre.

Kierkegaard's description of Beckmann's performance contains a fascinating reference to his own experience as a spectator. He refers to the "jubilation and clangor" in the upper galleries that occurs not just in response to verbal cues but is "a steady accompaniment, without which the farce could not be performed at all." In the midst of this uproar he experiences the performance differently from the working-class spectators in the galleries above him:

> Thus it was I lay back in my loge, cast aside like the clothing of a bather, flung beside the stream of laughter and merriment and jubilation which foamed past me incessantly. I could see nothing but the vast expanse of the theatre, hear nothing but the din in the midst of which I dwelt. Only now and then did I raise myself, look at Beckmann and laugh so heartily that for very fatigue I sank down again beside the foaming stream. (1941, 71)

Kierkegaard's experience in the theatre depends as much on the energy of the audience as on the performance of Beckmann, and he watches the audience almost as much as he watches Beckmann. He specifies earlier in the essay the desirability of having "a box alone by oneself," so he is part of the audience while nevertheless separated from it, and the other fascinating thing about his description is the way he maintains this distance, deliberately choosing a box from which he must crane to get a view of the stage, alternating exposure to the performance with experience of the crowd. It is as though he cannot bear too long an exposure to the upheaval produced in him by the paroxysms of laughter the performance provokes, but the tumult of the crowd all around him carries him along with it.

Arthur Symons, another very perceptive theatre spectator, describing Sarah Bernhardt in performance, also draws attention to the energy of the audience itself:

It was as if the whole nervous force of the audience was sucked out of it and flung back, intensified, upon itself, as it encountered the single, insatiable, indomitable nervous force of the woman. (1927, 151)

The mark of the great performer is that he or she is not only able to stimulate the audience to produce such huge amounts of emotional energy but is able to channel it and, in so doing, to augment it, "fling it back, intensified." As these two remarkable descriptions of performance make clear, energy does not simply emanate from the performer but is produced through the relationship between performer and spectator, and this can only occur when both are present in the same physical space.

My choice of premodern rather than postmodern theatre to illustrate this point about performance energy is to emphasize that this is not simply a quality of contemporary performance in which the bodily presence of performer and spectator has been foregrounded by the nature of the performance but that it is a potential of all live theatre, even if Artaud's grammarians and grocers do not know what to do with it.

There are a number of factors that contribute to the energy peculiar to a theatrical performance, besides the "nervous force" of the exceptional performer. There is, first, the fact that the performance is being created even as the spectators watch—and only because they are watching. Performance is always in process, never a finished product. As Hollis Huston puts it:

If writing tells of something happening, a performance of that writing then tells of and also is a thing happening, though the thing that happens is only a seeming, and is not the happening told about. (1992, 43)

The "thing told" may be familiar, the outcome may be known before the play begins, but the "thing that happens"' is unknown, cannot be known even if the production has been running for weeks, because it will happen only on that one night in exactly that way, and every moment is charged with possibilities of triumph or disaster. This is the fragility of performance, and it constitutes a large part of the fascination of theatre.

Knowledge of the essential uniqueness of each performance is another factor in the creation of the special energy that marks live performance, for it fosters in both spectators and performers a certain kind of awareness of the present moment, also a certain kind of alertness because what is missed is permanently missed (there is no rewind facility in the theatre, no turning back to the beginning of the book). The theatre experience is dependent on the relationship that gets set up between the performers and the spectators; every night this relationship has to be constructed, every night the task is different, not only because the composition of the audience changes from night to night but because the actors change too; they bring to the theatre each night their own moods, states of health, desires, etc., which are no more a constant than the composition of the audience.

A further aspect of the uniqueness of performance is that the actor in the theatre is unrecorded and unrecordable. In all other art forms there is either an artifact, a product, a permanent trace, of the artists' work, or others have developed methods of recording this work. Even conceptual artists, performance artists, body artists, and others whose works set out to subvert the dominant notion of art object frequently arrange to have their work filmed, photographed, or videorecorded so that there is in fact a visual trace, a more durable record (ironically, often a saleable commodity), of what they did. Actors, however, have been remarkably consistent in refusing to have their work videorecorded or filmed, knowing that the camera cannot capture what is really important in the live performance, and it is precisely in the intangible area of presence that this occurs. For musicians, on the other hand, sound recording has provided a multibillion dollar industry, and, even though live performance of music and recording are very different experiences both for the performers and the listeners, the results obtained through recording are such that the artists are prepared to collaborate fully in the recording enterprise.

Performance, as has been stressed throughout this book, is a relationship between performer and spectator, and, for such a relationship to occur, both must be present to each other. That is to say, both must be together in the same place. I have so far discussed the range of expressive functions fulfilled by the physical places in which performances occur (chap. 2), and, in focusing in the present chapter on the spatial reality of the performers, I have stressed their role as the mobile agents who activate and energize the performance space, thus rendering it meaningful. Spatial factors can also be seen to play a major role in the structuring of performance and in signaling such structuring to the spectators, and this aspect of spatial function is explored further in the next chapter.

4

Space and Performance Structure

In art it is always a question of arrangement of the material.
  —Vsevolod Meyerhold, *Der Schauspieler der Zukunft*

Theatre is the art of playing with division, introducing it into
space by means of dialogue.
  —Maurice Blanchot, *L'Entretien infini*

A theatrical performance, whatever its genre, is a physical event occupying a certain space and a certain duration. The duration may be a few minutes as in Samuel Beckett's *Not I*, or all night as in a *wayang kulit* performance, but whether it lasts the two to three hours that has become the accepted norm in contemporary Western theatre, or twelve hours or twelve minutes, the spatiotemporal continuum is necessarily structured in some way. That is to say, it is segmented into a number of component parts that are perceived as such by spectators and that set up relations of varying diachronic and synchronic sorts between themselves. This occurs most obviously at the presentational level in ways that involve the material reality of the performance itself, and it is for this reason that spatial factors play such an important part in the structuring process.

A traditional theatrical performance creates and presents a fictional world or worlds and the series of events occurring in these fictional worlds, or the series of actions presented, is also segmented, as the word "series" in both phrases indicates, and it is therefore itself necessarily structured. It can be argued, then, that there are at least two systems of segmentation at work in any theatrical performance, the presentational and the fictional. The structuring of the two systems is closely connected: they interact, construct each other, and yet remain to a certain extent separate. Depending on genre, period, and prevailing aesthetic codes, performance structuring may be more or less overt, more or less fragmented, or more or less artfully contrived so as to appear "invisible" or "seamless"[1] but, as will be argued in this chapter, it is always a vital part of the meaning-making process.

Furthermore, it can be shown that the connection between segmentation and meaning is of central importance at all stages of the creative process, that is, whether we approach the performance as a spectator in the theatre, or from the practitioners' perspective during the rehearsal process, or from the writer's perspective. A significant finding that emerges both from my observations of actors and directors in rehearsal and from work on spectators' perceptions of structure during and after the performance,[2] is that spatial elements, notably those activated by the actors' bodily presence in the presentational space, are of central importance in the construction and presentation of the structuring system, and in spectators' reception of this. It is for this reason that I have included such an extensive discussion of the topic in this study of spatial function.

To claim that performance segmentation occurs on two levels, the presentational and the fictional, is doubtless to invite the objection that not all theatre creates a fictional world, and it must certainly be recognized that in the performance practices of the avant-garde from Dada onward, the notion of fiction, and particularly narrative fiction, has been under attack. The experience of fiction is always precarious in the theatre due to the complexity and power of the stage reality and the fascination exercised by the presentational system, but I think it can be claimed with equal force that the theatre also functions very powerfully to fictionalize whatever it presents. As soon as the performer standing in the stage space says "I," we have fiction, or a blurring of fiction and reality, and even if the performer is Judith Malina playing herself we have, not simply Judith Malina, as Keir Elam pointed out in his discussion of the function of iconicity in the theatre (Elam 1980, 21–27), but "Judith Malina," a theatrically ostended Judith Malina.

Theatre is a place where fiction and reality come together to problematize each other. What is presented in performance is always both real and not real, and there is constant interplay between the two potentialities, neither of which is ever completely realized. The tension between the two is always present, and, indeed, it can be argued that it is precisely the dual presence of the real and the not real that is constitutive of theatre. My choice of the term *fictional* to refer to the events and actions presented during a performance is not an attempt to ignore the whole avant-garde endeavor, with its subversion and displacement of notions of character, story, and even acting, but a recognition of the problematical "reality" status of what is presented in performance and an attempt to draw attention to the ever present polarity.

In the theatre spectators are presented with a sequence of enacted events, ordered in space and time, and in their attempts to make sense of what they are experiencing, they respond to the events and to the way they have been ordered into a sequence as well as to the actual presentation. Thus it can be said that in the theatre the fictional is both ordered and constructed by the presentational system. The distinction that Gérard Genette makes between "story," "narrative," and the act of "narrating" is as valid and pertinent when applied to theatre as to the novel, whether or not the performance genre in question is overtly narrative, and his tripartite system of naming the structuring process as it functions in prose fiction is also useful in describing what occurs in the theatre:

> I propose, without insisting on the obvious reasons for my choice of terms, to use the word *story* for the signified or narrative content (even if this content turns out, in a given case, to be low in dramatic intensity or fullness of incident), to use the word *narrative* for the signifier, statement, discourse or narrative text itself, and to use the word *narrating* for the producing narrative action and, by extension, the whole of the real or fictional situation in which that action takes place. ([1972] 1980, 27)

The events and actions that I am calling the fictional parallel Genette's "story." It is the way that these events are dramaturgically shaped to form a narrative or organized into a sequence that parallels the "narrative," and this is an essential part of the fictional system and of the meaning-making process. The presentational system in the theatre is clearly more complex than the narration of a novel in that it involves multiple sign systems and media, but the physical performance in a given presentational and performance space of the events and actions can be seen, in structural terms, to fulfill a similar function to Genette's "narrating."

It is more difficult to account for the process as it occurs in the theatre than in the novel because the fictional content is subject to multiple shaping processes that may be widely separated in space and time and be the responsibility of different artists. In the novel it is the writer who produces both narrative and the narrating, whereas in theatre the authorial voice is necessarily divided between those responsible for the dramaturgical shaping of the material (the construction of the theatrical narrative) and its physical presentation (the narrating). While the play-

wright has, in the past, been seen to be more responsible for the dramaturgical shaping of the material, and the performers for the presentational shaping, there has been considerable slippage between these functions in performance practice in recent years. A further complication is
that the presentational shaping is itself extremely complex and involves
the input of numerous artists working with different materials. The
advent of the director has made us more aware of the authorial function
of the mise en scène, and accounts of the actor's process, such as those
provided by Stanislavsky (1967, 1968, 1981), make clear that a great deal
of dramaturgical shaping occurs during rehearsal, even where the work
revolves around a pre-existing written text that is already dramaturgically shaped.

It may be helpful, at this stage, to provide a more concrete illustration of the kind of dramaturgical shaping in question and its role in the
construction of meaning. A comparison of the same fragment of dramatic action (i.e., the same fictional moment) taken from two different
productions of Ibsen's *A Doll's House* will illustrate the way performance
segments the action and thereby shapes the events performed and the
meanings they convey. The different meanings produced in performance with the same moment of dramatic action provide insight into the
meaning-making process itself and demonstrate the function of performance segmentation in this process. My analysis is based on observation
of the rehearsal process for version one (a workshop performance
directed by Lindy Davies) and on my experience as a spectator in the theatre, supplemented by video documentation, for version two (Gale
Edwards's production of the play at the Belvoir Street Theatre in Sydney
in 1989). The fragment analyzed is taken from the beginning of act 1,
when Mrs. Linde comes to visit Nora.

The text of the two fragments, together with a brief performance
notation for the Edwards version, is set out in figures 12 and 13.[3] Lindy
Davies and her actors, working with the Michael Meyer translation, saw
the scene as composed of four "beats" (the term they used), with the "climaxes" (again their term) situated on the words indicated in bold format
in figure 12. The segmentation into beats thus functioned to foreground
a particular idea, selected by the director during a detailed exploratory
process in which the actors sought the emotional impulse for each phrase
of their text. As far as this play was concerned, the idea was always
encapsulated in a phrase or sentence from the text. At one stage the
director even gave the beats little descriptive titles, derived from their

ML:	Good evening, Nora.
N:	Good evening -
ML:	I don't suppose you recognize me.
N:	No, I'm afraid I - Yes, wait a minute - surely - I
	Why, Christine. Is it really you?
ML:	Yes, it's me.
N:	Christine. And I didn't recognize you. But how could I -?
	How you've changed, Christine.
ML:	Yes, I know. It's been nine years - nearly ten -
N:	Is it so long? Yes, it must be.
	Oh, these last eight years have been such a happy time for me.
	So you've come to town? All that way in winter. How brave of you.
ML:	I arrived by the steamer this morning.
N:	Yes, of course, to enjoy yourself over Christmas.
	Oh, how splendid. We'll have to celebrate.
	But take off your coat. You're not cold, are you?
	There. Now let's sit down here by the stove and be comfortable.
	No, you take the armchair. I'll sit here in the rocking-chair.
	Yes, now you look like your old self. Just at first I - you've got a little paler, though, Christine.
	And perhaps a bit thinner.
ML:	And older, Nora. Much, much older.
N:	Yes, perhaps a little older. **Just a tiny bit. Not much.**
	Oh, but how thoughtless of me to sit here and chatter away like this.
	Dear, sweet Christine, can you forgive me?
ML:	What do you mean, Nora?
N:	Poor Christine, you've become a widow.
ML:	Yes. Three years ago.
N:	I know, I know - I read it in the papers.
	Oh, Christine, I meant to write to you so often, honestly.
	But I always put if off, and something else always cropped up.
ML:	I understand, Nora dear.
N:	No, Christine, it was beastly of me.
	Oh, my poor darling, what you've gone through.
	And he didn't leave you anything?
ML:	No.
N:	No children, either?
ML:	No.
N:	Nothing at all then?
ML:	Not even a feeling of loss or sorrow.
N:	But, Christine, how is that possible?
ML:	Oh, these things happen, Nora.
N:	All alone. How dreadful that must be for you.
	I've three lovely children.

(*continued*)

MONEY, MONEY, MONEY.

ML: I'm afraid you can't see them now, because they are out with Nanny.
But you must tell me everything.
ML: No, no, no. I want to hear about you.
N: No, you start. I'm not going to be selfish today, I'm just going to think about you.
Oh, but there's one thing I must tell you.
Have you heard of the wonderful luck we've just had?
ML: No. What?
N: Would you believe it -
my husband's just been made manager of the bank.
ML: Your husband? Oh, how lucky -
N: Yes, isn't it. Being a lawyer is so uncertain, you know,
especially if one isn't prepared to touch any case that isn't - well - quite nice.
And of course Torvald's been very firm about that -
and I'm absolutely with him.
Oh, you can imagine how happy we are.
He's joining the bank in the New Year,
and he'll be getting a big salary and lots of percentages too.
From now on we'll be able to live quite differently -
we'll be able to do whatever we want.
Oh, Christine, it's such a relief. I feel so happy.
Well, I mean, it's lovely to have heaps of money and not to have to worry about anything.
Don't you think?
ML: It must be lovely to have enough to cover one's needs, anyway.
N;   Not just our needs.
We're going to have heaps and heaps of money.

Fig. 12. Beats and titles in Lindy Davies's *A Doll's House*

narrative content (The Arrival, The Welcome, The Widow, and Money Money Money), which have been included in figure 12. In this performance version the scene seems to be essentially about the contrast between Nora's happiness and fulfillment ("such a happy time for me," "I've two lovely children," "heaps and heaps of money") and the dignified sadness of Mrs. Linde.

Gale Edwards used a different translation, by May Brit Akerholt, which had some impact on the climax lines, and the scene as I saw it in the theatre was also made up of four segments (beats?) but rather differently constructed from those of Lindy Davies and her actors. In segment 1 both characters are standing at a distance from each other; in segment 2 Nora runs to Kristine, draws her into the room and bustles around her; in segment 3 both are sitting. This is a relatively long segment and it contains two of Davies's climaxes, neither of which receives particular

K: (1) Hello, Nora.

N: Hello.

K: I don't suppose you recognise me.

N: No, I...I'm afraid I...Oh yes, now I...Kristine.
It is Kristine, isn't it?

K: Yes, yes it is.

N: (2) **Kristine. And I didn't recognise you.**
Oh, but how could I? You've changed, Kristine.

K: Yes, I'm sure I have. It's been nine or ten years.

N: That long? Yes, it must be. These last eight years have
been such a happy time for me.
And now you've come to town (3).
You've made that long journey in the middle of winter.
How brave of you.

K: I arrived on the steamer this morning.

N: To celebrate Christmas of course. Yes, isn't it wonderful.
We're going to really celebrate this year. But do take
your coat off (4). Let's make ourselves comfortable.
No, no, in the salon (5). I want to sit in the rocking chair (6)*.
There, that's more like it.
Now I can see that you're like your old self again. It was just
that very first moment. But you're a little paler, Kristine, and
a little thinner perhaps.

K: And much much older, Nora.

N: Oh, a little older maybe. Just a tiny bit. Not much at all.
Oh, but how thoughtless of me, chattering away like this.
Dear Kristine, forgive me.

K: What for, Nora?

N: My poor Kristine, you're a widow now.

K: Yes. Three years ago.

N: Yes, I know, I know. I saw it in the papers. Oh, believe me,
Kristine, I often thought about writing to you. But I always
put it off.

K: I understand, Nora, really I do.

N: Oh no, it was very thoughtless of me. Poor thing, you must
have been through such a lot. And I understand he didn't
leave you much.

K: No.

N: And no children?

K: No.

N: So he left you with nothing.

K: Not even a feeling of grief or regret.

N: Oh, Kristine, that's hardly possible.

K: Oh yes, Nora, it's possible.   (continued)

N: So you're all alone. How difficult that must be. I have three
   lovely children. You can't meet them now. Ivor and Annie
   are playing in the park, and Bob, my little baby, is having his
   nap. You must tell me everything.

K: No, no. I'd rather you tell.

N: No, no, no. You first. Today I won't be selfish. Today I shall
   only think about your problems *. But there is one thing I must
   tell you. Have you heard about our wonderful stroke of luck?

K: No, I haven't.

N: Just imagine (7). <u>My husband has been appointed manager of
   the National Savings Bank.</u>

K: Your husband? Well, that is a stroke of luck.

N: **Yes, isn't it fantastic?** (8)
   <u>Oh, from now on our lives are going to be different</u> (9). We can
   do whatever we want. Oh, it's such a relief. Kristine, I'm so
   happy. It's wonderful to have lots of money and <u>not a care in
   the world, don't you think</u>? (10)

K: At least it must be wonderful to have enough.

N: No, no, no. <u>Not just enough but lots and lots</u> (11) *.

K: Nora, Nora, you haven't grown up yet. At school you used to be
   awfully good at wasting money.

N: Torwald says I still am. **But Nora Nora isn't as frivolous
   as you all think** (12).

---

* Audience laughter

MOVES
1. K enters, N stands centre stage
2. N runs to K, clasps her hands
3. N draws K into the centre
4. N bustles around K, taking her coat
5. K sits on couch
6. N fetches rocking chair and sits close
   to K.
7. N sits forward eagerly
8. N stands quickly, crosses down left,
   facing audience
9. N turns back to K, who turns on
   couch to face her
10. N turns back to face audience
11. N turns to face K, then back to face
    audience
12. N walks to end of couch, down left

Fig. 13. Moves and beats in Gale Edwards's *A Doll's House*

emphasis. In segment 4 Kristine remains sitting but Nora gets up suddenly and moves downstage to face the audience. Certain lines received special emphasis and this was always associated with a move or a big gesture as well as energetic vocal delivery ("Kristine. And I didn't recognise you," "There, that's more like it," "Manager of the National Bank / Yes, isn't it fantastic?") and these can, using Lindy Davies's phrase, be seen as the climax points in segments 1, 2, and 3.

In segment 4 Nora has her back to Kristine but she half-turns back toward her several times then turns away again quickly to face the audience. Each of the phrases thus marked receives a certain emphasis ("Our lives are going to be so different," "Not a care in the world," "Not just enough but lots and lots," "Nora Nora isn't as frivolous as you think"), and her nervous mobility seems to mark this micro segment as being particularly highly charged. The spectator is not aware precisely what is going on but, speaking from my own experience, begins to suspect that all is not quite as Nora is claiming.

As this analysis makes clear, a major factor in my perception of performance units was the proxemic relations between the two actors: segment 1 was marked by distance and stasis, segment 2 by proximity and mobility, segment 3 by proximity and stasis, and segment 4 by distance, stasis, and mobility. The spatial organization of the performance was thus the principal means of articulating and manifesting the segmentation of the dramatic action. In figure 13 I have used bold type to indicate the charged lines that climax each segment, and the phrases marked by Nora's turns in the final segment are underlined; the numbered references to moves and big gestures show how these occur in relation to the stressed lines. Following the example of Lindy Davies, it seemed that these four segments could be "named" in terms of the main idea conveyed. My suggestions (I have no idea how the performers conceptualized this scene nor of the rehearsal metalanguage) are as follows:

1. Nonrecognition (this creates a disturbance to the social fabric).
2. Re-imposition of social order (the emotional intensity given to "There, that's more like it," an apparently banal little phrase, shows how important this surface order is to Nora).
3. Sad past/happy past (the apparent contrast is between Kristine's sadness and Nora's happiness, but Nora's luck is "fantastic," and her brittle restlessness alerts us to the ambivalence—has Nora's past really been so happy?).
4. Fantasy future/real (hidden) past (here is another double title,

an increasing sense of ambivalence, the fantasy future that Nora predicts gives the lie to the happy past she has been claiming).

The scene in this production seems concerned essentially with Nora's attempts to remain in control and to maintain the fantasy of herself as the happy child-bride while being impelled, almost against her will, to tell someone the truth. While my analysis of this small section has been greatly assisted by several viewings of a video recording, the spectator in the theatre is equally assisted in perceiving important paradigmatic structures by the fact that they are always repeated, and by the elaboration from other sign systems. The "fantasy versus reality" and "social surface threatened by hidden forces" ideas I found in this scene received powerful support from Mary Moore's set design, with its massive ice floes forcing up the floorboards around the edge of the drawing room, which I have already mentioned in chapter 1.

Differences in the translation are an important factor in the meaning created. In the Gale Edwards version Nora made a big move on the line "Yes, isn't it fantastic?" and, as has been shown, the word "fantastic" was highly significant in the fantasy/reality contrast that I found fundamental to the scene as performed. Michael Meyer translates that line more blandly as "Yes, isn't it?" and it is hardly surprising that Lindy Davies and her actors did not pick that moment to explore further. The point I am making does not concern the accuracy of the translation nor the content of the original Norwegian, but the way actors use text in their construction of performance.

The titles Lindy Davies gave to her beats indicate the dominance of narrative factors, while my titles for the segments I perceived in Gale Edwards's version are perhaps more concerned with thematic content. This in itself suggests something about the way the segmentation functions in the production of meaning. Whether the emphasis is on the narrative or on the implications of the narrative, however, the main point to emerge from this example is that both from the perspective of the practitioners creating the performance and from that of a spectator viewing performance in the theatre, the segmentation of the dramatic action is a crucial part of the meaning-making process. The differently constructed segments (beats or micro-units), and the different lines of dialogue emphasized in the process ensure that a different "story" is told with the same raw material.

Equally important is the role played by spatial factors such as movement and gesture in constructing and signaling this structure to spectators. A different segmentation expressed in a different spatial organization produces different meanings. The particular fragment analyzed also draws attention to the role of language in theatrical meaning making, but while the *Doll's House* scene might be seen to exemplify the meaning-making process in a particular kind of text-based theatre, it can also be argued that the vast majority of theatrical performances consist of physical action and speech in some combination. The presentational system in theatre is, except in specific genres such as mime, composed of both physical and verbal material, and furthermore, the verbal is necessarily dependent on and constructed by the vocal. The paralinguistic features inseparable from vocal performance are an essential and inescapable part of the verbal content and of the meanings constructed. The structuring process can be represented in a schematic way, thus:

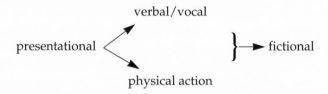

In traditional text-based theatre, a great deal of time is spent in rehearsal in carefully knitting together tiny fragments of speech and actions that motivate, illustrate, and interpret them. In other forms of performance the structuring process often involves a similar meshing together of words and action, though in some, words may be found only after the actions have taken shape, in others the words may exist only to be subverted by the action, etc.

While such propositions may receive assent from practitioners and spectators it is, in fact, no easy matter to describe the nature and function of performance segmentation, even in some particular pragmatic context, due to the ephemerality of the performance and the multiplicity of sign systems and modes of expression simultaneously in operation. As theatre spectators and practitioners know, any theatrical signifier is likely to belong to several orders of experience simultaneously and will bear a complex load of cultural inscription, and equally any signified is likely to result from the interaction of multiple signifiers functioning either simultaneously or sequentially. This is as true of performance segmentation as of any other aspect of theatrical function, and any theoretical formulation of the nature of this segmentation must take into account the multiplicity, simultaneity, and polyvalence factors that characterize theatrical semiosis.

The polyvalence can be glimpsed even at the level of popular usage[4] as indicated in the following three uses of the term *scene,* one of the most commonly used terms designating a performance segment. To say "the scene where Othello kills Desdemona was very well done," is to use the word to refer to an event or happening. In popular usage, a scene is usually a fictional event, but it is not necessarily restricted to theatrical or dramatic fiction, and a scene may be one of a series of events that have been transformed into a narrative sequence by being recounted. A phrase such as "the murder of Desdemona takes place in Act V scene ii," however, uses the word to refer to a structural unit, and this usage is normally restricted to dramatic works; the scene as structural unit is clearly defined in neoclassical dramaturgy, less clearly in Elizabethan and other periods, but it is nevertheless a distinct segment of dramatic action, signaled as such in the playscript by the playwright or editor. Yet another use of the word *scene* is to be found in a phrase such as "the scene of the murder is Desdemona's bedroom." Here the scene is a place, often but not exclusively a place of theatrical action. The way this spatial usage has been taken into non-theatrical contexts (e.g., "the scene of the crime") makes clear that a scene is not simply a place but, more precisely, a place where something happens. It may be, of course, that all that happens is that the scene is perceived as such by a viewer ("it was an idyllic scene").

The terminological slippage involved in these common uses of the same term is no coincidence but an indication of the multiple registers functioning simultaneously in the theatre. A scene is a fictional or dramatic event and a structural unit (i.e., it is a unit in both the fictional and the presentational systems), and it is also the place where the event occurs, and this should alert us to the likelihood that a comparable weave of factors will prevail in the composition of performance structures at other levels besides that of the scene. The inclusion of place is particularly interesting in that it points to the intimate connection between spatial factors and segmentation that is central to my argument in this chapter.

A good deal of interesting work on performance segmentation was done by theatre semioticians in the 1970s (Jansen 1968, 1973; Kowzan 1975; Pavis 1976; Serpieri 1981), and this was generally posited on the hypothesis that theatrical performance functions as a kind of language and that it should therefore be possible to break it down into minimal semiotic units on an analogy with verbal language. These hypothetical minimal units were conceptualized as being necessarily theatre specific notwithstanding the fact that they would be composed of sign systems in use in other areas of society. The theoretical and conceptual difficulties caused by reliance on the linguistic analogy and the limitations of the linguistic models in vogue at the time were compounded by the methodological strategies adopted by many researchers: the attempt to define structural units of a theatrically specific sort was conducted not in the theatre itself, nor in the rehearsal room where they were being constructed, but most frequently on the basis of the performance potential derived from a reading of playtexts, and sometimes on the basis of a completely different art form, such as film.

It is perhaps not surprising in the circumstances that the results of much of this work were rather inconclusive, but it was unfortunate that so many people abandoned the whole line of enquiry rather than reconsidering the conceptual framework. Keir Elam's conclusion in 1980 was that the minimal unit did not exist:

> If theatrical discourse were genuinely articulated into cohesive and well-defined units like language itself, then such units would be intuitively recognisable to both performers and audience as the conventional vehicles of communication. The difficulties involved in defining appropriate categories suggest that this is not the case. (1980, 48)

Anne Ubersfeld had already said the same thing three years earlier on the basis of the heterogeneity of theatrical signifiers:

> We know that there can be no such thing as a minimal unit in the theatre: the layering of differently articulated networks (of signifiers) prevents us establishing any moments where all the networks are interrupted except in the large units. (1977, 235)

The minimal unit *as hypothesized* was perhaps indeed Elam's "semiotic philosopher's stone," but we cannot therefore assume that performance is not composed of recognizable units. Observation of the rehearsal process, consultation with practitioners and written accounts of their creative practices all confirm that the structuring process occupies a good deal of rehearsal time and, as preliminary analysis of the *Dom Juan* material indicates, spectators do use these performance structures in their attempts to make meanings with what they see.

To explore this important aspect of theatrical semiosis and to

advance the theoretical understanding of how the medium functions it is
necessary to include the experience of the practitioners and to ensure
that theory is grounded in the pragmatics of detailed performance analysis. Textual analysis is useful, for the playtext is certainly an important
factor in the performance structures evolved in any performance created
with a preexisting written text but, even in this kind of performance, the
text is only one of a number of contributing factors. The answers to questions about performance segmentation will not be found in purely text-
based analysis, and a great deal more attention has to be paid to the
rehearsal process itself.

It is evident from watching rehearsals that most directors consciously divide the action into units of some kind. Furthermore, there is
a range of terms in use to refer to this segmentation. The terms vary considerably and over the last ten years I have heard all of the following: *act,
scene, episode, action, beat, bit, unit, image, idea, thought, point, sense block,
station, moment.* Actors might also say, "Let's mark this bit," and proceed
to discuss or run the proposed blocking of a small segment of action; this
suggests that there is a more refined level of performance behavior that
can be "marked" even if the individual components have not been conceptualized as named units of action.

Some of the terms cited are purely commonsense words, like *bit* or
unit, which could be used in many contexts; others seem to be more precisely defined and to incorporate an aesthetic philosophy. The
scene/beat/mark distinction is commonly used by actors and directors
trained in the dominant Stanislavsky-derived methods, but others, who
see such acting as too constraining or necessarily associated with a psy-
chologized, character-based narrative theatre, may prefer an aesthetic
based on terms such as *action, image,* and even *station.* Segmentation is,
however, an important factor regardless of the dominant aesthetic.

Even within a group with an accepted, shared performance aesthetic, the terminology in use may be very fluid and a number of different terms may be used for the same phenomenon, or the same name may
be used for apparently different phenomena. Notwithstanding the aesthetic and conceptual differences, however, rehearsal practice suggests
that, pace Elam, it is possible to talk about intuitive recognition of performance units, at least from the perspective of the practitioners within
the production process.

Performance segmentation is a recent academic concern, emerging
from the attempts to develop a semiotics of theatre, but it is interesting to

note that it is also a relatively recent concern amongst practitioners. While *acts* and *scenes* have been in existence for hundreds of years and are part of the dramaturgical structure provided by the writer, all the other terms I have cited as being in use among practitioners seem to have emerged during the course of this century. It is indeed only since the advent of the director that anyone has bothered to describe the production process or to theorize about it, and, of course, the process itself has evolved significantly due to the work of the director. If, as is claimed here, segmentation is an important part of the creation and communication of meaning, then it is important to know who does the segmenting and when and how. This is part of the constantly evolving question of authorial responsibility in the theatre.

Before presenting the speculations and tentative conclusions resulting from my own observations and analyses, it will be helpful to refer briefly to some influential commentaries on the production process and to some other attempts to account systematically for the segmentation of performance, and to relate these to the creative practices I have observed amongst Australian theatre practitioners.

Practitioners' Accounts of Their Own Practice

Stanislavsky was probably the first person to describe in detail the actor's creative process, and although the kind of acting he described (or prescribed) is no longer the dominant force in theatre that it has been, it is undeniable that a great deal of contemporary theatre practice still derives from Stanislavsky or from the kind of process he described. According to him the actor has to divide the play into "its main organic episodes" (1967, 111), and then extract from each of these episodes its essential content. This produces what he calls "the inner outline of the play," which is also referred to as "the spine" or "the through-line"; the procedures here, if not the terminology, converge in a revealing manner with later structuralist analytical method, reminding us that Stanislavsky and the Russian Formalists are products of the same cultural moment. The essential content of each episode has to be fleshed out with surface details and articulated in terms of the stage (proxemic relations, moves, gesture, business with props, etc.). Stanislavsky's extended metaphor of carving a roast turkey to describe the actor's construction process involving reduction of "the largest pieces to medium size, then to small and then to fine" (107–9) makes clear that his actor's starting point is a completed structure, the playtext, which has to be broken down and reassembled. The resulting performance is, however, made up of a hierarchy of "pieces" (fine, small, medium, and large) that together construct "organic episodes."

Brecht is another influential director who has provided a detailed description of his rehearsal process and, while his system or "model" serves a very different aesthetic and political philosophy from that of Stanislavsky, the performance segmentation that they both describe is strikingly similar. Brecht, like Stanislavsky, would have the actor begin by dividing the play into episodes on the basis of plot, establishing the "nodal points," defined as "the important events that carry the plot a stage further" (Brecht 1964, 240–42). The objective is to bring out the social and political significance of the events, their "social gestus" rather than the psychological insights of Stanislavsky's "inner outline," but the first stage of the work process for both is a careful textual analysis and dramaturgical segmentation.

Brecht's second stage involves a similar micro-segmentation to that of Stanislavsky: each episode has to be worked through in terms of stage actions, positions, movements, groupings, business with carefully selected props, etc., in order to express the social Gestus of the acts and situations that make up the episode. Brecht's notes on the "Representation of sentences" (106) indicate that the micro-segmentation can be very detailed indeed, recalling Stanislavsky's "fine" pieces, and they suggest that the actor must work sentence by sentence, even phrase by phrase in the process of stage realization.

Stanislavsky, as actor and director, is primarily concerned in the texts quoted with the task of the individual actor particularly in relation to the creation of character; the perspective of Brecht, playwright and director, is somewhat different in that he describes a collective process that, while involving detailed individual work, is concerned with the play as a whole and is designed to achieve an ideologically calculated totality. It is significant that in relation to performance segmentation, notwithstanding their very different aesthetic philosophies and their different practice orientations, there are such obvious similarities in what is proposed. For both, segmentation occurs on a number of levels, results in a hierarchy of different types of unit, and is based on a combination of narrative content (derived from the text) and the physical realities of the stage and the bodies that people it.

Stanislavsky and Brecht both provide insight into the way practitioners utilize text and other elements in their elaboration of performance structures. Working from the perspective of an earlier performance tradition and one that is not based on a preexisting written text, Tim Fitzpatrick provides striking corroboration of the dual basis of performance segmentation, both fictional and presentational, its organizational function and its multileveled nature. Fitzpatrick has analyzed the commedia dell'arte scenarios of Flaminio Scala, and posits a two-level performance structure: first, the "scene-units," defined as in neoclassical dramaturgy on the basis of entrances and exits, which form the "basic organizational unit of plot and dramatic action," each of which can be further divided into a second level of subunits that "answer the question 'Who does/says what, to whom, next?' and so can be distinguished as constituted by a single act or speech-act combined with a change in deictic orientation" (1989b, 182–83).

In commenting on the key role played by the *commedia* in the subsequent development of European dramaturgy, Tim Fitzpatrick makes the very pertinent observation that the scenarios, by virtue of their schematic nature, can be seen as "the most direct and simple notation of what are essentially performance-units (the subunits constituted by a single act or speech-act)"; in the full playtext, however, these "performance-units are atomized into even more microscopic units of dialogue-utterance and individual gesture" (185). As the *Doll's House* example illustrates, in contemporary theatre practice it is the work of the actors and director in rehearsal that constructs the performance-units of their production, utilizing among other things the verbal and presentational structures provided by the playtext. Analysis of stage practice at a certain remove from the literary complexities of the written playtext reveals the basis for what are the units intuitively recognizable by practitioners and spectators that Elam hypothesized.

Alessandro Serpieri and his group of academic researchers shift the emphasis from the combination of fictional and presentational in the construction of performance-units, and stress the presentational. In order to specify the textual units "at work in the production of meaning on stage," they suggest that "one should not segment the 'story', but rather identify what will be termed here its indexical-deictic-performative segments and their iconic self display" (Serpieri et al. 1981, 165). They point out that theatrical language functions differently from literary language in that it produces meaning in relation to a pragmatic context. While questioning whether literary language is really so different from theatrical language in this respect, it can nevertheless be acknowledged that the language of playtexts seems to be even more radically unstable in the meanings it conveys than other forms of written language. The meaning of a theatrical utterance is always to be constructed within the performance context by the actors and the mise en scène, and it is never simply a given of the playtext.

Serpieri's proposal of segmentation based on shifts in deictic orientation and his functional categories of "deictant" (the producer of the deixis), "deictee" (the addressee), and "object of the deixis" provide a useful framework for exploring the relationship between text and performance or verbal component and performance. Attempts to apply the method systematically produce what may be thought an excessive degree of fragmentation: in the examples given in the article cited, the researchers proposed thirteen units in thirty-four lines of *Macbeth,* and eleven in one-third of a page of prose dialogue, and, as each unit is composed of multiple sign systems (linguistic, gestural, stage), the task of the notator attempting to analyze a whole play is rendered very cumbersome. Such a degree of fragmentation is, however, entirely compatible with the actor's work process as described by both Stanislavsky and Brecht and this is borne out in my observations of rehearsal practice where actors do indeed work with tiny fragments.

It is unlikely that the extremely fragmented micro units based on deictic shifts will all be perceived and, as it were, processed by the spectator in the theatre but they are doubtless present in some form to the spectator's consciousness. It is certainly difficult, if not impossible, to make sense of such a flow of detail and practitioners and theorists alike agree that in order to make sense of the myriad details that compose the performance, the spectator has to group the details into larger units. The performance itself provides guidance in how to do this. In performance genres where narrative coherence is important, the Stanislavsky-derived notions of objectives, super-objectives, through-lines, etc., assist both the actors in their attempt to relate their individual performances to the mise en scène as a whole, and the spectators who are attempting to make sense of the performance. In other forms of performance, too, spectators will find clues to the reception process the work demands.

Lindy Davies, describing to students her work process, talked of the risk of creating too many beats and thereby "shattering the text." In her experience excessive fragmentation is a problem and it is the director's job to ensure that the rich detail of the individual performance does, in Stanislavsky's terms, "fuse into larger units" (1967, 110).

The theoretical problem is the recurrent one of the basis upon which this fusion occurs. Serpieri and others acknowledge that it must happen and claim that the minimal semiological units they have defined can be "set out in larger units, which can be called (still in performative-deictic terms) microsequences, according to a coherent design. The microsequences are in turn organized into macrosequences, which might coincide with the scenes" (Serpieri et al. 1981, 170). So the micro units, which are composed according to a principle that explicitly excludes "story," ultimately fuse into macro sequences (scenes) whose basis is essentially narrative. The authors do not discuss how or at what stage nonstory becomes story. The mistake is probably to claim that story is ever excluded, even though the fragments involved in their deictic performative units are doubtless too small to figure even as the minimal elements of the kind Gerald Prince (1973) theorized.

Anne Ubersfeld, writing from the perspective of the spectator and reader, also proposes a hierarchy of units. She speaks of the performance as composed of major, medium and micro sequences (1977, 225–39), and her choice of the term *sequence* indicates that at each of these levels the performance segments are composed of yet smaller units. Her major and medium sequences equate approximately with the acts and scenes of neoclassical dramaturgy, so that the major sequences are signaled by a cessation of all performance signs for a period, medium sequences are signaled by important shifts in the groupings of characters present in the stage space, or by shifts in the type of exchange presented (the example she gives of a major sequence is the division of the kingdom in *King Lear*, which is made up of three medium sequences: Lear and his daughters, Lear and Cordelia, Lear and the husbands/suitors). Both of these types of unit are substantially derived from the text and are characterized by the fictional and presentational factors other commentators have mentioned.

The definition of the micro sequence is, as she admits herself, more problematical; her minimal definition is "that fragment of theatrical time (textual and performance) during which something happens which can be isolated" (236). Although Ubersfeld sees this system of segmentation as part of the temporal structure of the performance, my perception is that it is manifested essentially in terms of space (entrances and exits, movement and proxemic relations of all sorts). The happenings can be actions, interactions, even something as indeterminate as "an idea," and they are articulated by the content of the dialogue, content within a single speech, the nature of the utterance (prayer, order, question, reply, etc.), or by gestures or emotional shifts (these too are usually indicated by syntactical shifts, although not exclusively the deictic markers singled out by Serpieri and his group). Ubersfeld stresses that, although this segmentation of the performance may be based in part on the linguistic signifiers of the playtext, it is nevertheless not contained or inscribed in the text but has to be constructed by the performance. The beats I have noted in the *Doll's House* scene are doubtless the kind of thing Ubersfeld would consider a micro sequence.

She does not in *Lire le théâtre* consider anything smaller than the micro sequence but in a later work she introduces the idea of the "stage act"; this, she claims, is the basis of the actor's work and these are the units of semiotic/semantic import that need to be recorded in any performance notation. Her definition remains, predictably, fairly imprecise:

> in each sequence there will be for each actor a number of stage acts composed of the speech acts and physical actions which s/he carries out in the course of the sequence in relation to the stage acts of the other actors. (Helbo et al. 1987, 160–61)

She acknowledges that we do not have any precise, "scientific" method of notating or even of clearly distinguishing these acts, and suggests that all the analyst can do is to describe as carefully as possible what each actor does, taking into account the relationship between gestural and paralinguistic features of this doing, and ensuring that each actor's "acts" for a given segment of performance are considered both in relation to each other and to those of the other participants in the segment.

This notion despite its vagueness is much more promising than some of the proposals of the 1970s in that it evidently relates much more closely to the actor's work process and to the kind of thing that is elaborated during rehearsal and, in part, noted by the stage manager in the prompt book. The notation needed is a development and refinement of a system that already exists, rather than something totally extraneous to the practices of performers and production crew. Furthermore, the stage act as described does not involve any artificial separation of signifiers as was often the case with the earlier proposals.

There are still a number of problems. The examples of stage acts that she suggests to illustrate the concept ("Hamlet kills Polonius,"

"Hermione curses Oreste who has avenged her," "Don Juan (in the Vitez production) caresses a dove while Elvire's brothers try to tear each other to pieces") consist of a variety of categories of action and do not seem particularly minimal. "Hermione curses Oreste" for example may involve a single speech, but that speech would certainly be divided into sub-units of some sort by the actors in performance, while "Hamlet kills Polonius" could as easily be seen as a micro sequence in her own terminological system. The examples cited make no distinction between the fictional world and the stage reality and conceptualize "Hamlet kills Polonius" as a stage act equivalent to "Don Juan strokes a dove," and this is equally problematical in my view.

More work is clearly needed before the nature of the micro segmentation of performance can be theorized with confidence, or statements made about the relationship between micro and macro segmentation. To pursue these questions further it is certainly instructive to enquire of actors and directors themselves how they conceptualize the performance and its component parts.

Rex Cramphorn was a director who worked very intensively with text and his productions, usually of classic works, were always an illuminating meditation on and around the text. His preparatory work, before the actors began their reading phase, involved a minute analysis of the play in terms of both its physical staging requirements, particularly the detail of the coming and going within the presentational space, and in terms of the progression of ideas presented by the text. He used these two systems together to compose what he called "sense blocks," and his concern was as much with the actors' future work process (making "bite sized chunks for the actors" as he put it in conversation), as with the construction of a meaningful progression of ideas that would be part of the spectator's experience.

He divided the whole play into sense blocks, and he pointed out that the process indicates very interesting differences between playwrights in terms of the actual quantity of words they typically devote to an "idea." This can vary tremendously, and while some playwrights (like Racine, for example) provide a very even and regular structure, others may be very irregular (Shakespeare is the outstanding example); with Shakespeare, there is no regularity even within a given play, and as Cramphorn put it in conversation with me, Shakespeare may "endlessly elaborate a single idea, and then introduce a major new idea in very few words, maybe less than a line." The physical dimensions of the sense blocks are major factors in the rhythm of the ensuing performance.

The segmentation into sense blocks would be discussed and modified by the actors during the days spent reading and talking through the text (a substantial part of any Cramphorn rehearsal process), and it would form the underlying structural basis for the actors' work in the early stages of the rehearsal. As the process evolved, however, there would be less reference to this level of segmentation while the actors grappled with character, emotion, action, words, the space, each others' bodily and emotional presence, etc. The segmented structure with its dual physical/abstract basis, its inscription in stage space and in the imaginary would, however, continue to function as the director's guide in his overriding concern for the totality being constructed with the ever evolving, endlessly proliferating detail provided by the actors, and the designers of costume, set, props, and lighting.

Further evidence about the perception of performance units by both actors and by Rex Cramphorn himself, and their status at different stages in the work process is provided by the *Dom Juan* project that has already been mentioned, in which Rex directed an extract from Molière's *Dom Juan* (act 2, scenes 2–3, in his own translation). In the preliminary discussions, the extract was divided into twenty-one segments on the basis of its narrative content and manifest staging requirements. While Rex may have thought of these as sense blocks that term was not stressed, and the actors used words like *bit, idea,* and even *unit:* (notes taken during this process include such phrases as "what's the next bit?" "that's a new idea," "that really makes a new unit," "no, the break doesn't really come there"). There was general agreement about the segmentation, but it did not seem to figure significantly in the rehearsal discussions that ensued day by day as the scene took shape. Interestingly, one unit of action (Don Juan's physical examination of Charlotte) was from the very early stages of the rehearsal conceptualized as a unit, and named "the horse trading" which indicates the way they played it. Yet this unit was not seen as a separate segment or sense block at the reading stage when it was incorporated in a bigger sense block conceptualized as "Don Juan's first declaration of 'love'."

When the performance was being documented I asked the actors to do a walk-through, stopping for a photographer to take a shot of each moment that, in their view, illustrated a unit of action. The director was not present for this session, but he did his own series of shots at a later session, again in an attempt to provide a photographic record of the dramatic progression as manifested in that production. The actors recorded twenty-seven moments, which was very close to the original twenty-one sense blocks, but departed significantly from that schema to stress some of the physical business that had evolved. A unit like "the horse trading" rated a photograph, as did Don Juan's gesture on "What I say is from the bottom of my heart" (both in the same original sense block). The first speech by Don Juan, which composed a single sense block in the original segmentation rated two photographs, one for each of the two bits of business that punctuated it: Sganarelle finding a fish in his shoe, and Don Juan slapping Sganarelle for his clumsiness in lighting him a cigarette.

The director's record consists of seventy-five shots. He was clearly recording quite a different level of performance detail from the actors (for instance, his record of "the horsetrading" consists of four shots). It seems that the actors chose to record a different order of segmentation from the director: their segmentation is essentially that based on the narrative content extrapolated from the text in the reading phase of the rehearsal process, while the director recorded the fine detail of the performance (the presentational system, in the terminology I am using). Of course, fictional and presentational factors always interweave in practice and indeed each figures in the construction of the other.

The photographic record provides a double perspective on performance segmentation from the practitioners' point of view, from which it can be seen that multiple factors contribute to the elaboration of the segmentation and that it serves different functions at different stages of the creative process. This practical experiment also provides empirical evidence that performance segmentation is multileveled, for the director's "units of action" were so much more detailed than those selected by the actors as constituting the operative structure of their performance. It is significant in terms of the concerns of this study, that the factors that signal the segmentation, whether based essentially on the fictional or the presentational or the verbal, are overwhelmingly spatial: moves, gestures, physical orientation, position within the space, and use of objects.

It was perhaps slightly surprising that it should have been the director who recorded the fine detail of the actors' performance, while the actors noted the major stages in a dramatic action, for it is clear that the finest level of micro structuring (the level Rex Cramphorn documented in his photographic record), is very much the domain of the actor, which is perhaps why it has hitherto been so little theorized, and indeed so little explored. The actor may be the principal creative focus in performance but as far as scholarly discourse is concerned, it is the input of playwright, director, and even architect that has been documented and privileged, and we still have a great deal to learn from and about actors.

Norman Price, the director and writer of a play called *Dust Covers*, asked the two performers (Michele Finnegan playing "X" and Catherine Milne playing "Y") to write an account of their individual performance, and the two were included as an appendix in the Master's thesis he wrote on the genesis of the work (Price 1989). A sample page from each "score" is reproduced in figures 14 and 15, with the kind permission of the authors. Catherine Milne calls the account a "map" and sees it as made up of the "lines of their journey." These spatial metaphors are highly pertinent, for the actors present in schematic form their movements within the presentational space as well as a shorthand indication of their major actions, gestures, and the stages of the emotional experience they go through each time they perform the work.

As demonstrated in the sample page reproduced in figure 14, Michele Finnegan's very systematic account is arranged as a series of numbered "Points," each of which is segmented into a further series of numbered units. Her moves within the rectangular presentational space are noted, together with directional arrows and her stopping points. The term *point* that she uses to refer to the first level of performance segmentation is interesting in that in its normal usage it can refer both to position in space and the abstract level of ideas.

Finnegan's "Points" are each composed of a number of moves and positions but seem to refer also to stages in an emotional progression; it seems likely that from her point of view the bodily experience of the space and the emotions and ideas being communicated are so tightly interconnected that they cannot be separated.

The second level of segmentation includes a range of differently conceptualized units: some refer to a single act ("seeing gloves," "bow in deference to power"), others to a more complex action, such as "take Y to center and roll out" (this refers to the fact that Y was lying on the ground rolled up in a sheet of red cloth; she only enters the performance when dragged to the center by X and "rolled out" of the cloth). Some of these units refer to emotional states rather than moves ("rejoicing," "admon-

1st point

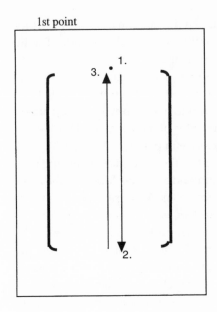

1. a. Waiting for light.
   b. Feeling light, growing, bathing,
      rejoicing.
   c. Seeing technician.
   d. Seeing gloves.
   e. Bow in deference to power.
   f. Rise with hands prepared.

2. a. Travel to gloves.
   b. Put gloves on - LIGHT.

3. Ready to begin.

2nd point

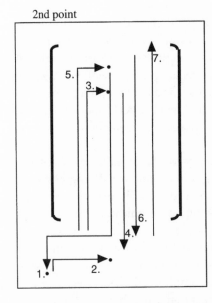

1. Rock a bye - get Y out.

2. Take her to centre and roll out.

3. Pineapple towards centre.

4. Takes Y so she can view performance.

5. Backs up to perform.

6. Father story performance.

7. Admonishing Y yet her own defeat.

Fig. 14. *Dust Covers:* Michele Finnegan's performance map

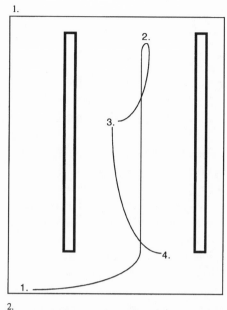

1. Under the stairs.

2. Stretched out - tense/looking/sensing.

3. First movement - an instinctive jerk away from X - (repulsion) and to seize the host which is a symbol of my potential wholeness.

4. Dragged down to centre by X (so far - except for 3. only been <u>acted</u> upon by X - a sense of biding my time, gathering my forces, back straightening, purpose becoming clearer) to watch her.

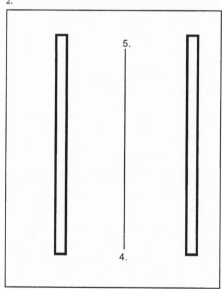

5. Advancing upon X - holding snake up to her, then pointing it at her, accusing her. Walking looking over my shoulder back at her.

5.continues - Me standing there alternately forcing then willing her into snake story - pulling the cloth up to the end/centre.

Moment of confrontation at end/centre.

(I'm still quite stationary at this stage - movement does not come easily until I go into corridor. (Also something to note after seeing Michele's map - my lines of journey / my maps much cleaner and clearer than hers))

Fig. 15. *Dust Covers:* Catherine Milne's performance map

ishing Y yet her own defeat"), and some are themselves divided into a further level of segmentation (unit 1 under first Point consists of five subunits, unit 2 has two).

The function of the verbal text in relation to this performance map is also very interesting, as the performance is not conceptualized in terms of the detailed structures of the verbal text. Whole sections of the text are referred to in a kind of shorthand form ("Pineapple" is her account of being chosen to be the "Pineapple Queen" in a parade, "Father Story" is another lengthy textual segment). Michele Finnegan did not, as it were, graft the account of her performance onto the printed trace of the verbal, but incorporated her verbal "performance" into the score composed of her actions, moves, and the experiences of her character X. The presentational aspects of the performance are foregrounded in this account and the verbal component is conceptualized in terms of units of performance.

The account by Catherine Milne is set out in a similar way with diagrams mapping the moves and a written account of the content, physical and emotional, of each of the numbered stages in her dramatic progression. Both actors adopt a two-level system of performance notation but the way they conceive the component parts is slightly different. Milne does not use the term "point" and her macro level is indicated simply by the numbered series of diagrams. She has eighteen of these, while Finnegan's performance consisted of ten Points, and Milne numbers her sub-units consecutively for the whole performance (forty in all) while Finnegan begins the numbering afresh each time.

It is evident that Michele Finnegan's ten Points are very much stages in a progression (indeed, in another document included in the appendix to Norman Price's thesis, an account of X's relationship to the dress she wore, Michele Finnegan uses the joint term *Point/Stage*), and the account makes very clear her sense of ten phases in an emotional journey, whereas Catherine Milne's account does not articulate very clearly how her eighteen macro units relate to the forty points that compose them. It seems possible that the eighteen-unit segmentation relates more to the amount of movement that can be conveniently illustrated in one diagram, and that the forty units of action are the equivalent of Finnegan's Points, the stages marking Y's journey.

Milne conceptualizes the verbal content of her performance in a similar way to Finnegan but her account focuses more on the emotional content of her actions and interactions with X, although this is still very much bound up with the physical moves that articulate it. The page of her score reproduced in figure 15 is a representative example of the way she combines commentary on the physical moves themselves ("move to her spot," "first circle around her," "bend to whisper in her ear"), the emotional color of both verbal and gestural behavior ("insidious," "forceful," "disturbing her, threatening her"), and the fictional situation ("open up her space—invade it, break into her frail circle of self"). It is also interesting to note that she uses the first person throughout her commentary, the actress and character are one being, and the only *she* refers to X. Michele Finnegan uses virtually no personal pronouns and her language indicates a third-person distance ("turns back," "is repelled," "her own defeat").

These accounts, with their similarities and their different emphases, provide fascinating insight into the way actors work with each other, with physical actions in a given space, and with emotional states and energy levels, in order to create the performances that will allow others to make the emotional journey. The position of the text in the work process thus "mapped" is due in part perhaps to the fact that it did not predate the rehearsal period but evolved out of it. A significantly different view of textual function is provided by the working notes taken by another actor, Lyn Pierse, who played Masha in a workshop production of *The Three Sisters*.

The photocopied pages of Chekhov's text (in Elisaveta Fen's translation) were pasted into a large exercise book, Masha's words highlighted, and all around Lyn made notes to herself as the rehearsal progressed. The different notes added day by day as the scene was reworked, or as she worked on the script at home, convey an indication of the development of the role and of her understanding of it and attitude toward it, and the document constitutes what could be seen as an archaeological site in which the actor's work is revealed in its temporal dimension. A sample page reproduced in figure 16 has been touched up and slightly reconstructed, but only so as to make legible the actor's comments etc.

A detailed analysis of the single page of working notes reproduced here would require many pages of commentary, but for the purposes of this chapter's discussion of performance segmentation we need to stress simply the minutely detailed level at which the actor's notation occurs. Lyn Pierse's working method is clearly derived from Stanislavsky; she reiterates her super-objective for this segment of the scene: "to confess" and "to confess I love Vershinin," the obstacle to this: "morality" and

Objective   To Confess I love Vershinin

Obstacle - MORALITY - Class - Inspira a - Tituulative

To light - mock   Natasha

Setting up   [TO CONFESS]
out of bed - as of beauty.

To blow / mock
To slice / erase
eradicate
- get picking up things
to break
- check for someth

shab congo do about it.

Posture inspire in Natasha to audience
- L save book: reason -

Object - Olga - think about it, Instead

Affect - Irma - to nothing, soothe

COURAGE   Up on the top of the head!
        — Need to speak.   Courageous enough to say it
CONQUEST of fear

WILL WON'T!

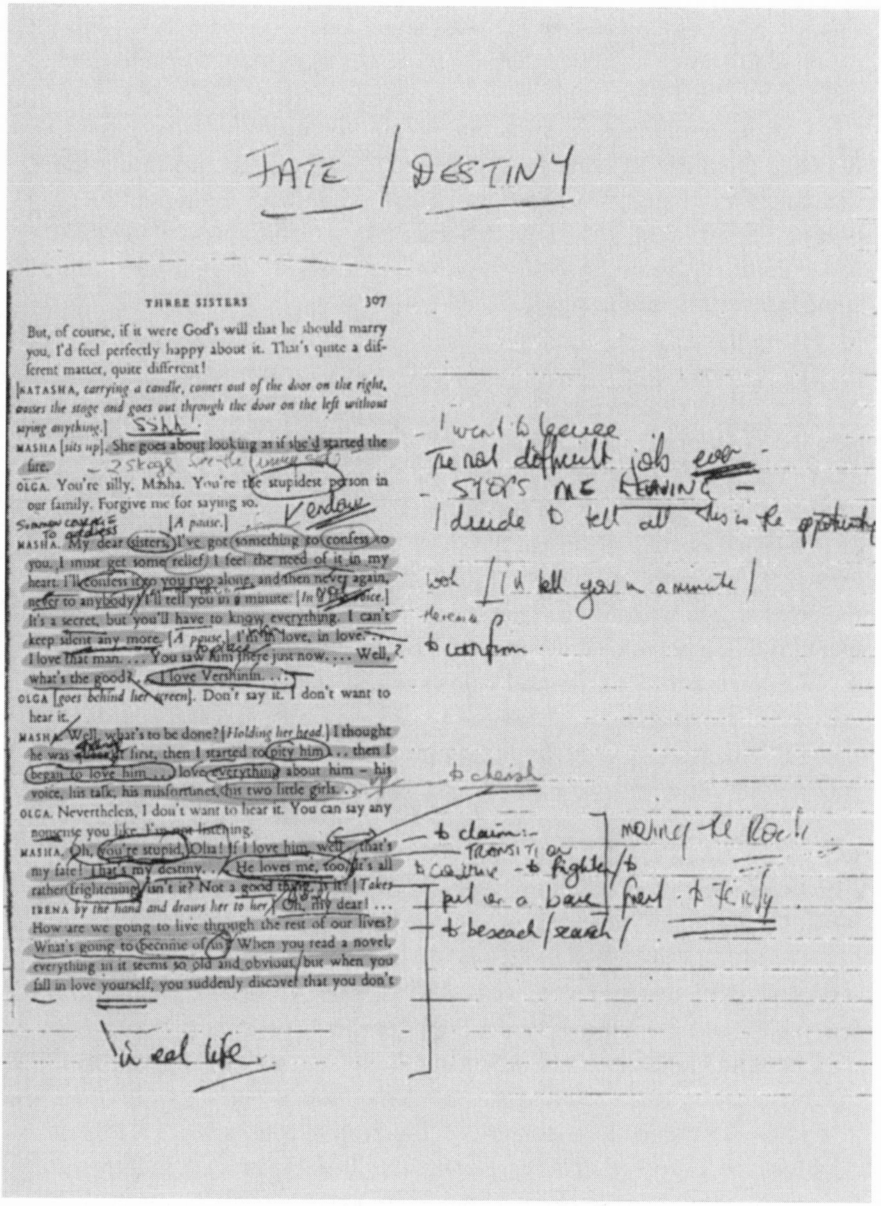

FATE / DESTINY

But, of course, if it were God's will that he should marry you, I'd feel perfectly happy about it. That's quite a different matter, quite different!

[NATASHA, *carrying a candle, comes out of the door on the right, crosses the stage and goes out through the door on the left without saying anything.*]

MASHA [*sits up*]. She goes about looking as if she'd started the fire.

OLGA. You're silly, Masha. You're the stupidest person in our family. Forgive me for saying so.

[*A pause.*]

MASHA. My dear sisters, I've got something to confess to you. I must get some relief. I feel the need of it in my heart. I'll confess it to you two alone, and then never again, never to anybody. I'll tell you in a minute. [*In a low voice.*] It's a secret, but you'll have to know everything. I can't keep silent any more. [*A pause.*] I'm in love, in love.... I love that man.... You saw him here just now.... Well, what's the good? I love Vershinin...

OLGA [*goes behind her screen*]. Don't say it. I don't want to hear it.

MASHA. Well, what's to be done? [*Holding her head.*] I thought he was strange at first, then I started to pity him.. then I began to love him... loved everything about him - his voice, his talk, his misfortunes, his two little girls...

OLGA. Nevertheless, I don't want to hear it. You can say any nonsense you like, I'm not listening.

MASHA. Oh, you're stupid, Olia! If I love him well, that's my fate! That's my destiny. He loves me, too, it's all rather frightening, isn't it? Not a good thing, is it? [*Takes* IRENA *by the hand and draws her to her.*] Oh, my dear! ... How are we going to live through the rest of our lives? What's going to become of us? When you read a novel, everything in it seems so old and obvious, but when you fall in love yourself, you suddenly discover that you don't

Fig. 16. From Lyn Pierse's script for *The Three Sisters*

"class"; she establishes numerous subordinate objectives usually expressed through an active verb (*to cherish, to beseech, to claim,* etc.) and subordinate obstacles ("she stops me leaving"); there are other indications of the emotional reading she is constructing—the FATE/DESTINY removed from her text and emblazoned across the page, indicating the thematic importance of the idea and her struggle with the repetition of two such nearly related and yet different terms, elaborations of her subtext ("yourself" underlined in the text and glossed "in real life") and some information about physical actions ("sitting up," "out of bed," "go to pick up things").

The most striking thing is the way all of this apparently chaotic mass of interpretive information is posited on or interwoven with extremely detailed notations concerning speech. Information to herself concerning intonation, stress, rhythm, and emotional energy is mapped onto the text in a bewildering profusion. It seems that for an actor working in this sort of text-based narrative theatre the work process involves an extremely intensive exploration of the textual structures, and it is also evident that the actor works with minute fragments of emotional/textual/narrative material that have to be embodied and physically manifested.

Another form of segmentation emerges from John Gielgud's account of playing Hamlet (Gielgud [1939] 1974, 103–5). Having played the part in so many productions over a number of years, he was able to encapsulate the experience in a two-page description that establishes what might be termed a "score" of the work process involved. This provides a structural breakdown of the actor's task in performance and constitutes a sort of graph of the energy levels involved. It records a very different level of detail from that noted by Lyn Pierse on her script.

These accounts of rehearsal practice and of actors' individual work processes share a significant amount of common ground. The evidence from all the sources cited indicates that there are several levels of performance segmentation functioning in any theatrical performance, and that the construction of the units of this segmented totality involves different artists, working at different stages of the creative process. It is also evident that the composition of these units is multi-factorial both in terms of the variety of sign systems and codes involved and of the principles according to which the elements are combined.

A Schema for the Analysis of
Performance Structure

Reflecting on my own experience as a spectator responding to the spatiotemporal reality of performance and the narratives it presents, and on the insights into the production process acquired from all the sources mentioned above, it seems that we are necessarily dealing with at least four levels of performance segmentation. In choosing to call these simply levels 1, 2, 3, and 4, I am attempting to foreground the abstract, analytical nature of such a perception of performance structure and deliberately to distance it from any particular performance aesthetic or creative practice.

Level 1

Level 1 refers to the most obvious level of segmentation where, as Ubersfeld has pointed out, units are usually indicated by a significant interruption of the performance for a period of time. Conventions govern the manner in which the interruption is signaled and the degree of severance from the fictional or performance world. Devices commonly used include, for example, a blackout for a few seconds (not enough to encourage relaxation of attention or conversation amongst spectators), a blackout onstage followed by raising the houselights slightly (enough to return the spectators to awareness of the performance space but not enough to signal permission to leave it), lowering of stage lights/absence of actors/presence of stage hands adjusting the set (here the fictional world may be tantalizingly both present and absent, and the presentational space fascinatingly reveals its own processes).

In older theatres that are still equipped with a front curtain this can be used to effect a temporary withdrawal of the presentational space, and in such cases the mere signaling of performance structure is overlaid with a conscious statement about cultural tradition and past practices. Even with a front curtain, contemporary audiences will need the additional information provided by the level of auditorium lighting to know whether they can move from their seats or not. Music or sound effects may be used, alone or in combination with visual signals, to indicate a break, or the signal may even be as minimal as the actors freezing in their positions for a few seconds. The most complete interruption is provided by the interval, when spectators are allowed or encouraged to leave the performance space altogether usually for fifteen to twenty minutes.

The number of these macro units, the length of the interruption, the behavior expected and encouraged (vacating one's seat or remaining quietly seated, talking or not talking, consuming food and drink, and even such apparently extraneous factors as the degree of relaxation or agitation related to this ritual consumption), are all important for the global impact of the performance. It is evident from what has been said that even at this macro level there is a potential hierarchy in terms of duration of unit and completeness of the cessation of performance signs. Social conventions and economic necessity[5] govern the nature and length of performance breaks in today's theatre. The length of the performance itself is also governed by social convention and custom, and has changed considerably over the years; all sorts of transgressions and self-conscious play are possible with the prevailing norms but these do nevertheless prevail, even in a period marked by its questioning of all norms.

It is most common in contemporary Western dramatic theatre to have a two-part structure at this level, at the most a performance might have two intervals, thus creating a three-part structure. This now conventional two-part division often overrides a different macro segmentation inscribed in the playtext itself. Classical and neoclassical dramaturgy favored a five-part structure, in the nineteenth century four acts and three were common, and the question of where to place the interval and of the way a two-part performance macro structure will relate to or affect a five-, four-, or three-part structure functioning at the dramaturgical and textual levels are important production decisions.

The term most commonly used to refer to this level of performance segmentation is the *act*, and there are significant differences between playwrights, and between performance practices at different periods of theatre history, in the way such segmentation has been used. In a neoclassical play by a writer like Racine, for example, the situation does not change or develop significantly between the acts, while in Shakespeare, Brecht, and many others fictional time passes, and major events may be deemed to have occurred within the fictional world: the baby Perdita has been found by shepherds, has grown into a beautiful young girl, and has caught the eye of the king's son between acts 2 and 3 of *A Winter's Tale;*

in act 1 of *The Three Sisters* Andrei declares his love for Natasha, in act 2 they are married and she has already had their first baby.

Performance segmentation at this level may be used for a variety of dramaturgical, aesthetic, and even social functions. The gaps between the units may be exploited within the fictional world (as in the examples cited), or they may be used rather for metatheatrical purposes (in Molière's *Malade imaginaire* the three acts of dramatic action are intercut with prologue, interludes, and finale that draw on many different performance genres—opera, ballet, farce, pastoral—to elaborate in different registers themes presented in the dramatic part (McAuley 1974); a completely different but equally metatheatrical function is exemplified in David Williamson's *What If You Died Tomorrow,* in which the actor playing Andrew remains onstage in full view of the audience throughout the interval, continuing to build an elaborate structure with children's building blocks that he has begun to construct toward the end of act 1. For the spectators at the Sydney Theatre Company's 1973 production who remained in their seats, as I did, mesmerized by the actor's absorption in the meticulous task, and then by the structure itself, the edges between fictional world and performance reality became blurred, and the presentational became a fascinating end in itself. For those who went out to chat and drink and who came back to find that there had been no interruption and that the character had gone on "living" in their absence, the impact must have been reversed: for them the fictional world must have gained a new kind of authenticity that would take precedence over the presentational.

The interstices between level 1 performance units may be exploited socially, as in court masques, for example, in which spectators joined the actors and danced during the interludes, or in the 1970s productions of *Hair* or, more recently, in Gale Edwards's production of *The Rover* (Aphra Behn). In all these examples there is an element of metatheatricality involved with the social experience: if the spectator dances with an actor in costume is it the character or the actor who is dancing, does the fictional or the presentational level dominate, and what happens to the performance when the dancer/spectators sit down and become spectators again while the dancer/actors move back into the fictional world?

These examples indicate the importance of the level 1 units in the global performance structure and of the way they may be conceptualized in relation to the narrative. The signaling devices (blackouts, curtain,

absence of performers) are part of the physical vocabulary of performance, and the experience of the spectator in being returned, if only
briefly, to full awareness of the performance space, ensures that these
performance units function very strongly at the presentational level. It is
nevertheless also true that, in text-based theatre, the structure is usually
strongly indicated at this primary level by the playwright and is very
much part of the play's dramaturgical shaping of narrative content.

Notwithstanding the playwright's role in providing a dramaturgical structure at this level, it has to be acknowledged that the demands of
the performance and the dominant presentational conventions of the
day normally take precedence over the writer's structure. A five-unit
structure will normally be experienced in two parts by contemporary
audiences, and the differences between a five-unit and a four-unit structure become blurred when both are severed by a single interval. Contemporary theatre practice offers compensations for this sort of loss of
structural clarity: developments in the physical possibilities offered by
the stage and shifts in viewing conventions provide playwrights with
new potential. For example, the flexibility of lighting signals as compared with the performance closure effected by the literal closing of the
curtain has made a hierarchy of macro structures possible without sacri-
ficing concentration and intensity.

Level 2
Acts and scenes have traditionally been acknowledged as the primary
and secondary units of dramatic structure, and it can be argued that the
scene, as defined in neoclassical dramaturgy,[6] is also one of the principal
structuring devices at the presentational level. The second level of performance segmentation, as I have observed it from both production and
reception perspectives, involves units constructed essentially along the
lines of the neoclassical scene, on the basis of actorial presence within the
presentational space. Documentation of spectators' response in the *Dom
Juan* project already mentioned provides corroboration that from the
spectator's point of view, any entrance or exit constitutes a performance
event that signals a new structural unit. These units, constructed and signaled largely through the presentational system, intersect with and
make manifest a narrative structure, as Stanislavsky and Brecht have
emphasized.

It is significant that the neoclassical "scene" has nothing to do with
fictional place. A change of scene does not mean a change of place, as it

frequently does in Shakespeare's plays, for example, but is purely a structural unit in a dramaturgical progression. Fictional place is not involved, but presentational space is critical, for it is the entrances into and exits out of the space that mark the units and enable the pattern of combination and alternation to be constructed.

A good deal of the structuring of dramatic material at this level has already been done by the playwright, so that actors who are working with text, whether they are dividing the level 1 units into "organic episodes" or finding the "nodal points" that will enable them to interpret and comment on a connected series of events, are essentially involved at this stage of the process in exploring, interpreting, and appropriating a dramaturgical structure.

It seems to me that we can go further and claim that even when the performance is not concerned to create a fictional world or to tell a story, even when its main aim is the radical subversion of narrative coherence, the actors' task at this stage is fundamentally similar whatever kind of texts they are working with. The material to be presented may be fragments of a number of different stories, the fragments may be so small and so disconnected that they defy incorporation into a coherent whole, the events may have only the most tenuous connection with any fictional world, but the actors must still establish the series of actions or episodes that constitute the performance, and establish their order, rhythm, and sequence. The spectators, too, in their response to the performance, work from a perception of the segmentation created at this level by the entrances and exits and other major proxemic shifts, to an awareness of the implications of this segmentation.

Level 2 segmentation is concerned essentially with the construction of the "narrative," to use Genette's terminology, that is to say with the dramaturgical shaping of the material to be presented. Whether the shaping process is the work of the writer or whether it is substantially undertaken by the director, dramaturg, and actors during the rehearsal process, whether or not it is inscribed significantly in a preexisting written text, its physical manifestation in performance will utilize the actors' movements into and out of the presentational space as a major signaling device. It can thus be claimed that it is the spatial factors in theatrical performance that enable the structure of the performance to be made manifest.

"Episode" and "scene" are the most common terms used to describe the units at this level of segmentation and there is a considerable degree of agreement amongst theorists and practitioners about its dependence on both the fictional and presentational systems simultaneously. There is clearly a good deal of Elam's "intuitive recognition" that, at this level, theatrical performance is composed of units of dramatic action that are signaled physically through major proxemic shifts, in particular the entrances and exits. The narrative system and the fictional world it is conveying are interwoven with the scenic reality of bodily presence within a particular spatio-temporal framework. At this level the interweaving is coarse enough for analysts to see more or less clearly how the factors interrelate, and the breaks or shifts occur in all contributing systems simultaneously: an exit, for example, marks a major shift in all the presentational systems and it is the end of an interaction in the fictional world.

Level 1 and level 2 may together be seen as constituting the macro structures of performance. Indeed the distinction between the two can at times be difficult to establish. A performance of *Britannicus* presented with a single interval would seem to me to consist of two level 1 units, each divided into a number of level 2 units on the basis of the entrances and exits, and the decision to situate the interval between acts 2 and 3 or between acts 3 and 4 would have significant repercussions on the overall experience. A performance of the same play, such as the one directed by Rex Cramphorn in Sydney in 1980 that had no interval but which marked the ends of the acts with a drum roll and a pause to accentuate the momentarily empty stage, is clearly composed of five level 1 units, each divided into level 2 units on the basis of Racine's "scenes." Such a performance experience accentuates the internal coherence of the five-part structure.

Level 3
With level 3 and level 4 we come to the micro structuring of the performance, and to the substantive work of the director and actors during the rehearsal process. Level 3 units are comparable to the "beats," familiar from Stanislavsky-derived production processes, or Rex Cramphorn's "sense blocks," and as was demonstrated in the *Doll's House* analysis presented earlier in this chapter, the way the units at this level are conceptualized and constructed is crucial to the meaning conveyed. It can make the difference, for example, between taking Nora to be saying "You are sad but I am happy" or saying "This (fantastic) stroke of luck means that now I shall be able to be truly happy," and there are obvious implications

for the construction of character and motivation, relationships of power and thematic content in this kind of decision. These significant differences emerged in practice from the way the conversational flow of the dialogue was articulated into topics (i.e., from the segmentation) and signaled through the blocking, and the phrases that were foregrounded in the process.

Substantial indications of level 1 and level 2 segmentation are written into the playtext, and even though the mise en scène may reinforce or subvert these (depending on the nature of the playwriting and the degree of authorial function taken on by the director), the dramaturgical structuring involved at these levels in text-based theatre is very much the responsibility of the writer. The micro structuring of level 3 seems, however, to be much more the task of the director and the actors. It is here that directors really begin to construct their authorial vision, begin to exercise a dominance over the text they may nevertheless claim to be serving. The text certainly feeds this process, but equally it is the process that constructs the text as it will function in that production, as was illustrated in the *Doll's House* example.

Many terms exist to name the units that are being constructed and manipulated (beat, idea, unit of action, action, sense block) and this in itself indicates that the processes involved are reasonably well understood, even codified, although they may not have yet been theorized with any precision. With the emergence of the director as a major force in theatrical creation this dimension of the process has been brought to the fore, demystified to an extent and established as critically important in the artistic process.

The segmentation of the action or narrative and the progression of ideas it articulates has to be physically manifested; the process actors call "blocking," which was discussed in chapter 3, is essentially the construction of this physical manifestation. The level 3 units of performance are the outcome of the blocking process and, as with the level 2 units that are constructed and signaled essentially on the basis of movement into and out of the presentational space, so in the case of level 3 units, too, movement is the critical factor (displacement moves within the presentational space or heavily marked shifts in orientation). In both cases the creation and communication of meaning in the theatre is heavily dependent on space, for it is the space that makes movement possible and enables spectators to locate and "read" such movement.

Level 4

The level 4 segmentation is perhaps the level of detail the early proponents of minimal units were looking for, and I presume it is comparable
to what Stanislavsky had in mind when he referred to the "small and fine
pieces" of the actor's role and to what Anne Ubersfeld is calling the
"stage acts." One of the problems for analysts and theorists is that the
detail involved is indeed so fine, and the whole performance aesthetic
may be designed to cover the traces of the construction process so that
everything flows "organically." The difficulties of notation and even of
observation at this level compound all the other problems.

Level 4 is truly the micro level, and it is the domain of the individual actor, which, as I have already suggested, may explain why it is
much less talked about, less well understood, and less well theorized
than the other levels of segmentation. There seems to be no terms in common use to refer to the detail of what actors are working with at this
level, and the nature of the work is such that it may not be really appropriate to refer to its different components as though they were separate
units nor to conceptualize the fragments of action as though they had a
discrete existence. At this level of the performance the actors work in
detail with minute fragments of bodily behavior, emotion, thought,
impulse, energy, and speech, as has been indicated in the documents
provided by Lyn Pierse, Michele Finnegan, and Catherine Milne. All of
this myriad detail has to be carefully timed and knitted together with the
detail of the other actors' work, and the best place to observe it is in the
rehearsal room, when it is in the process of being constructed.

Actors' use of the phrase *marking* has already been mentioned, and
it is particularly interesting in that it indicates that elements that will
later flow smoothly and seamlessly together are indeed separately conceived. The process in question involves establishing in meticulous
detail the timing of physical action in relation to the verbal, and while it
provides a striking illustration of the interconnectedness of all the elements of movement, gesture, and business, it also demonstrates their
separateness. A director might also say that something should be "bigger" or "smaller" and some even use the notion of an energy scale (using
phrases like "I'd like that at 2.5" or "Force 10 for this bit"). This kind of
metalanguage certainly indicates a conception of the physical actions
and the emotional states they are embodying as mini units that can be
repeated at varying strengths, unpicked and recombined, or, to use

another metaphor, "fine-tuned" (a phrase used by Lindy Davies to describe the director's work in the final phase of rehearsal).

Some actors have questioned the existence of a level of performance unit below that of the beat (or whatever term they use to describe what I have called a level 3 unit), but Aarne Neeme working with actors on Pinter's *Old Times* referred to "scenes," "beats or units," and "moments," and his three-part hierarchy can be mapped almost exactly onto my level 2, 3, and 4 units. In his terms the beat is a transaction or a completed action, while the moment is a thought, an act, or a speech act, which seems to imply that a beat involves interaction between two or more participants, while the moment is more likely to be something internal to the individual actor. He claimed also that the moment was determined by the actor's breathing: essentially what has to be said in one breath. This very perceptive observation is borne out by Hollis Huston who also uses the notion of the moment in talking about performance structure. For Huston "a moment is that portion of time bounded by a breath," and he quotes numerous experts from different disciplines to corroborate his perception that the normal quiet breath has a duration of between three and five seconds (Huston 1992, 29). He extrapolates from this that the normal quiet breath relates to the "smallest amount of time in which we can receive a stimulus, analyze it and frame a response to it" (175).

In terms of the argument I have been advancing in this chapter, the most interesting thing about the notion of the moment and its dependence on the bodily reality of the actors' inhalation/exhalation is that it indicates that even at the micro level of performance segmentation there is the same kind of interplay between textual triggers and presentational realities that I have observed in the other three levels. Elements that may seem to be a given of the text are in fact determined by spatial and bodily factors deriving from performance.

In certain kinds of performance this sort of fine detail in the performance structuring may not be of crucial importance, but in text-based narrative theatre it is critical to the meanings created. For example, in the *Dom Juan* project that has already been mentioned, two groups of actors both worked on the seduction scene from act 2. The narrative sequence provided by Molière's text entails that Don Juan and his servant Sganarelle should meet Charlotte, that Don Juan should successfully woo her, and that Sganarelle should ineffectually disapprove. Rex Cramphorn and his actors, working within this narrative frame, created a cynical, aloof misogynist seducing a pathetic peasant girl for the pleasure of shocking his servant. Beverley Blankenship and her actors meanwhile produced a virile womanizer and a lusty peasant girl single-mindedly pursuing their mutual pleasure while a bumbling servant ineffectually tried to dissuade both.

These differences are so great that they raise questions about the extent to which one can truly say that the two scenes are presenting the same narrative. The fact that the same play can be seen to mean such radically different things has been one of the revelations of the so-called director's theatre of the last fifteen to twenty years. While other factors besides segmentation are involved here, it is what I have called the level 4 segmentation, namely the physical and emotional detail produced by the actors in their work with the reality of text, bodies, space, and each other's subjectivity, the minutely detailed correlation of speech event and physical action to articulate fictional experiences that is crucial to the construction and communication of this kind of meaning.

In other performance genres, however, the meaning may reside more in the repetition or the duration of a particular action sequence than in its precise detail. For example, in *Stages of Terror* (a postmodern piece conceived and performed in Sydney in 1993 by a group of women performers), one sequence required two performers, clad only in athletic singlets and briefs, to run at high speed for several minutes on end around the outer edges of the rectangular performance space, behind the spectators, and up and down the central presentational space, repeatedly colliding with each other, and repeatedly transforming the collision into an embrace. The important elements of this sequence seem to have been the exact repetition, the physical endurance of the performers, and the connections set up between this repeated, apparently arbitrary action and other apparently arbitrary actions by other performers occurring simultaneously in the space. In terms of the nomenclature I have adopted, the *Stages of Terror* performance was working very intensively with level 3 segmentation, while the two versions of the *Dom Juan* scene differed so radically from each other due to the detail of the actors' input at level 4.

This discussion of the levels of segmentation and the nature of the units that make up theatrical performance has drawn attention to the shaping and structuring processes involved, which, as Meyerhold points out in the phrase I have quoted as epigraph to the chapter, are crucial to the creation of any work of art. Another important fact to emerge from this analysis is the way that primary responsibility for the structuring process shifts from level to level and is shared in differing ways among writers, directors, and actors. My analysis also demonstrates that it is the combination and interaction of fictional events, actions, or verbal utterances and the presentational means that construct and present them, which mark the segmentation process at all levels. Maurice Blanchot, in the other epigraph, draws attention precisely to the interplay between language and space, to dialogue as spatialized language, but just as dialogue is the means whereby the physical space is divided, activated, and made meaningful, so too is the verbal made meaningful through its location in space.

The levels and different types of segmentation must always be conceptualized as feeding into and constructing each other: it is the myriad detail of level 4 that builds up the next level and so on. Practitioners working from a preexisting playtext begin with partially constructed units at an upper level, as the playwright will usually have incorporated a good deal of dramaturgical and some presentational shaping of the material into the text. The task for the performers in this kind of theatre is to explore, break down, and appropriate the playwright's segmentation in order to reconstruct it and give it the form they wish it to have. In other forms of creative practice where performance is constructed from improvisations done during the rehearsal process, for example, or in the task-based performance associated with artists like Richard Foreman or Robert Wilson, the units of action are built up by the practitioners in different ways. Even in text-based theatre, as the example of *Dust Covers* suggests, not all performers conceive of the relation between verbal and physical in their performance in the same way. The experience of the spectator is not, however, necessarily radically different in these different kinds of theatre: spectators must work from the detail of the micro levels, from which they construct larger units of action. For the spectator it is the interconnection of the verbal/vocal and the physical performance, notably the proxemic and kinesic features, that constructs the action and gives it the particular meaning it carries in that performance, whatever the relative status of verbal and physical action in the construction process.

The vocal/physical elements that make up the presentational system and the fictional/action system that is presented do not work in synchrony at levels 3 and 4 to make discrete units. At these levels a transition in the verbal may be overridden by the vocal, a major vocal shift (change of speaker, change of energy level, intonation,) may occur within complete stasis at the physical level, etc. In these cases we get the sense of a subunit embedded within a larger unit.

At levels 1 and 2, however, the verbal/vocal and physical systems and the fictional actions they present all function in tandem, articulations are normally marked by simultaneous shifts in all three systems, and the performance continuum is structured in ways that spectators cannot avoid perceiving and which are relatively easy for the performance analyst to notate. At the finer levels the systems interact more subtly and the possibilities of variation are practically infinite, which is, of course, why no two productions of a given play are ever the same, why such different meanings can be produced with what is ostensibly the same material, and why the performance process is so endlessly fascinating.

This chapter has stressed the interconnectedness of the systems in play but also the primacy of the spatial function in constructing and signaling the performance segmentation and structure. It is the bodily presence of the actors in the presentational space, their movements and behaviors, even the pattern of their breathing, and the spectators' experience of their energy output that shape the performance and segment it into related parts. These elements enable the spectators to construct both a fictional series of events and an interpretation of those events. The performance space that is so central to theatrical expression (but not to the dramatic) and the presentational space that is that part of the performance space energized by the actors' presence have been shown to be key factors in both the structuring and the way it is communicated. In the next chapter I consider the multiple functions of objects in modern performance practice, as here, too, it is the spatial reality of live performance that enables the object to acquire its expressive force.

5

Objects in Performance

Each item
In her stock is hand picked: straps and belts
Pewter boxes and ammunition pouches; hand picked too
The chicken and the stick which at the end
The old woman twists through the draw rope
The Basque woman's board on which she bakes her bread
And the Greek woman's board of shame, strapped to her back
With holes for her hands to stick through, the Russian's
Jar of lard, so small in the policeman's hand; all
Selected for age, function and beauty
By the eyes of the knowing
The hands of the bread-baking, net-weaving
Soup-cooking connoisseur
Of reality
　　　—Bertolt Brecht, *Weigel's Props*

Actors have always used hand props of one sort or another (one thinks immediately of the miser's purse and the quackdoctor's potions in medieval farce, the daggers in *Macbeth,* swords and poisoned wine cups in *Hamlet,* Desdemona's handkerchief, and Prospero's staff, of the ladies' fans in Restoration comedy and of the zanni's slapstick in commedia dell'arte), but objects have come to play an increasingly important part in contemporary performance practice. The emergence of the object as a major signifying element in theatrical performance dates back to the middle part of the nineteenth century, with the work of people like Madame Vestris and her husband Charles Matthews at the Olympic in London (1831–38), and most notably with the so-called cup-and-saucer comedies staged by Squire and Marie Bancroft at the Prince of Wales in the 1860s and later at the Haymarket. The development of naturalism, particularly in the work of André Antoine at the Théâtre Libre in Paris (1887–94) and Stanislavsky at the Moscow Arts Theatre (from 1898), took reliance on objects to new heights, but, as Anne Ubersfeld has pointed

out, it is in recent years, and with the abandonment of illusionistic staging, that the object has come to the fore as at no earlier time:

> Rather than blending with the background, (the object) has taken on its
> own autonomous identity as an element in both the dramatic action and
> the overall meaning of the work. Its mobility permits it to become flexible
> and multifunctional for it ceases to be a single thing and becomes what-
> ever the actor and the dramatic action require it to be on any given
> moment of the performance. (1984, vii)

Madame Vestris introduced the box set and, as Sybil Rosenfeld has
described it

> . . . gave verisimilitude to everyday rooms by furnishing them with real,
> not painted, furniture of taste and quality. She took pains to supply good
> carpets, fine draperies, real blinds over practicable glass windows and
> props such as clocks, fireplaces, mirrors and even actual door knobs.
> (Rosenfeld 1973, 113)

It was Tom Robertson, however, a generation later, who found a dramatic use for such detail, for in his productions the props and objects that
furnished the stage were not merely there to provide a credible background for the dramatic action but were the pretext for stage business
designed to express emotion and convey complex interpersonal relationships in ways that dialogue alone could not have done. The famous stage
direction for the scene in *Caste* in which Polly Eccles serves tea to Sam
Gerridge and Captain Hawtree makes clear the class and power relations
between the characters with humor and a certain delicacy:

> Sam cuts enormous slice of bread, and hands it on point of knife to
> Hawtree. Cuts small lump of butter, and hands it on point of knife to
> Hawtree, who looks at it through eye-glass, then takes it. Sam then helps
> himself. Polly meantime has poured out tea in two cups, and one saucer
> for Sam, sugars them, and then hands cup and saucer to Hawtree, who has
> both hands full. He takes it awkwardly, and places it on table. Polly, hav-
> ing only one spoon, tastes Sam's tea, then stirs Hawtree's, attracting his
> attention by so doing. He looks into his tea-cup. Polly stirs her own tea,
> and drops spoon into Hawtree's cup, causing it to spurt into his eye. He
> drops eye-glass and wipes his eyes. (Robertson 1980, 162–63)

The connection between Robertson's practice and that of the artists
who later developed stage naturalism (notably Antoine and Stanislavsky) is evident. The chairs and tables, cups and saucers, ornaments,

books and other objects that furnished the sets came increasingly to fill a number of related functions. They enhanced the impression of reality created by the set and were, thus, somewhat akin to the "reality effects" that Roland Barthes was later to describe in prose narrative (1966, 1–27). They provided indications of the social context, or milieu, that the naturalist movement saw as a crucial factor in determining character and behavior. As Antoine put it:

> In contemporary plays, written in the spirit of truth and naturalism, where theories concerning milieu and the influence of external factors have come to play such a large part, is the decor not the indispensable complement to the work? (1921, 198–203)

They were a means through which an actor could express a character's emotion even when the playwright had provided no words, beautifully exemplified in the following description of business devised by Henry Irving in his production of *Othello* in 1881. Irving played Iago, and, in the scene in which his character watches Cassio and Desdemona together, he

> marked his contempt for such folly by eating grapes and spitting out the seeds 'as if each represented a worthy virtue to be put out of one's mouth' in Ellen Terry's words. (Rowell 1981, 16)

Finally, they provided actors with opportunities to devise the sort of expressive interactions between characters that Robertson wrote into his script. Looking back over his practice at the Théâtre Libre from the perspective of 1903, Antoine realized that this was the most important result of the new kind of staging, for once the stage set was realistically furnished, the actors gradually adjusted their acting, which "unwittingly and almost in spite of themselves, became more human, more intense, more full of life in terms of attitude and gesture" (1903, 607). The new acting, required for the new writing, thus emerged from the physical organization of the stage, and what Robertson had had to specify in somewhat laborious detail was later developed by the actors themselves in rehearsal. Indeed, as the Irving anecdote indicates, the "lifelike" behaviors and gestures elicited by props and objects affected acting styles throughout the repertoire and not simply in the modern, realistic drama.

Naturalism was certainly the major factor in the development of the use of objects in modern theatre, but naturalism has long been transcended and, in contemporary performance the set no longer functions simply to provide a more or less realistic setting for the dramatic action, and the objects that appear in the presentational space are no longer selected exclusively in relation to the ostensible fictional place. Objects have acquired a measure of autonomy and can be expressive elements in their own right. In Grotowski's early work, for example, objects provided what Ludwig Flaszen described as a "dynamic orchestration" of the dramatic action; in the Theatre Laboratory's production of *Akropolis* (loosely based on Wyspianski's play) objects were no longer things placed within the set but things that, by their placement, constituted the set:

> There are no "sets" in the usual sense of the word. They have been reduced to the objects which are indispensable to the dramatic action. Each object must contribute not to the meaning but to the dynamics of the play; its value resides in its various uses. The stovepipes and metallic junk are used as settings and as a concrete, three-dimensional metaphor which contributes to the creation of the vision. (Qtd. in Grotowski 1969, 75–76)

The objects that played such an important part in Richard Foreman's productions in the 1970s and 1980s were not simply those that were "indispensable to the dramatic action," as Flaszen says of Grotowski, but anything that "seemed suggestive" or potentially able to "add an interesting second level to the scene" (Foreman 1992, 19). The function of the apparently heterogeneous collection of objects on the stage in his productions was to open up the text, to assist the spectator to perceive the range of associations it evoked, and he claims that although he sometimes toyed with the idea of presenting his plays without the elaborate mise en scène that has become such a significant part of his practice, he always rejected the option: "then I realise that such a naked space does not allow the text to ricochet between levels of meaning, which is my obsession" (65). The objects he gathered together in his productions and the ways in which the human performers interacted with them were crucial to the dynamic meaning-making process. People Show, another group working in the 1970s, generated their productions around found and constructed objects rather than using objects to express what was already contained in a preexisting written text. Victoria Nes Kirby described the group's working method in an article in the *Drama Review*, telling how members of the group continually collected costumes and materials:

> Often when they see a particular costume or object, they have a definite idea of how and when they want to use it, but more often than not they

take it because they like it and sense its potential . . . Sometimes an object becomes a focus for their actions or it suggests a series of related images. The props, costumes, and the elements of a set become equal in importance to the performers themselves. (1974, 57)

This sort of practice is no longer the exclusive domain of the avant-garde, and objects have come to play an increasingly expressive part in the production of mainstream theatre in recent years.

Anne Ubersfeld is quite correct to point to the connection between the abandonment of the dominant proscenium arch style of theatre in the 1960s and 1970s and the development of a new aesthetic concerning the object in performance. When the presentational space no longer has to create a credible image of a fictional place, when the dramatic action no longer needs to be situated in a particular fictional place, when the illusion of being somewhere other than the theatre is no longer a central requirement, then the object is liberated to fulfill multiple expressive functions. The object, being physically present in the space, necessarily serves to shape and define that space and, equally necessarily, has an impact upon the human users of the space.

Naturalistic business of the sort devised by Antoine and his actors (emotion expressed through upsetting a cup or twisting a pencil nervously in one's fingers) requires a small theatre and proximity between actors and spectators and it is significant that the Prince of Wales Theatre, where the Bancrofts presented Tom Robertson's plays, was exceptionally small by the standards of the day, seating less than 600 spectators. While this sort of acting may seem to us now to be crying out for the close vision provided by the camera, it nevertheless marks an important stage in the development of theatre, and in the skills required of actors, and is evidence of the close connection between the performance space (its nature, dimensions, and physical organization) and the kinds of communication that can occur there.

If objects have played an increasingly important role in the theatre and in performance more generally over the course of this century, the same can be said about their role in the social world beyond the theatre. In a number of recent studies, sociologists, economists, and anthropologists have commented on the complex role of the object in contemporary life. Baudrillard has pointed to the fact that human beings in industrialized societies are surrounded by a profusion of objects that constantly need to be replaced, either because they have broken and it is deemed uneconomic to repair them, or because they have been superseded by new technology. Appliances bought a few years previously are regarded as museum items when a replacement part is required, and whereas in earlier generations it was the things that outlasted the human beings, now the situation is reversed: "Urban societies are marked by an increasingly rapid turnover of products, appliances and gadgets, compared with which human beings have come to seem a particularly stable species" (Baudrillard 1968, 7).

Arjun Appadurai, in a collection of essays significantly titled *The Social Life of Things* (1986), argues that we need to distinguish between things, commodities, products, goods, artifacts, and objects, and shows that a given thing can move between some of these categories, can move in and out of commodity status over its "life." Igor Kopytoff, in the same collection, uses the term *cultural biography* to refer to the way a thing or class of things can acquire and shed value in different circumstances. The point emerging from all these studies that I wish to retain here concerns the complex status of objects in contemporary society, the multiple roles they play and the multiple perspectives from which they can be experienced, for this necessarily affects their expressive functions in the theatre.

For Abraham Moles the object is not a naturally occurring substance or thing, but something manufactured by man or, at least, selected by man for use in some connection: "In our culture, the object is hardly natural. We do not speak of a stone, or a frog, or a tree as an object, but rather as a *thing*. The stone becomes an object only when selected for use as a paperweight" (Moles 1969, 1–21). Baudrillard goes further and argues that the important thing about any object is not so much the object itself or its ability to perform a given operation (which he sees as its denotative level of significance), but the connotative level "whereby the object acquires value, is commercialised, personalised, through which it becomes useable and enters into a cultural system" (1968, 14). The objects a person buys, possesses, displays reveal a good deal about that person, and they exist, in Baudrillard's view, less as material things than as signs in a system of signs: "The object can go beyond its primary function and attain a secondary function, can become an element of combination, calculation or play in a universal system of signs" (77).

All this is highly relevant to the use of objects on the modern stage, where they are frequently used to convey information about character, social context, place, lifestyle, status, period, etc., but can equally be used to baffle attempts at associating the presentational space with any familiar environment. They can be used as part of a critique of the contemporary fetishization of possessions or, as Artaud foresaw but never managed to bring to realization, to move away from the social toward the metaphysical.

Before discussing in more detail the variety of functions performed by objects on the contemporary stage and in the creative process, it will be helpful to define more precisely what I understand by the term *object*. The terminology traditionally employed in the theatre refers to *properties*, usually abbreviated to *props*, sometimes glossed as *hand props*; as the term suggests, hand props are those small enough to be carried by a particular actor, or intended to be touched, used, manipulated, by the actors. They may be associated with a given character (Gayev's box of sweets in *The Cherry Orchard*, Solange's rubber gloves in *The Maids*), or a particular bit of business undertaken by a given actor (e.g., Irving's bunch of grapes in *Othello* or Jouvet's umbrella in Copeau's production of *Les Fourberies de Scapin*). Certain hand props may be seen as part of a character's costume though their function in performance exceeds that of costume (e.g., a lady's fan in a Restoration comedy). The term *prop* includes objects far larger than those that come into the category of hand props, and may even include furniture or any other potentially moveable element of the set. Such elements necessarily demarcate sub-spaces within the overall presentational space and, while in some productions objects are there essentially to furnish the space, or to enhance the realism of the fictional place it presents, in others they are there for the contribution they can make to the "dynamics of the play," as in Grotowski's production of *Akropolis*. Even when their major function is to indicate the nature of the fictional place, however, contemporary acting methods ensure that any object present in the space is likely to be incorporated into the action at some time during the performance.

The words *prop* and *property* convey in themselves a suggestion of the range of functions objects have traditionally filled: both a support (or prop) to the actor and a means of bodying forth certain qualities (or properties) pertaining to a character, place, or situation. The French term *accessoire* suggests an additional factor: it implies that props are in some sense a secondary means of expression, they are accessories, things that can assist the actor but that are not essential to the communication that is occurring. It is evident from what has already been said about artists like Richard Foreman and the People Show that contemporary practice entails rethinking some of these assumptions, and this is one reason why many theorists prefer the more neutral term *object* to the familiar *prop* or *property*, which bring with them the connotations of former, perhaps outmoded practices.

In general it can be said that the stage object is inanimate, and it is either brought into the presentational space by an actor, or is already present. Furthermore, it is of such a nature that it can be touched, moved, or displaced by an actor. The crucial factor in defining the stage object is thus human intervention, as Abraham Moles has asserted in relation to objects more broadly considered. A thing on the stage becomes an object if it is touched, manipulated, or even simply looked at or spoken about by an actor. This means that items that would normally be seen as part of the set (doors, furniture, pictures) can become objects, elements of costume can become objects if touched by someone other than the wearer, and the wearer, too, can transform an element of his or her own costume into an object by taking it off or using it in some way beyond its customary vestimentary role. The distinction between object and nonobject is thus fluid and unstable, and in much modern theatre and performance the goal is less to tell a story or present a character than to explore the shifting boundaries between decor and object, body and object, costume and object, and this in itself tells us a good deal about contemporary human experience.

For some analysts the body of the actor is an object, indeed the primary object onstage (Erikson 1995), but I would say that, although a part of the body, or even a whole body, can become an object if so treated (touched, carried) by another actor, it is unhelpful to assimilate the inanimate and animate, to place into the same category subject and object. The scandal of treating a person or animal as object is muted if all bodies are routinely classified as objects. Modern performance practice delights in blurring the distinctions (Stelarc piercing his own body with hooks and having himself suspended by these hooks, Glenda Jackson/Charlotte Corday transforming her hair into a whip in the flagellation scene in the *Marat/Sade*), and indeed this blurring goes back a long way (e.g., Tom Snout as "Wall" in *A Midsummer Night's Dream*), but the device can only work if it is underpinned by a clear recognition of the distinction between human being and object. Actors who warn of the dangers involved in appearing onstage with animals are aware that the animal exercises a power of fascination by virtue of the very fact that it is animate, that it does possess a will and desires of its own (however carefully it may have been trained), and that at any time it may, to the invariable delight of the audience, do something that the human organizers of the performance have not planned.

The stage object is physically present in the performance space and this means that it can appeal to senses other than the visual. Theatrical performance in general appeals most intensively to the spectators' sense of sight and hearing but objects, by their nature and by virtue of their material presence, provide great scope to practitioners who wish to bring into play the other senses. Another factor to be considered in relation to the object is, thus, the sense to which it makes its predominant appeal, the mode in which it offers itself to be experienced by the spectator. Sound can be very important and, indeed, Grotowski's choice of objects in *Akropolis* was as much for their acoustic as for their visual qualities: "metal grating against metal, clanging of the hammers, creaking of the stovepipes through which echoes a human voice" (Flaszen, in Grotowski 1969, 76). Spectators can be invited, even obliged, to touch a particular object if it is passed around or thrown amongst them, and food consumed onstage or shared with spectators can be a means of stimulating their sense of smell and taste (in Entr'acte Company's production of *The Last Circus* in 1988 a performer situated to one side of the presentational space was engaged throughout the performance in making bread, mixing and kneading the dough and then baking it; the smell wafted through the space and at the conclusion of the show the performers divided the bread and shared it with the spectators). The object has become an important means whereby theatre artists can go beyond the visual, extend the auditory beyond the spoken word, and engage the spectator in a bodily experience.

To claim that human intervention transforms things into objects means that in the theatre we are dealing with a multi-level form of objecthood. Before the actor/character can use a thing in the way that has just been mentioned, that thing first has to have been selected, usually by someone else, and placed on the stage, usually by yet another person. That is to say that there is a primary level of human intervention that necessarily applies in the theatre, and the framing function that has already been described as a necessary attribute of the performance space (see chap. 2) ensures that any object placed on the stage functions first of all to signal its own status as theatrical sign. The chair onstage is first and foremost *onstage*, and before it conveys any information about the fictional world or the real world outside the theatre it presents itself to the spectators as a theatrical chair. Depending on the style and genre of performance, this primary level of significance may be almost entirely (but never completely) masked by the secondary level according to which the object exists within a fictional world about which it conveys information and this information depends upon the spectators' knowledge of similar objects in the real world. A chair may indicate the fictional location of the dramatic action (school, cafe, palace, indoors as opposed to outdoors, etc.), it may provide information about the social class of the characters, and it creates an expectation of a certain behavior (at some stage someone may sit on it). Veltrusky called this expectation the "action force" of the object, and he described it as follows: "[The prop] has a force (which we call the action force) that attracts a certain action to it. As soon as a certain prop appears on the stage, this force which it has provokes in us the expectation of a certain action" (1940, 88).

During performance both primary and secondary levels of significance may be overtaken by the role the object comes to play in the dramatic action. Developing the example given by Veltrusky, a dagger in a holster worn by a particular character will be seen as part of that character's costume, and it will convey information about period, masculinity, class, and so on; its 'action force' prepares us for violence and if it is indeed used within the fiction to kill someone then its status will be overlaid with the significance of that act; it will become a signifier for the murder, and may acquire further symbolic significance (guilt, vengeance, betrayal, cowardice, heroism, etc.) depending on the way the stabbing is presented in the dramatic action and in the production.

Although the theatrical "frame" necessarily transforms any object placed within it into a sign, the object in the theatre is always simultaneously a real, material presence. Indeed, its semiotic status is frequently ambivalent insofar as there may be no distinction between sign and referent: when Polly Eccles pours a cup of tea for Captain Hawtree the actress may actually be pouring a cup of tea, which is to say that the sign for a cup of tea is a cup of tea. The practice in contemporary theatre is very varied in this respect, ranging from the most literal realism to pure fantasy: a cup of tea may be real and we may see the steam rising from it, equally it may be an empty cup from which the actor mimes the act of drinking, it may be a cup into which tealike liquid is poured; in another style of performance it could be some other object altogether that the actor says is a cup of tea (a word is sufficient to transform an object onstage into some other object), or indeed there may be no object at all and the actor may mime the presence of cup and tea. This spectrum of practices reveals another fundamental truth about the stage object: like everything else onstage it is subject to the working of denegation, it is both real and not real, and its function and even its identity can be transformed at will by the actor.

Insofar as it is real, the object onstage exists in relationship to the world outside the theatre and it derives much of its expressive power from this fact. Objects in the world contain their own gestural demands, impose certain gestural behaviors on their users, exist in relation to corporeal and social practices, as Marcel Jousse pointed out when he coined the phrase "the gesture of things" (*le geste des choses*): "This is because we really know things only to the extent that they perform or 'gestualise' themselves (*se gestualisent*) in us" (1974, 61). This goes beyond Veltrusky's "action force," which is simply the expectation the object creates in the spectator that a certain action will occur, for according to Jousse the object actually elicits the behavior or gestural practice. A good example of "le geste des choses" is provided by the costumes Antoine Vitez chose for the cycle of Molière plays he mounted in 1978; he wanted the costumes to be accurate replicas of seventeenth-century dress, not so much for the constraints on movement and behavior that period costumes impose on the bodies of modern actors, but for the time it took the actors to put the garments on and get them fastened, and for the fact that no one playing an upper class character could dress without assistance. The clothes thus not only required from their wearers certain bodily behaviors, but, more important, they affected the social practices of the group in significant ways. In this instance, Jousse's "geste" became a "Gestus," for the bodily behaviors and social practices imposed by the garments expressed something about the interpersonal relations and power hierarchies prevailing in the society where such clothes were worn.

In the second part of this chapter I discuss the variety of functions performed by objects in modern theatre practice. Anne Ubersfeld is the critic who has most extensively theorized the object, both in an appendix to the chapter on space in *Lire le théâtre* (1977), and in a full chapter in *L'Ecole du spectateur* (1981). In keeping with her semiotic framework, she perceives the object as a sign that can fill iconic, indexical, and symbolic functions, that can be metaphor or metonym, and she claims furthermore, applying a linguistic analogy, that there is a syntax of the object according to which they can be seen to function as subjects, objects, adverbs, and adjectives in relation to the verb provided by what the actor does with them or to them or what they do to the actor (Ubersfeld 1981, 148–52). These functions frequently overlap, but the feature that is most typical of the theatre is that, due to the transformability of the object in the theatre that I will discuss in more detail below, all the functions that I have just listed can be performed by the same object in a given production.

For instance, in Peter Kingston's brilliant production of Richard Barrett's play *The Heartbreak Kid* at the Stables Theatre in Sydney in 1988 (later a rather ordinary feature film, made in a purely realistic mode), there was a soccer ball that was used in numerous ways throughout the production. The schoolboy characters bounced the ball between them with virtuoso skill, energizing the whole space immediately before the performance began, and making it evident that soccer was a central feature of the boys' lives. The presence of the ball was an indication of fictional place: school playground, football pitch (the set was not otherwise modified apart from shifting the position of a bench and battered dustbin that were the only other objects present). It was sufficient for the ball to be bounced into the audience space for the spectators to be transformed into schoolchildren for the school assembly scene (indexical and metonymic functions). The soccer ball also signified the marginal status of Niky within the school, and within Sydney society more generally, soccer being the football code played by European migrants and despised by the rugby and Australian Rules players of Anglo parentage (symbolic function). Furthermore, the ball was a real one and thus, like so much else in modern theatre practice, it conflated iconic and referential functions. It was also the means of signifying Niky's transgressive behavior and his alienation from the dominant school community, both within the fiction and in a broader metaphorical way in the performance itself. In the tiny space of the Stables Theatre, the size, weight, and smell of the ball, the noise it made bouncing on the wooden floor, and the way it penetrated the audience space, violating the spectators' assumption of pure observer status, suggested something about the anarchic force of the central character, his adolescent sexuality and physical energy, and the underlying element of danger that this represented for the institutions trying to control him.

Its transformation in the scene where his family wins a prize in the lottery was an irresistible touch of pure theatricality: Niky's mother, in apron and slippers, sits watching television, waiting for the draw, while Niky and his friend, doubling both as the compere and hostess in the

popular lottery show, and as the machinery through which the numbered balls are selected before the gaze of the public each week, threw
the soccer ball across the space, catching it in the battered dustbin that
had earlier served to symbolize the school environment and calling out
the "number" it represents. The exuberance and skill with which this
scene was performed was remarkable, but the main point being made
had little to do with the ostensible plot and much more to do with the
theatre itself. It was as though the actors and director were intoxicated
with the power of theatre to transform anything into something else, and
at the same time wanted to celebrate the centrality of the actor and the
joys of actor-based "poor" theatre.

It is this complexity and economy of function, conferred upon the
object by modern theatre practice, that makes it so expressive, and it is
evident from the example of the soccer ball in *Heartbreak Kid* that I have
presented at such length, that not only do the semiotic functions overlap,
but that the overlapping itself is part of the meaning. Furthermore, it is
the fact that the object is physically present in the performance space that
permits such a range of semiotic functions to operate.

Reality and Nonreality of the Object

The object is able to function in this way because it is both real and, subject to the theatre's law of denegation, not real. It is doubly real in that it
is, first, a real presence in the presentational space and, second, in that it
connects actors and spectators to the real world beyond the theatre
through its action force and all the connotations deriving from its referential functions. And, at the same time, it is a mere sign, able to be transformed into something else through the intervention of the actor. This
reality/nonreality status merits more elaboration, for it is the means
whereby the object acquires its peculiar versatility in the theatre.

For Brecht and his collaborators, the object was profoundly real and
its reality derived from its existence outside the theatre. Just as Neher
insisted that actors learn how to handle objects with respect for the gesture they contain, so Brecht was fully aware of the connection between
an object and the lifestyle it presupposes, and they would both surely
have approved of Igor Kopytoff's notion of the "cultural biography" of
things. It was this awareness that led Brecht and the actors of the Berliner
Ensemble to take such pains to select appropriate objects and why he

preferred things that brought to the stage their own past history of work
and human use, rather than artificially constructed, purely theatrical
props. I chose his poem, *Weigel's Props,* as epigraph for this chapter
because of the triple link it makes: first, between the object and the world
of work and gesture it contains within it; second, between these gestures
and the life of the character that they can convey; and third, between the
object and the actor whose insight and skill enables it to express so much.
The poem is a celebration of the people whose daily gestures have given
the objects this patina of use, of the actor who has chosen them, and of
the theatre itself as the place where homage can be paid in this way to
ordinary human beings.

The reality of the object has, however, always raised certain problems in the theatre. From the earliest days there have been spectators
who were disturbed by the contrast between painted scenery and real
objects, and, of course, it was immediately obvious that the real bodies of
the actors destroyed the illusion of reality created by the perspective
painting of the set if they came into close contact with it. An astute comment in the *Spectator* in 1711 about such practices ends by asserting that
"Scenes which are designed as the Representations of Nature, should be
filled with Resemblances, and not with the Things themselves" (qtd. in
Rosenfeld 1973, 66). As practitioners like Antoine and Stanislavsky provided more and more realistic scenery, more and more of the "Things
themselves" for actors to incorporate into their acting, a major paradox
became increasingly apparent: in the theatre, and perhaps in art more
generally, incorporation of the real works against realism.

Naturalism poses this paradox with peculiar clarity, and particularly in relation to the object. In Mike Leigh's *Greek Tragedy,* performed at
the Belvoir Street Theatre in Sydney in 1989, the scene was the kitchen of
a suburban house in Sydney and characters (migrant women engaged in
the drudgery of home-based piece work for a local shirt manufacturer)
made themselves cups of coffee at regular intervals. While the set was
meticulously realistic, I found myself continually distracted from the fiction by the mechanics of the set: the fact that water had been piped to the
sink, that the fridge and kettle were real and were plugged into real
power points, registered in my mind and indeed took precedence over
the dramatic fiction to the extent that they have remained in my memory
while I have forgotten nearly everything else about the production.

Meyerhold's criticism of the profusion of small objects that cluttered
the sets in Stanislavsky's productions was that they were ineffectual,

being too small to be seen by spectators without opera glasses. While it was argued by directors like Antoine that the value of such detail was rather in the impact it had on the actors, that the realistic detail encouraged a new style of acting, the inescapable problem of naturalism in the theatre was that any sense of reality seemed to recede in direct proportion to the quantity of realistic detail that was added. The sides of beef hanging from hooks in Antoine's production of *Les Bouchers* in 1888 may have dripped blood authentically onto the sawdust scattered on the floor beneath them, but the response they provoked from the audience ranged from outrage to gasps of delight, both equally inappropriate if the experience Antoine intended to evoke was simply that of being in a butcher's shop.

As usual in the theatre, it takes a generation or so for practitioners to find an artistic necessity for a technical innovation and it was probably not until Brecht began to explore the expressive potential of well-worn tools and domestic utensils that the naturalistic prop came to fulfill a profound and totally convincing artistic purpose onstage. It is significant that in Brecht's theatre such props were not placed in a credible, naturalistic setting where, of course, they would in a sense become invisible, but they were able to "speak" of the real world of human work precisely because they had been removed from it.

Even more important than its connection to the real world, is the fluidity or transformability that the theatrical frame confers upon the object in the theatre. Meaning in the theatre is crucially dependent on what the actors say and do and this means that the way an object is used by the actor can transform its function and even its identity. In the cinema, the camera and editing process may seem to have liberated objects from their dependence on human agency: an extreme close-up of a simple object, say a door handle, can strike terror into the heart of spectators even though no human being is present in the shot. This independence, however, masks a rather literal communicative function (the door handle is frightening because of what we imagine is on the other side, but it remains a door handle). In the theatre, by contrast, objects can be transformed at will, by a word or gesture, into other objects.

Grotowski, working in the early days of the "poor theatre" to eliminate all objects that had a life of their own, that is to say that were capable of expressing or representing something independent of the actor's activities, discovered how gesture could create or transform any object into something else, how "by his controlled use of gesture the actor transforms the floor into a sea, a table into a confessional, a piece of iron into an animate partner" (1969, 21). Richard Foreman has told of his fascination with "the notion that objects might invade and acquire the qualities of other objects" and says that he particularly enjoys "generating a mise-en-scène out of a character's attempts to use a prop in a way that suggested the two separate objects the prop seemed to be at once" (1992, 86). These practices are not the preserve of the twentieth-century avant-garde, however, but exist in different forms in many ancient theatre traditions. In the No, for example, the most versatile object is the large fan carried by each performer, painted to match the performer's costume, which might at first glance be considered part of the costume. As René Sieffert explains, it is far more than an element of costume: "In the hands of the actor it can suggest a weapon or a flask, a pine branch trembling in the breeze or the full moon rising above a mountain peak" (1960, 23).

Jindrich Honzl, in an article entitled "The Dynamics of the Sign in the Theatre" written in 1940, described what he called the "changeability" of the theatrical sign, the way the actor's body can function in the place of scenery, furniture, or props, the way a sound can suggest a place and a thing can become a character, and he claimed that this changeability whereby the sign "passes from material to material with a freedom unknown to any other art" (qtd. in Matejka and Titunik 1976, 86) is unique to the theatre, and indeed it is, in his view, one of the defining characteristics of theatre as an art form. The dynamism Honzl described affects all signs in the theatre, but it is around the object that it achieves its greatest impact, and it is no coincidence that contemporary theatre artists have paid so much attention to the expressive possibilities of the object.

The striking feature of the theatre is that the mobility, transformability, changeability (all these terms have been used by different translators and commentators in reference to Honzl's perception), of the object is always introduced through the actor, is anchored in the actor's skills and bodily presence. There is always a human agency, unlike animation or special effects in film, and, furthermore, the transformation requires the imaginative participation of the spectator because the object itself is unchanged. If the function of the object has been transformed, while the object is nevertheless still present in its original form, yet another level of potential meaning can emerge as earlier meanings leave a trace in the later functions that may be introduced. If the gap between two different functions attributed to the same object is very wide, or if a given object undergoes frequent transformation, then it is the transformation process itself that will be foregrounded. In such a case it is likely that the performance will function to celebrate the power of theatre rather than to tell a story or present an action.

Food onstage, particularly food that has to be consumed, represents a rather special case that poses in an acute form the question of the reality status of the object in performance. The food provided can be either artificial or real. If it is artificial, it can either be overtly artificial (the roast chicken can be obviously made of plaster of Paris) or it can be a convincing artifice. In both cases, however, the fact that the actors cannot eat it brings into question the reality status of the whole performance. If the food is real, there is a further choice for the actor who can either pretend to eat it or really eat it. If the actor also has to speak there is likely to be a logistical problem as the incompatible demands of chewing and swallowing and voice production have to be met simultaneously. If the character is supposed to be enjoying the meal, but the actor is not in fact eating very much and the plates are removed still obviously full of food, then there is a credibility problem. If the decision is made that the actors must really eat real food in realistic quantities, then the eating will tend to become an end in itself, the fiction (if any) will be overwhelmed and the performance will be that of eating a meal. In several recent productions that have explored the question of food the spectators were invited to eat the food that had been produced, but it is significant that in every case the participation of the spectators effectively ended the performance.

Food is an object that poses the question of reality so acutely because the bodily demands it makes necessarily transcend and exceed enactment, and it is doubtless for this reason that contemporary theatre practitioners seem so fascinated by its potential in performance. Stage managers usually detest plays in which food has to be produced, especially if it has to be served hot, ready to eat at a given moment. The reason is, of course, that the physical demands of food preparation, notably the time imperatives, are in practical terms incompatible with those of theatrical performance, and the stage manager in such a production is the person who must ensure that these conflicting imperatives mesh seamlessly together. While film time is infinitely adjustable, and we can see the cook sifting flour into a bowl and then a second later removing the cake from the oven, and a second later again we see the same cake, beautifully iced and decorated, being served to assembled guests, the reality of food in the theatre means that real time must prevail. The real time involved in food preparation is what the Entr'acte Company exploited to such good effect in *The Last Circus*.

The Object in Performance

In the narrative/character/text-based theatre of the mainstream Western tradition, objects function to indicate facts about the fictional situation, place, or time but, as Antoine foresaw, they have come increasingly to serve the actor as an instrument through which a character's state of mind or emotional state can be articulated, and interaction between characters can be motivated. In this kind of theatre, in which meaning is constructed in conjunction with a preexisting text, one of the major functions of the object has come to be the means whereby the actors can body forth the interpretation they are giving to a particular phrase or passage of dialogue. That is to say that the object is used intensively in rehearsal and in performance to bring together words, bodies, and space, to place words meaningfully within the space, and to make manifest the interpersonal relations in force in a given physical space. Major shifts of meaning can be created from the same line of dialogue from one production of a play to another through the object, that is to say that the same line of dialogue can come to mean radically different things depending on the object the actor has chosen to use and what he or she is doing with it.

In physical theatre or performance, where there may be only a minimal fictional content and where there is no preexisting text to be interpreted and made meaningful, objects have an even more powerful part to play. The physical presence of the object, its role in defining the performance space and the opportunities it provides to the performers to display different physical skills can be as important as its connotational levels of meaning. If the fictional level is greatly reduced then these connotational levels will work directly in relation to the referential context (i.e., a chair is not King Lear's throne *and* a chair but simply a chair, with its action force implying a given range of actions, and with its similarity to chairs in other contexts, hospital waiting room, suburban living room, or whatever).

The power of the object to transform meaning in text-based theatre, and the magnitude of the meaning shift that could be produced through a minor alteration of timing, or a small gesture were vividly demon-

strated to me one day in rehearsals for *Miss Julie*. In the scene at the very
end of the play, where Julie first thinks of suicide as a solution to the
problems created by her sexual liaison with Jean, there is a cut-throat
razor on the table. The text, in Elizabeth Sprigge's translation, is as follows:

> *Julie:* If you were in my place, what would you do?
> *Jean:* In your place? Wait a bit. If I was a woman—a lady of rank who
> had—fallen. I don't know. Yes, I do know now.
> *Julie:* (*picking up the razor and making a gesture*) This?

As the actors were developing the scene, Julie picked up the razor while
Jean was speaking so his "Yes, I do know now" was a response to her
implicit suggestion that she then makes explicit with her gesture. On one
occasion the actress failed to pick up the razor in the usual way and Jean
looked at it before she did. The meaning of the moment was transformed, and with it the relationship between the two characters. It took
the smallest change in timing and a single look to produce a radically different meaning from the one they had been working with, for now it
seemed that he put the idea of suicide into her head.

The richest source of material at my disposal through which to
explore the functioning of the object in performance is the comparative
project on *The Maids* that has already been referred to in chapter 2. The
play is one in which objects have an important part, for Genet has imagined a situation in which Madame's possessions take on ritual significance for her two maids and he provides actors with scope for a good
deal of work around these objects, but the value of the project for my
present purposes is also that it was comparative. The actors (John
Howard, Warren Colman, Robyn Gurney, and Elaine Hudson) produced four different performance versions of the same scene, using the
same words, and at least beginning with the same two spaces, furnished
with the same objects. Analyzing the performances after the event,
reflecting on the meanings produced, watching the video recordings to
pinpoint the moments that made a difference, revealed the centrality of
the object in the actors' work.

The actors were provided with two spaces, one an end stage with
box set and naturalistic decor that followed Genet's stage directions as
accurately as the budget permitted, the other an open stage surrounded
on three sides by raised seating and a very stylized set, consisting simply
of a white floor covering that also ran up the back wall, framed by black

drapes at the two sides. The realistic space contained a dressing table with mirror, jewels, make up and perfume, lace curtains, a bed with cushions and frilly pink cover, a wardrobe containing ball dresses, and a little table with lace cloth, a silver tray, and a fine tea service. In the stylized space only two objects had been selected from the profusion that constituted Madame's bedroom in the realistic space: the white ball dress, which was hung against the back wall at one extremity of the space, and the poisoned tea, now in a gigantic (but still fine porcelain) teapot and placed on a high stand diagonally opposite the white dress. The actors, working in pairs with the partner of the same sex, each produced the final scene of the play (from the exit of Madame) in both spaces. These performance versions will be referred to here as MR (male actors, realistic space), FR (female actors, realistic space), MS (male actors, stylized space), and FS (female actors, stylized space). In the following section I list some of the ways in which, in these performances, objects functioned in relation to words and gesture in the creation of theatrical meaning and which seem to me to exemplify modern theatre practice in respect of the object.

Same Object / Different Meaning

First, the meaning of the object was modified by a gesture or action involving it. When Claire decides to recommence the "game," as the only solution to the situation created by Madame's departure, she puts on the white ball dress, thereby indicating to Solange that she has become Madame. In both the MR and FR versions the actor playing Claire in fact held out the dress, indicating that they wanted assistance in putting it on, but their gestures were very different (figs. 17–18). In FR the dress is simply a dress, and Claire's gesture reveals a proprietorial attitude to both her dress and her "maid." Warren Colman's gesture in MR valorizes the dress, it is held up as some special object and although it is still a dress there are already overtones of some kind of ritual and a certain fetishism of the dress itself.

There were two large vases of flowers, one placed on the dressing table, the other on the cupboard containing the ball dresses. When Solange imagines the funeral cortege for herself as murderer of Madame/Claire, she mentions the profusion of flowers. In MR when John Howard said "So many flowers" he was still out on the balcony with his back to the room, and spectators may or may not have looked at the real flowers in the bedroom at that moment. When he came in, he had his back to the real flowers and looked only at Claire as he said "She was

Fig. 17. *The Maids*—FR: the dress as object. (Photography by Raymond de Berquelle.)

Fig. 18. *The Maids*—MR: the dress as fetish. (Photography by Raymond de Berquelle.)

given a beautiful funeral." In FR, by contrast, Solange (Robyn Gurney) came back into the room before the reference to flowers, and spoke while looking at the real flowers on the dressing table and breathing in their perfume. She then took the vase and placed it at the head of the bed, crossed over to the cupboard, took the other vase and placed it at the foot of the bed, and then said the line "she was given a beautiful funeral" looking down at the floral tomb she has made (fig. 19). Claire later took up the fantasy and transformed it into a reality by choosing to die as Madame on that bed, still bedecked by flowers.

The lace curtains were simply curtains for the male Solange, he thrust them apart on "Let me go out," and the gesture showed only the urgency of Solange's need to escape the confines of the room. In FR, Solange used the curtains in a way that revealed that they, too, were part of Madame's domain, they too possessed the power to transform. Coming back into the room, determined to kill Madame (or Claire), she spoke the line about Madame's lovers through the lace curtain (fig. 20), thus vicariously dressing herself in something of Madame's finery, and for a fleeting moment assuming Madame's existence.

Same Words / Different Meaning

A second function of the object is to create meaning with the dialogue, and the same words can be radically transformed by the object that is brought into play or the gesture that accompanies them. Before the pseudo-murder Solange says, "With you I shall, perhaps, find the simplest way, and the courage, Madame, to save my sister and at the same time to cause my own death." It is not clear whether she is talking to Claire or to Claire in the role of Madame (Claire is already wearing Madame's dress), or to the real Madame (meeting her lover in Paris), nor is it clear who is included in the *you* (*vous* in French can be either plural or the polite form of the singular). In MR the line was addressed directly to Claire, already on her knees, awaiting some form of punishment (fig. 21). Claire thus became an unwilling ally in Solange's scheme. In MS the sense of the "vous" was reversed, for Solange here spoke the line to the red dress, holding up the white dress as sacrificial victim (fig. 22), while Claire lay prostrate on the floor. In this version Solange's ally is not Claire but Madame, or Madame's power or the spirit of evil (or whatever else is included in the image of the red dress).

At the end of Solange's monologue she asserts to an imaginary police inspector and to Monsieur and Madame, whom she imagines dis-

Fig. 19. *The Maids*—FR: the floral "tomb." (Photography by Raymond de Berquelle.)

Fig. 20. *The Maids*—FR: Solange speaks through the lace curtain. (Photography by Raymond de Berquelle.)

Fig. 21. *The Maids*—MR: "With you I shall find the way to save my sister." Solange (John Howard) speaks the line directly to Claire (Warren Colman). (Photography by Raymond de Berquelle.)

covering the dead body of Claire, that the crime she has committed (killing her sister) has conferred upon her a new identity. She says, "Now we are Madamoiselle Solange Lemercier." In FR this was a moment of triumph for Solange, watched pensively by Claire, who was excluded from it (fig. 23), and the plural *we* was simply a form of self-aggrandizement—the royal *we*. In FS Solange spoke the line staring fixedly into Claire's eyes (fig. 24), and the *we* seemed to include them both. They had become a composite person, and indeed from Claire's reentry into the action from the end of the monologue she spoke all Solange's lines in unison with her. In MR Solange spoke the line to her own mirror image (fig. 25) and the "we" thus became an indication of her divided self. Having vanquished Madame (the distorting mirror whose beauty reflects only her abasement) and Claire (the hated double of herself) she immediately divided herself yet again. This then motivated her next line, the recognition of failure ("Claire, we are finished"), delivered as she slowly slumped forward, her head on the dressing table.

Three times in the monologue Solange refers to herself as wearing red, the red garb of the criminal—"You see her dressed in red"—but she is in reality wearing the black dress of the servant. In MR she gestured

Fig. 22. *The Maids*—MS: the same line, spoken here to the red
dress. (Photography by Raymond de Berquelle.)

toward her own clothes on this line, and this was the traditional valet
garb, it was this that became valorized, becoming the "red garb of crimi-
nals." This gesture indicated that the maids' strength comes from assuming their servant role and playing it through to its logical conclusion. In
MS each reference to Solange wearing red found her positioned in front of
the red dress, and the triumphant nature of the gestures became more
pronounced with each occurrence. The power of crime and perverse
reversal of accepted moral categories was thus accentuated in this version. In FS Solange stood, pathetically tugging at her black penitentiary
dress, and the gesture marked a forlorn counterpoint to the words. The
crime in this version has not liberated Solange, and there was no triumph.

Fig. 23. *The Maids*—FR: "Now we are Mademoiselle Solange Lemercier"—the royal *we*. (Photography by Raymond de Berquelle.)

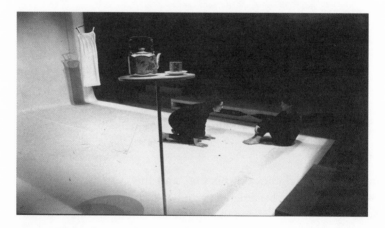

Fig. 24. *The Maids*—FS: "Now we are Mademoiselle Solange Lemercier"—the composite *we*. (Photography by Raymond de Berquelle.)

Fig. 25. *The Maids*—MR: "Now we are Mademoiselle Solange Lemercier"—*we* as divided self. (Photography by Raymond de Berquelle.)

The Absent, Invisible, or Misused Object

There is such a wealth of references to objects in Genet's text and a major effect of this in performance is to set up a tension between the objects that are physically present onstage and those whose existence is purely verbal. The actors devised numerous ways of exploiting this feature of Genet's text, either miming objects that are mentioned in the dialogue then or at some other time but that are not present on the stage, or creating what might be called invisible objects (things that are not mentioned in the dialogue) or using real objects (present onstage) against their normal function, or using a different object (physically present) from the one mentioned in the dialogue. In all these ways the disjunction between the real space and the maid's fantasy or ritual is emphasized.

The Absent Object
In FS, in her buildup to the murder, Solange mimes the gesture of pulling on rubber gloves (fig. 26); these are not mentioned in the dialogue until after the murder (when she says: "Madame is dead at last. Strangled with the washing up gloves"). The gesture here with all its sinister overtones built up suspense about what was going to happen as well as furthering the idea that Solange was locked into some inner hell of her own

Fig. 26. *The Maids*—FS: the rubber gloves. (Photography by Raymond de Berquelle.)

imagining. The fact that there were no gloves indicated the level of para-
noia at which the scene was being relived by the character.

The Invisible Object

Even more powerful was the invisible object that was neither spoken nor
evoked in relation to an earlier physical presence but that existed purely
in the paranoid domain of the characters' fantasy. In the MS version,
when Claire is attempting to incite Solange to action after the departure
of Madame, she wrenches her head back by the hair and assaults her
physically in other ways; at the end of the play, when Solange is again
prostrate and Claire is again imposing her will, this time from a distance,
she seemed to pull at an invisible rope, forcing Solange against her will
to rise up (fig. 27). Claire was standing in the position of power, erect
before the red dress, the gesture was a reminder of the hair pulling and
other torments from earlier in the scene, but the impression of violence
was even greater than when these were realistically acted, and the
"invisible rope" was a powerful image of the bonds that link and bind
the two sisters.

The Misused Object

A very powerful example of the object used against its normal function,
or used against the verbal reference occurred in another production of

Fig. 27. *The Maids*—MS: the invisible rope. (Photography by Raymond de Berquelle.)

The Maids, this time by Igor Persan, also with male actors playing the female characters. When Claire playing Madame in the first scene tells her maid to bring her the emerald necklace, the actor playing Solange/Claire produced, not a necklace but a piece of plaited cord, yanking it violently between his hands as he stood behind her, then offering it submissively when she turned around. The violence latent in the object, the danger evoked by the gesture was all the more disturbing in that there was close proximity between actors and spectators and it was evident that the rope was frighteningly real and we could see the strength in the actor's wrists.

Sartre claims that the object in the theatre is always in one sense absent. He says that the reader of a novel imagines the character's surroundings as described by the novelist and the relations between character and objects in terms of his own relations to similar objects, and in the cinema the camera and editing process tell the spectator when and how to look at a given object, but that in the theatre the spectator is obliged to look, as it were, without seeing:

> In the theatre I don't see the object, because seeing it would bring it into my world where it would figure as a tree made of cardboard; seeing it would mean seeing it as something painted on a support or on some object

or other. My only relation to the decor is through the gestures of the characters, the only way I can be in a relationship to the tree is to see a character sit down in its shade. (Sartre 1973, 27)

The reality of the object (whether this be painted cardboard, a cunningly constructed, lifelike, three dimensional model of a tree, or even a branch of a real tree) is precisely what the spectator cannot "see" if he wants to believe in the character's experience.

What Sartre perceives with such acuity is that, in the theatre, it is the actor's bodily gestures that create the fiction, while the objects themselves belong to what I have called the presentational realm and, indeed, may not even be present at all. He mentions approvingly the practice of Jean-Louis Barrault for whom objects and even the character's surroundings can be created without recourse to anything beyond the actor's body: a man on horseback, a man swimming across a river can be performed without horse or river. What Sartre does not see so clearly, however, is the power of theatre to hold both the fictional and the presentational in some kind of tension. When Barrault performs the action of riding a horse his body becomes both rider and horse, but at the same time it remains a human body and the spectator's pleasure in the performance is enhanced because of this. The rubber gloves are still present in Solange's gesture, but the gesture reveals more than the gloves, it suggests the murderous power of her hands. The piece of rope is also a necklace, we see the rope but hear the word *necklace*, and the deadly weight of Madame's possessions, the jealous rage of the maid, is made manifest for a fleeting moment. The actor's gesture liberates the object from its material function or even replaces the object, creates the idea of the object disconnected from its material reality; the theatre is, thus, able to sunder signifier from signified, showing both as well as the gesture that connects/disconnects the two.

The Arbitrary Object

There is another use of the object in contemporary theatre that needs to be mentioned here: the arbitrary object for which any link to a referent in the real world has been obliterated. In *Le Théâtre et son double*, Artaud suggests on several occasions the power of such objects and, like Grotowski after him, he planned that they would replace decor and set:

> No decor. Hieroglyphic characters, ritual costume, thirty foot high effigies
> of King Lear's beard in the storm, musical instruments as tall as men,
> objects of unknown form and purpose are enough to fill this function.
> (Artaud 1970, 76)

It is the rupture with the real world, the inability to ascribe function, the
realization that the object can be neither understood nor controlled that
gives such surrealistic objects their power.

For Artaud the intention was to stir people, to jolt them out of their
smug, positivistic self-assurance into some awareness of the chaos he
knew surrounded us: "Another example would be to have a fabricated
being appear, made of wood and cloth, completely invented, resembling
nothing, able to reintroduce onstage the slightest intimation of the great
metaphysical fear underlying all ancient theatre" (53). Contemporary
directors and performance makers may not all share Artaud's metaphysics, but the use of troubling objects, of arbitrary or inexplicable
things that seem to have no function in the performance but which
remain to haunt the spectator's memory is a striking feature of much
contemporary theatre. These can be simply bizarre, like the polar bear
that strolled quietly across the back of the stage in Matthias Langhoff's
production of *The Dance of Death* at the Comédie Française in 1996 (which
was, indeed, so arbitrary as to provoke in me the suspicion that he was
mocking the play, his own production of it and the whole institution of
state subsidized theatre).

Such objects can also be highly poetic images: in Lynette Walworth's production of her own play, *God, the Doctor and the Impossible
Body* at the Performance Space in Sydney in 1992, there was a wardrobe/
chest of drawers, the drawers partially opened, down which water
began to cascade. The homely, familiar nature of the object, the incongruity (scandal even) of water running down the polished wood, the
incompatibility of the connotations of indoors and outdoors that were
nevertheless both strongly present, made it a highly compelling spectacle in itself, but in the context of the whole performance (derived from
stories told by women patients to Walworth during her year as an artist
in residence in a specialized cancer hospital) it seemed to take on more
and more emotional power. She used the myth of the Little Mermaid to
evoke the experience of women trying to come to terms with the reality
of bodily mutilation involved in surgery, and there were other images of
water: a birthing tank placed in the center of the space in which a mer-

maid character "swam" around for nearly the whole duration of the performance, and a live goldfish swimming around in its bowl, which was beautifully lit and suspended on invisible wires from the ceiling. The chest of drawers/waterfall was a very powerful means of evoking the impossible, incompatible nature of the Mermaid's desires, and by extension the impossible nature of the Woman's conflict in the play.

The arbitrary and the absent object represent opposite extremes in terms of the reality/nonreality status of the theatrical object. In the one case, the object is a material presence but its connection to referential reality has been severed, and in the other the denegation that always threatens any theatrical reality has been taken so far that the material presence of the object is obliterated. In both cases, it is only due to the spatial reality of performer and stage that the object can function in the ways described.

The Object in Rehearsal

Modern actors have gained a great deal of experience with objects and even in plays that do not seem, on the face of it, to require any objects they may suggest to director or designer that a particular object would help them. Watching actors at work in the early stages of rehearsal has been extremely revealing in terms of the value of objects in helping an actor to define his or her character, to articulate motivation at a particular moment, and to help find the physical actions that will body forth an emotion or intention. Rehearsals for *God, the Doctor and the Impossible Body* revolved around objects, perhaps because Lynette Walworth (the writer and director) is primarily a visual artist. Her practice was to bring some object to each rehearsal that the actors would handle, look at, and discuss and later use in their improvisations around a segment of text. Some of these objects did find their way into the final design, others did not but nevertheless left traces in the performance they had influenced.

An object introduced into the action at some stage during the rehearsal may then acquire other uses, and indeed may turn out to be decisive in the interpretation of a whole scene or even more. An example of this occurred in Beverley Blankenship's work with actors on the seduction scene in Molière's *Dom Juan*. Charlotte and Pierrot were played with broad Australian accents and the dialogue had been amended to reflect the Australian vernacular. Gillian Hyde was developing Charlotte as a down-to-earth character and decided that she wanted her to be discovered at work when Don Juan and Sganarelle come onstage. Furthermore, she wanted this to be a dirty, unglamorous occupation (she is, after all, supposed to have dirty hands) and, after some discussion, it was agreed that she would be digging vegetables in a field. A patch of earth, fork, sack, and an assortment of somewhat phallic root vegetables were provided by the stage manager and much comic action was developed. In the preceding scene, between Pierrot and Charlotte, Pierrot tries clumsily to kiss her hand and it was decided that if she were to wear gardening gloves, she could snatch her hand away leaving him holding only the glove. This was done, providing Pierrot with more comic business for his exit (taking the glove with him, kissing it, and singing, "All you need is 'glove'"). In early rehearsals for the pushing and shoving scene between Pierrot and Don Juan (when the latter has been discovered kissing Charlotte's hand) the actors developed some rather realistic violence, but this tended to overwhelm the comedy. It was decided to bring in the glove in order to "make a connection with the earlier scene" (although it was never specified what this connection should be, nor why it was desirable) and to provide Don Juan with a less threatening weapon than his stick. In the final version Pierrot came on, still clutching the glove, singing, "'Glove', 'glove' me do," intervened when he saw Don Juan kissing Charlotte's hand, only to have the glove snatched from his hand and used to slap him around the head. While the degree of violence was less, the humiliation of Pierrot was the more complete in that the glove had earlier represented his amorous triumph. When he was finally crushed, he sank to his knees in the dirt of Charlotte's vegetable patch and Don Juan threw the glove down beside him in a gesture that suggested precisely what would happen to Charlotte herself as soon as he had completed the seduction. As this example shows, a prop can acquire a life of its own, it can inflect the meaning of a scene or interaction, and it can make explicit what is only a suggestion in the dialogue.

A different prop can produce a different gesture that can lead to a different characterization emerging: Don Juan armed with a sword is a different figure from Don Juan carrying a swagger stick. A different prop, producing a different action, can change the relationship between two characters or create a very different moment. At an early stage in rehearsals for a scene in Pinter's *Old Times* in which Kate offers Anna a cigarette, no props were available. Sue Lyons (Kate) mimed the act of picking up a cigarette box from the coffee table and proffering it in a gesture that kept Anna at arm's length. Later, Deeley offered Anna a cigarette, but Brandon Burke, playing Deeley, did not use the box mimed by Sue Lyons. He mimed reaching into the pocket of his jeans for a packet, and the difference between the two gestures involved, the proximity between Anna and Deeley created by the small packet as opposed to the distance the box created between Anna and Kate, made Deeley's offer seem extremely personal, and the sexual overtones were almost tangible. Even though this was a very early stage of the rehearsal process, it was evident that from one small piece of business a great deal of insight into relationships and sexual tensions could be derived, and that the choice of container for the cigarettes would make a big difference.

The connection between object and human user, the "gesture" that, in Jousse's term, is contained in the object, means that directors can modify the objects or their placement in the space in order to modify the behavior and even the bodily presence of the actors. In his introduction to *Symphony of Rats*, performed by the Wooster Group, Richard Foreman tells a story that perfectly illustrates this aspect of the object's function:

> there were standing microphones all over the stage for the actors to speak into, but all through rehearsal when they came to speak into the mikes, they seemed suddenly drained of life. Then I lowered the mikes a bit, so in order to speak into them the actors had to crouch slightly. This energised not only their bodies, but their whole emotional being. (1992, 209)

Caspar Neher taught Brecht about the gestic force of objects and furniture, and in Brecht's essay on "Stage Design for the Epic Theatre" Brecht tells how Neher designed objects precisely so that the "action force" in them would serve the dramatic moment:

> With what care he selects a chair, and with what thought he places it! And it all helps the playing. One chair will have short legs, and the height of the accompanying table will also be calculated, so that whoever eats at it has to take up a quite specific attitude, and the conversation of these people as they bend more than usual when eating takes on a particular character, which makes the episode clearer. And how many effects are made possible by his doors of different heights! (1964, 231)

Egon Monk reports that actors referred to Neher's tables and chairs as being at "Neher-height," and, although this could vary from production to production, it was usually "about 5 to 10 centimeters below normal" (qtd. in Willett 1986, 113).

Creative Agency and the Object

In view of the importance of objects in the expression of meaning in modern theatre that has been described in this chapter, it becomes interesting to consider which of the many practitioners involved in the production process is primarily responsible for them or, in semiotic terms, who is the subject of the utterance in which they figure as signs. The situation of the object is, in fact, particularly interesting in that responsibility for its introduction and exploitation can be claimed by many different artists, notably the playwright, the director, the designer, and the actor. Furthermore, it can be introduced at very different stages into the creative process, and this all adds to the wealth of expressive potential that surrounds the object in contemporary performance (whether in mainstream or avant-garde practice) as well as to some serious problems.

The object can be written into the performance by the playwright, whose instructions to the actor can be more or less detailed, more or less explicit, more or less compelling, as can be seen in the practice of writers from Tom Robertson or Feydeau to Chekhov, and later in the work of writers like Ionesco, Pinter, and Beckett. The stage direction already quoted from *Caste* rivals those of Beckett's *Happy Days* for precision, leaving little room for innovation by the actor, and in Pinter's plays, too, the timing of gestures involving the apparently harmless objects of any domestic interior (a cup of tea, a newspaper, a glass of water, and so on) is very accurately encoded in the writing; after working on a production of Feydeau's *On Purge bébé* at the Sydney Theatre Company, Rex Cramphorn told me that when the actors tried to improvise new business it usually did not work, and they found that Feydeau had already mapped together dialogue and business involving objects with such meticulous care that their task was simply to execute with equally meticulous care what was clearly indicated in the text; Chekhov's habit of giving certain characters a particular object that comes to constitute a kind of signature for that character is equally compelling to actors, even though here they must explore for themselves how often, when, and how to use the object in question. Other kinds of writing assume the existence of certain hand props, such as the fan or snuff box (Restoration comedy), or the cigarette (Noel Coward and other playwrights of the 1920s and 1930s) without specifying their presence, and in performance based on this kind of writing it is up to the actor to find the most appropriate ways to use the prop to punctuate and segment the verbal flow, and to create additional levels of meaning.

The power of the cigarette to create subtext was brilliantly demonstrated for me during rehearsals for *Phèdre;* the translation being used was by John Cairncross and the actors had remarked on what they saw as the "frozen, English quality of the text," and had been struggling to find a performance where, as Gillian Jones (playing Phèdre) remarked "you expect the metre to carry the meaning and it doesn't." At the end of a rather frustrating work session on the scene where Phèdre first confesses to Hippolyte that she loves him, the actors launched into a Noel Coward pastiche. Phèdre poured herself a stiff drink before launching into the confession, and she punctuated her first speech (appeals to Hippolyte on behalf of her child, now that she believes her husband is dead) with lighting a cigarette, and taking a number of puffs. The effect of this was immediately to cast into doubt the sincerity of her words: as she inhaled deeply after saying, "I come to tell you of a mother's fears" or "You, only you, can see to his defence," it seemed evident that she was not concerned about the child, and even the way she inhaled the smoke suggested self-indulgence rather than agitation due to the danger afflicting her child. In the event, the final performance built on this pastiche, and in later rehearsals I saw Gillian Jones "place" the sips of gin and drags at the cigarette so that they punctuated that speech in several different ways, but always the effect was to undermine the sincerity of what she had just said.

One of the major tasks of the early directors, like Antoine and Stanislavsky, was to ensure that the sets were appropriately furnished and to encourage actors to exploit the expressive possibilities offered by a naturalistic set and the objects it contained, and modern directors have developed this aspect of the work considerably, frequently using objects as a means of articulating their own interpretation of a classic text and, as the quotations from directors as divergent as Richard Foreman and Brecht have indicated, in order to elicit a certain style of acting or bodily behaviour from the actors.

The designer has become an extremely important figure in the contemporary theatre, and the current fashion for extravagant, musical spectaculars like *Phantom of the Opera* has given designers massive resources and star billing, and it has shifted the balance away from the performers during the creative process. Some designers work with a pic-

torial imperative that can create problems for the performers if their bodily needs have not been adequately provided for, or if the demands of the
dramatic action have been subordinated to the aesthetics of the picture.
Bertrand Tavernier, after much experience as a director in both theatre
and cinema, claims that designers always provide too much detail:

> I have learned to fight the art director and the set designer who always
> want to do too much. Whether it's on stage or on screen, visual austerity is
> vital. In my opinion, the film maker should always divide by ten the num-
> ber of props suggested by the set designer. (1996, 23–24)

It is, of course, the actor who works most closely with the object, and
as has been argued throughout this chapter, it is the actor who confers
meaning upon the object, who brings object and word together to make
new meanings with both, and who can replace the object by gesture or
transform it into something else. The object is so closely associated with
its human user, can have such a powerful impact on bodily behaviors
and on the interpersonal relations developed between characters that it
seems evident that the choice of stage objects, their quantity, placement
etc., should emerge from the actors' work in rehearsal. All the more surprising to discover that in a great deal of modern theatre this is not the
case at all.

The actors' ability to improvise and innovate may be curtailed by
the prescriptive nature of the writing, as in the example of Feydeau and
Beckett that has already been mentioned. Such writing gives little scope
to the actor to do anything new, and even when the play is a masterpiece
like *Happy Days* it is possible that the result will be to discourage new
productions of the play. Problems are always likely to arise if the actors'
task is reduced to that of finding ways to use what has been imposed on
them from without, whether by writer, director, or designer, rather than
emerging from their own work in developing character and motivation,
and using the space fully. If objects are seen merely as decorative background to the action, if their presence is controlled by pictorial rather
than theatrical imperatives, and if their use does not emerge from the
actors' work, then a valuable and potentially very powerful means of
expression is being underutilized. Antony Sher was aghast when he discovered that the tombstones provided for the first scene in Bill Alexan-
der's production of *Richard III* were not going to be strong enough for the
actors to climb on them:

Apparently a lot of money will be saved on the budget if they're built much lighter. This seems crazy to me. How do we know yet that we won't want to climb on them? . . . With them dominating the set like they do, surely they're crying out to be used somewhere. (1985, 171)

An object that cannot be used is, literally, of no use to an actor even though the pictorial design in which it figures may be deeply satisfying to the designer. Designers and even directors, working in realistic mode, may use objects very much as Antoine described his own practice at the beginning of the century, in order to create a credible sense of the characters' milieu, to provide a sense of place or atmosphere, and to create a context for the action. Actors are much less interested in this kind of "big picture" and, even in realistic mode, will use objects in relation to the detail of the dramatic action. As has been demonstrated through the examples drawn from work on *The Maids* and *Phèdre*, actors use objects intensively in relation to the verbal text, to tease out meanings from it, even to impose meanings on it. A designer who is not working closely with the actor in rehearsal may provide objects that the actor does not wish to use or that are no help to him in the performance he is elaborating.

Sydney actress, Kris McQuade, has commented on the frustrations regularly felt by actors in television where the first time they see the set in which they are going to perform is usually the day they arrive at the studio for the shoot. She said that on one occasion there was such incompatibility between the living room set provided by the designer and the character she had developed (whose room it was supposed to be) that she felt unable to continue. After some argument, and with little understanding by the production team of the nonfrivolous nature of her protest, ornaments and nicknacks were removed, a vase of fresh flowers substituted, and the shoot proceeded. Even in the theatre, in which actors are so much more central to the communicative process and where their creative process is taken so much more seriously than in either television or film, the actor is frequently the last person to be consulted about the set design. For Antony Sher, and for many others, the contemporary practice of designing the set before the actors have begun to rehearse severely reduces the actors' ability to develop interesting and innovative performances. If the set takes precedence over the actors, their task will be reduced to that of servicing the set, and instead of depth and complexity in the performance audiences will be offered a glittering surface.

An example of the problems that can arise from a design with which the actor is not in sympathy arose in *The Maids* project that has provided so much material for this chapter. The women were perfectly happy working in the stylized space as created before the project began (i.e., white floor covering, white dress hanging at one corner, poisoned tea in a gigantic pot diagonally opposite on a high stand). They developed a strong sense of imprisonment in the final scene, and the spectator was not sure whether Claire was really present or if she was there only as a figment of Solange's imagination. Both by its whiteness and by its openness the space itself suggested the opposite of imprisonment so the idea of an imagined, perhaps psychotic, state was created, the idea of a person trapped by memory, by the past. The two objects proclaimed the space as being under the dominance of Madame but there was nevertheless a powerful opposition between them (Madame's life/Madame's death, Madame's innocence/the maids' guilt) and the actors created a further opposition between the objects and the characters by their decision to play the whole scene virtually on the floor, crouching, writhing, rolling over each other. The objects seemed thus to have usurped the human position of verticality, and the humans were in thrall to them.

The men were given the same space with its two objects but found it impossible to work with them. After a day and a half's increasingly anguished creative impasse, the breakthrough came when they introduced the second dress. They abandoned the teapot on its high stand and instead set up a polarity between the two dresses: the red chiffon was hung in the center of the back wall, in a grotesque combination of altar piece and frock shop window display, and they hung the white dress directly opposite at the top of the steps in the audience space. The most interesting thing about the men's inability to use the poisoned tea is that, at the thematic level, it can be argued that the white dress and red dress together constitute a paradigm that functions in practically identical ways to the white dress/poisoned tea coupling: innocence/guilt, life/death, Madame/Maid (by this stage in the action Madame has given the red dress to Claire, thereby divesting it of much of its value as a Madame-signifier). The major difference is, of course, that the dresses are associated with the female appearance, the female body, while the teapot is merely a utensil. In their work in the realistic space, too, the men had concentrated on objects associated directly with the female body (the dresses and makeup), while the women had used all the objects (those associated with the space itself—lace curtains, flowers, bed cover—as well as those associated with the body of Madame). In both male versions the actors developed a performance revolving around the fetishization of the female body, but this would have been blocked in the stylized space if the director/designer had insisted on the original design and refused the introduction of the crucial second dress.

Actors can, of course, get carried away by the power over the dialogue that props bring with them. A performance can be imposed on, rather than emerging from, the words the playwright has provided, which is why the term *a props solution* is usually used by theatre practitioners in a pejorative sense. This refers to a moment for which the actors have not found a satisfactory meaning, and so construct one with the use of props (as in the example of the cigarettes and gin for Cairncross's translation of the scene in *Phèdre* that I mentioned earlier). In a good rehearsal process, in which ideas that come up are fully explored and especially one in which actors are encouraged to make proposals, it is likely that numerous objects will be requested, their potential explored, but that only some of these will find their way into the actual performance. I have heard an actor say "this is getting a bit proppy," meaning that things were taking precedence over dramatic action, that instead of elucidating and bodying forth the action they were becoming an end in themselves.

In the theatre it usually takes a considerable amount of time before practitioners find ways to use new expressive possibilities provided by advances in technology, and even longer before they become an artistic necessity. The object is no exception in this respect, but as this brief account of its historical trajectory has shown, the theatre has come a long way artistically in the hundred years or so that separate Mrs. Bancroft's "cup and saucer comedies" and, say, the work of Vitez, Planchon, Sobel, and Strehler, that was documented in the volume of *Les Voies de la création théâtrale* devoted to productions of classic texts (vol. 6, 1978). The object is now a vital element in theatrical meaning making, and the task of the actor in particular has evolved to take account of the new possibilities it has brought with it. The problems to which I have drawn attention in this final section of the chapter arise only where one or other of the creative agents involved in the production process gains too much precedence over the others. In respect of the object, as in so much else in the theatre, the most artistically satisfying work occurs when the artists involved are listening to one another, when the aesthetic imperatives of each of the art forms involved are held in creative tension with each other, and when the centrality of the actor in the performance process is acknowledged and valued.

The object has come to play an extremely important part in both text-based and non-text-based performance at the latter end of the twentieth century, whether the performances involve classic plays or new works, whether or not the intention in these works is to suggest a fictional world, and whether or not objects played such a part in the performance tradition from which the work derives. It is evident from the analyses and commentaries in this chapter that space is once again the medium that permits the expressive function that has been described. It is because the objects are located in space, present to the spectators through visible/audible/tactile/olfactory means, that the actors can utilize them in such varied ways and that they can function so intensively in the meaning-making process.

6

Space in the Written Text

In the way of singing itself the space is codified. One sings differently in the mountains and in the plains.
—Jerzy Grotowski, *Tu es le fils de quelqu'un*

Most of our fundamental concepts are organised in terms of one or more spatialisation metaphors.
—George Lakoff and Mark Johnson, *Metaphors We Live By*

Language exists in the theatre as speech, even if it has been written before being spoken, and this means that words in the theatre convey layer upon layer of information in addition to meanings that can be derived from their written form. A further corollary of the bodily source of language in the theatre is that words are thereby necessarily located physically within the performance space, and this too contributes to the meaning they convey. Whether the words spoken are monologue or dialogue, naturalistic conversation or a lyrical flight of fancy, the speakers must be placed somewhere; their bodies must necessarily be in some relation to the bodies of other performers, to the space as a whole, and to the spectators. In film or television the aptly named "voice-over" makes possible speech that is unlocated within the fictional space, even though it is relayed through the same loudspeakers as the voices of the characters speaking from within the fiction. In the theatre even an offstage voice is physically locatable (it comes from the right or left of the spectator, in front or from the rear, from near or far off), and it will be associated by spectators with whatever fictional situation has been constructed by that production as connected with that "localized off" space. In a nonnarrative, nonillusionistic performance in which there is no fictional place, an offstage voice may create awareness of the offstage space as practitioner space or perhaps simply as a space that is invisible or otherwise off limits to spectators. Whatever the function or status of the space thus activated, the voice is physically located, and the meaning of the words spoken is inflected by their location.

Dolby surround sound has given filmmakers the possibility of physically locating the source of the sound at different points in the cinema, but the effect created is frequently disconcerting. In the theatre the fiction is located in the actor, and so an actor entering through the audience, speaking from the back of the auditorium, or calling from offstage activates the spaces he or she temporarily occupies and takes them over for the fiction. In the cinema it is the image on the screen that is the site of the fiction, and sound alone does not seem sufficient to transform another part of the spectators' social space into a secondary site for the fiction; in a film such as Gillian Armstrong's *Little Women*, for example, my first reaction on hearing a woman's voice apparently calling from the back of the auditorium was that the person calling was a spectator or usherette. When I realized that it was part of the fiction I was even more disturbed because the voice had activated a space the fiction cannot occupy in the cinema; it functioned, thus, to draw attention for no discernible purpose to the nonreality of the screen image precisely when my pleasure most depended on being able to forget this fact.

Words in the theatre are physically placed by virtue of being spoken, and even offstage, amplified, or recorded voices tend to acquire some spatial location (e.g., the phonographs in Cocteau's *Mariés de la Tour Eiffel* or the reel-to-reel tape recorder in *Krapp's Last Tape*). Some of the implications of this spatialization of language in the meaning-making process have been explored in the preceding three chapters: the gestural content of the individual actor's delivery and the impact of proxemic relations on the meanings conveyed (chap. 3), the role of spatial factors such as movement in segmenting the performance continuum and therefore determining structure (chap. 4), and the use of objects as a means of linking the space and its human occupants and of conferring precise meaning on particular words and phrases (chap. 5). As these chapters have shown, the spatialization of language that is so fundamental to theatre enables the words spoken to function in relation to larger signifying structures, enables meaning to extend far beyond the verbal.

While these chapters have focused on ways in which the physical, bodily realities of performance function to situate the verbal in relation to a given space and on how this contributes to the meanings conveyed, it can equally be argued that written texts contain their own indications of spatiality and that these constitute another important dimension of theatre space. The spatiality I am interested in here concerns the material reality of the performance space, not the abstraction of dramatic space (to use Ubersfeld's term) that has been so perceptively studied by critics such as Stanton Garner (1994), Una Chaudhuri (1995), and Ubersfeld herself (1964). My purpose in this chapter is, rather, to consider what kind of spatial indications are contained in the written text, how they are encoded, how compelling they are to practitioners engaged in their own spatialization process—in other words, how space in the text relates to the spatialized words of the performance.

The relationship between written text and theatrical performance has been an area of significant controversy during the course of the current century. Antonin Artaud was not the only person in the 1930s to argue against the dominance of the literary text in the theatre, although he has certainly been the most influential. Gaston Baty, one of the so-called cartel of directors of art theatres in Paris in the 1930s, wrote frequently of the deleterious effect great writers have had on the theatre. As he saw it, for example, the plays of Racine exist in such a complete form as written texts that they make performance redundant:

> Everything is in the words, every detail concerning the characters, every emotional nuance, their physical appearance, their facial expression, their costume, and even the decor, the environment, the atmosphere. Academics get very excited about this and claim it reveals profound understanding of theatre! The opposite is true; Racine knows about only one of the elements that makes up dramatic art: language. He makes words convey many things that could be expressed as well or better by other means. (1949, 107–8)

Baty, developing the new art of mise en scène, was searching for a kind of playwright whose writing left room for the particular creativity of the actor and the director, and he thought that the moments of greatest achievement in the European theatre (he cites Greek tragedy, medieval mystery cycles, and Elizabethan theatre) came about when there was a balance between poetry and spectacle:

> At these times everything is in balance, the text does not take up the whole space, nor does the visual spectacle prevent the text from delivering its full value. All the collaborators—writer, performer, designer—contribute on an equal footing, to the extent that their particular craft can serve the communal goal. (214)

Artaud was not interested in this kind of balance, and his critique of a theatre dominated by literary texts was differently motivated and led to a very different position from that of Baty. Because that which is written is already fixed in a physical form, it was, as he perceived it, already dead, and his interest in the theatre was that, precisely because it involved live performance, it was the one art form that could escape this encroaching deadness and enable us to tap into the live sources at the heart of existence:

> And just as masks, once used in magic rituals, are no longer fit for anything but to be put in museums—in the same way, the poetic effectiveness of a text is exhausted—theatre's effectiveness and poetry is exhausted least quickly of all, since it permits the action of movement and spoken things, never reproduced twice. (Artaud 1970, 59)

It is evident why Artaud would reserve all his scorn for those who subordinated the performance, theatre's unique strength, to the dead and ineffectual text, but many of the practitioners and theorists in the 1960s and 1970s, who took up Artaud's arguments with such enthusiasm, were less concerned with the metaphysics underlying his polemic than with their own attack on bourgeois culture, or, more simply, with an attempt to shift the authority of authorship from the playwright to the director or performer.

Successive generations of experimental, avant-garde, and alternative performance makers have often taken up a radical position vis-à-vis the written text, either privileging the expressivity of body, space, and object over that of language, as in physical theatre or theatre of image, or refusing to work with preexisting texts and developing their own (with or without the assistance of a writer) at a later stage in the creative process, and of course postmodernism has led, in the theatre as elsewhere, to the subversion of narrative and character, mainstays of the textual tradition that has been under attack for most of this century. Although there has been so much criticism of the role of the written text in the performance process and notwithstanding the conviction of academic/practitioners such as Richard Schechner that the text/narrative/character-based theatre of the mainstream Western tradition is moribund, kept alive only by the conservatism of academic instititutions and funding authorities, "the string quartet of the 21st century" (1992, 8), it is interesting to note that the directors who have dominated theatrical production in Europe in recent years have not rejected this tradition. Direc-

tors have emerged as the dominant creative force in the theatre of this
period to the extent that it has come to be known as "director's theatre,"
yet they have not used this undoubted creative supremacy to develop
their own material, as has been the custom in alternative theatre. They
have, on the contrary, drawn on the traditional repertoire, radically
rethinking and reinterpreting plays from the past, borrowing from the
traditional repertoires of neighboring cultures, and thereby entrenching,
if not actually inventing, the notion of the classic. Roger Planchon has
pointed out that there is a link between the development of the classic
and the development of the director as the dominant force in modern
theatre:

> The emergence of the classic brings with it the birth of a dubious charac-
> ter. He presents himself as a museum curator; leaning on Molière and
> Shakespeare, he levers himself into a position where he is running the
> whole show. We may lament the fact, but the two things are linked: the
> birth of the classic gives power to the theatre director. (Qtd. in Bradby and
> Williams 1988, 6)

Notwithstanding the polemics of the past decades concerning the
tyranny of the written text, the fact remains that theatre is an art form
that gives a very special place to language. Marguerite Duras, inter-
viewed in 1996 for a documentary about her work that was broadcast on
French television, said "Theatre is an exhibition . . . exhibitionism . . .
exhibition of the word." She was clearly thinking aloud as she spoke, and
in her attempt to formulate the thought she draws attention both to the
centrality of language in the theatre experience and to the fact that language in the theatre is made visible, displayed, located in space. Audiences hear as much as they see, sometimes more, but the important thing
is that in the theatre the verbal is always situated in relation to the visual;
it exists through the vocalization of the actors but only for a fleeting
moment, which is why language in the theatre is able to escape the dead
fixity feared by Artaud. It is acknowledged by all that verbal meaning in
the theatre does not reside in the words themselves but in how, where,
and to whom they are spoken, and, while a lazy or incompetent actor can
fail to delve beneath the surface to discover the performance possibilities
a text has to offer, it is also well recognized that a really good actor can
utterly transform the words he or she speaks. As David Warrilow put it:

> I found that an actor can bring something to language that is unfath-
> omable, it's not knowable on a certain level of experience, it just appears.

> When it appears, it can illuminate words, phrases, sentences, paragraphs, chapters, scenes, in such a way that you almost don't know if it's great writing or perfectly ordinary writing. (Zarilli 1995, 314)

The actor brings something to the playwright's language, but language certainly also brings something to the actor. While this may not be evident to people reading a play as they would read any other kind of text, it will emerge for the actor who "works" the text rather than simply reading it. Louis Jouvet used the analogy of a baker kneading the dough to refer to this aspect of the actor's creative process and insisted over and over again in his classes at the Paris Conservatoire that the task for the actor is not to act the text, that is, to impose meaning on it, but to find in it the rhythms, the patterns of breathing it demands, to feel it physically in his mouth and in his lungs, for then, and only then, will he find meaning and emotion:

> You'll only feel the meaning of the text by trying to speak it, not by acting it. If you try to act it, you'll puff it up, you'll breathe in a certain way that doesn't correspond to the words. It's through the physical sound of the words, through the respiration necessary to speak those words that you'll find the feeling, and that feeling won't be the one you bring to the text through your own little personal emotions. (1965, 14)

The actor, working from a written text, must first transform that written material into speech, must internalize it, experience it corporeally. Louis Jouvet again: "For professors at the Sorbonne, texts provide material for grammatical exercises, but for actors the text is above all a written form of breathing" (104). Breath is essential to the actor, and I have argued in chapter 4 that it can be seen as central to the construction of the smallest units of performance, and hence to the overall structure; in Jouvet's experience actors working on texts, especially those written by Molière (for he was an actor and he wrote as an actor) have to "breathe" the text, and only through this physiological, corporeal reality are they able to find their character's emotions or thoughts.

Jouvet's insight is borne out by many other anecdotes recounted by actors and teachers of acting. As John Harrop puts it, dramatic dialogue may have a whole world of behavior "printed within it," and it is because actors work physically with text (speaking it, breathing it, pacing up and down, moving it around) that they discover this. He gives the example of Noel Coward's sophisticated comedies written in the 1920s and 1930s in which cigarette smoking "is part of the punctuation of the language, predicated upon the inhaling and exhaling of smoke, and the flicking of ash" (1992, 72). Jouvet and Harrop are talking about performance indicators that the individual actor can find in the written text of the dialogue, but Jacques Copeau, writing at the beginning of the producer movement in the theatre, went much further: for him the playtext, provided that it is written by a dramatist who truly understands the theatre, contains its own mise en scène:

> The born theatre practitioner, by some mysterious complicity, takes possession almost without effort of the work of the born playwright. In what is for the outsider just a series of words, black on white, the disjointed phrases of a dialogue, he discovers almost at first glance a world of shapes, sounds, colour and movement. He does not invent these things. He discovers them. They are the movements, colours, sounds and shapes that were more or less present in the mind of the poet as he wrote. That is why I think that for a work that has been genuinely conceived for the stage there is a single, necessary *mise en scène*, the one inscribed into the text by the author, like the notes on a musical score. These notes do not speak to the eyes of the profane, but the musician's gaze makes them sing. (1974, 268–69)

Copeau's assertion that there is only one mise en scène inscribed within the play text is certainly open to objection, both on the pragmatic grounds that each different director approaching a given text seems to "find" and construct a different mise en scène and in terms of the postmodern critique of the view of language and meaning making that, it would seem, underpins Copeau's claim.

It would be easy to see Copeau here as an authoritarian director who, in setting himself up as the mystically endowed interpreter of the playwright's text, was seeking to assume the playwright's authorial power as well as his own and to see in him the forerunner of so many other authoritarian directors who have used their self-proclaimed knowledge of the playwright's "intentions" and a vocabulary posited on the notion of "serving" the play in order to exercise complete power over the creative process. There may, indeed, be an element of truth in this, but Copeau in his directorial work succeeded in bringing many plays to the stage that had been deemed unstageable by his contemporaries (e.g., Molière's farces, Shakespeare and other Jacobean writers, Claudel). It seems that his practice of heeding the mise en scène implications he found in these great works of the past rather than imposing on them the staging customs of the day enabled many plays that had long been consigned to the library to come to life and speak urgently to contemporary audiences about contemporary issues.

If we dismiss Copeau too hastily here, I believe we miss gaining a profound insight into theatre work and into the function of written texts in the performance process. No one could call Grotowski a traditional theatre maker nor a text-based director, yet he, too, claims that certain kinds of traditional song contain very specific indications of bodily movement and, in the article quoted in the epigraph to this chapter, extends this even to the geographical space inhabited by the singer/composers. According to Thomas Richards, "Grotowski told us that encoded in each ancient song is a way of moving, *only one way:* each song contains, hidden inside itself, its own distinct way to move" (1995, 22). The striking parallels between the various claims that I have quoted here, notwithstanding the differences in the performance genres involved, suggest that the relationship between written text and performance created with and around that text is perhaps more complex and more interesting than contemporary theorists (of both performance and language) have been prepared to admit. Practitioners are, in general, rather vague about precisely which textual features convey the performance indicators they claim to find there or how the text can be made to render up this knowledge, but my observation and documentation of actors in rehearsal suggest that it emerges from a prolonged, physical (i.e., corporeal and spatial) work process, closer to Jouvet's idea of kneading dough than to Copeau's instant insight. That is to say that it is a pragmatic process, involving kinesic, proxemic, and cognitive factors and carried out, as actors say, "on their feet." Comparing academic textual criticism with an actor's work on a text, I suggest that no amount of close reading, semiotic analysis, or textual deconstruction will yield the knowledge that actors gain, for actors ask different questions of a text, make different demands on it, they experience it as a physical rather than a mental reality, and their knowledge is acquired through their bodies, which is, doubtless, why actors so typically find it difficult (or unimportant) to put into words what they have discovered.

It can be argued, of course, that all texts contain a great deal of spatial and bodily information due to the nature of language itself. Lakoff and Johnson have drawn attention to the all-pervasive presence of orientational metaphors in English and other languages, and phenomenologically inclined thinkers from Marcel Jousse onward have stressed the connection between the human body and human processes of thought.

The bilateral structure of the human body, the position of our eyes and ears, and the fact that we walk upright but sleep lying down are fundamental in determining the way we perceive and experience the world around us and the way we conceptualize, order, and even talk about our experience. For instance, we structure our arguments in terms of the body's bilateralism ("on the one hand," "on the other hand"), we conceptualize time in terms of space and our body's orientation (the future is "in front of us," the past is "behind"), and thought becomes spatialized in the very process of talking. In addition to the spatial and bodily metaphors that pervade natural language, human societies have usually attributed value and symbolic significance to certain positions and orientations. The fact that these values differ from one society to another indicates the extent to which culture intervenes to confer meaning upon the bodily experience.

For Jousse human bilateralism occurs on three different axes, and the phenomenological experience situates consciousness in a sort of ideal space at the center:

> Man is in effect a triply bilateral being who feels himself to be the centre of the mechanism he constructs. As the Greek philosopher remarks with profound wisdom, "man is the measure of all things" . . . And this is the great mechanism of the Divide. There is the right and there is the left. There is the front and the back. There is up and there is down. And at the centre, there is man who creates this divide. (1974, 216–17)

The body at the center of these axes of perception "teases apart the world of our lived experience," as Edward Casey expresses it (1993), but at the same time it acts as the middle ground between the overlapping fields created by its own physical presence.

In the circumstances it is not surprising that written texts of all sorts contain a great deal of spatial imagery and spatial metaphor, but dramatic texts are particularly interesting in this regard, although the indications of spatiality might not occur where one would most expect them. For instance, it has frequently been observed that, compared with the novel, descriptions of place in playtexts are often so rudimentary as to make the term description inappropriate. Shakespeare and his contemporaries certainly provided wonderful evocations of place and atmosphere, and this so-called acoustic scenery was a function of the bare platform stage of the time. Once painted, and later built, scenery became the norm, however, detailed descriptions of place became redundant, for the impression of fictional place could then be created by the scenery, lighting, and other stage effects. Typical indications of place such as "Lady Sneerwell's dressing room" or "The action takes place in Rome, in a room in Nero's palace" or "A country road. A tree. Evening" are terse to the point of inexpressivity, but this very inexpressivity is evidence that in the theatre the work of creating an idea of place occurs not in the text but on the stage. The directions thus function more as instructions to the practitioners than as descriptions of place. Naturalism emphasized the importance of milieu in determining character and action, but naturalistic playwrights vary considerably in terms of the amount of description of place they include in their plays: Strindberg normally gives a great deal of detail at the beginning of each play, but Chekhov typically provides only a few brief sentences specifying the number of doors and windows and their relation to the localized off-spaces. Modern playwrights tend to describe the presentational space rather than fictional place, and again the real work of making place an expressive category occurs in the staging rather than in the writing. Pinter's *Old Times* begins with the following words: "A converted farmhouse. A long window up center. Bedroom door up left. Front door up right. Spare modern furniture. Two sofas. An armchair. Autumn. Night." This makes it clear that he has calculated the mechanics of the dramatic action in terms of the stage, but he leaves it to the director and set designer to find a way of conveying the idea of a converted farmhouse and to decide what sort of "spare modern" furniture Deeley and Kate would have, how the sofas and armchair should be placed in relation to each other, what other objects to include, etc.

Playwriting is a particular form of writing in that most plays are not intended primarily as works to be read, but as the verbal component of a performance which is itself the primary means of communication. It is a form of writing designed to generate a spatial practice, or at the very least to lend itself to exploitation within a spatial practice. The nexus between writing and theatre goes back a very long way, for, as Walter Ong has pointed out, before the advent of tragedy in ancient Greece, poetry and narrative existed only as oral performance, not written text, and it was the complexities of theatrical production as compared to performance by a single poet that required a written text: "Greek drama, though orally performed, was composed as a written text and in the west was the first verbal genre, and for centuries was the only verbal genre, to be controlled completely by writing" (1982, 142). While one might query

Ong's choice of the word *controlled* here (can it ever be said that text controls performance? has it not always been more a question of transformation, incorporation, and interactive processes?), the important point is
that from the very beginning theatre has involved interaction between
the written and the oral. It is indeed an interesting paradox that the first
lengthy texts ever to be composed in writing were not addressed to readers as such but to theatre practitioners, for whom they formed the basis
of another kind of oral performance. Something of this ambiguity as to
the addressee remains in theatrical writing to this day, and this is evident from the stage directions quoted earlier, in the slippage between
evocation of fictional place and instruction to practitioners concerning
arrangement of the presentational space.

The playwright, as the etymology of the word suggests, is not conceptualized primarily as a writer but as a "wright," that is, a builder or
maker of plays. As theatre practice has evolved over the centuries, the
playwright's contribution has increasingly become a matter of writing,
but, as has been indicated already, it is writing that exists not as an end
in itself but in order to make possible a performance. The extent to which
the potential performance has been imagined and inscribed in the text,
and the extent to which such detail is prescriptive and constraining to
performers vary from period to period and from individual to individual. The extent to which practitioners heed the writer, allow their performance to be constrained by the text, also varies from period to period
and, in particular, since the rise of the director to authorial status sur-
passing that of the playwright.

In English the commonly used term to refer to what theatre practitioners do with the playwright's text is *produce*—to put the play on stage
is to "produce it," and a particular text gives rise to many "productions."
The implication is that, in its written form, the play exists only in some
virtual way and that it has to be produced before it can become a reality.
The playwright provides the words the actors will speak, but the words
as written convey only a small part of the information they will convey
when produced (i.e., performed and staged). Not only does oral expression necessarily convey a great deal of additional material through the
paralinguistic features that are an inescapable component of speech but
also the fact that a speaker necessarily has a body means that the gender,
age, and appearance of the speaker become part of the content, vocalization means that factors such as class and region are introduced, and the
context and the presence/visible reaction of interlocutors add further

levels of meaning. The dialogue as written is speech from which all the factors that make it speech have been removed; the actors' task in rehearsal, when working with written text, is to re-oralize the written (if such a term can be permitted), to fill in the gaps that the fact of writing created. This process, as has been demonstrated in the preceding chapters, can completely transform what the words on the page seem to mean.

Wolfgang Iser claims that the reading process is an interaction between reader and text whereby the reader, responding to the "indeterminate, constitutive blanks" in the text, is moved to "acts of ideation" that then construct the meaning the text has for that reader:

> Blanks indicate that the different segments and patterns of the text are to be connected even though the text itself does not say so. They are the unseen joints of the text, and as they mark off schemata and textual perspectives from one another, they simultaneously prompt acts of ideation on the reader's part. (Suleiman and Crosman 1980, 112)

If Iser is correct, then the theatre process must be an exemplary act of reading, for this is precisely what happens in rehearsal for a text-based work, but in the theatre process the practitioners' "acts of ideation" are manifested physically and spatially rather than remaining virtual, as in silent reading.

The playtext typically contains two different kinds of writing: first, the dialogue, that is the words that will be spoken by the actors and heard by the spectators, what Ingarden called the "Haupttext" (the primary text) and distinguished from the "Nebentext" (the secondary text): the stage directions, list of dramatis personae, prefaces, or other commentary concerning the writer's intentions, ideas in relation to staging or earlier productions, and so on (1931, 209–10). There is virtually no secondary text in plays published in the sixteenth century and very little in plays of the seventeenth century apart from prefaces when plays were republished later in a well-known writer's career or dedications expressing fulsome gratitude to noble or royal patrons; playwrights such as Beaumarchais in the latter part of the eighteenth century began to include detailed stage directions concerning particular moments of the dramatic action, but it was in the nineteenth century that it became the norm for playwrights to provide substantial indications of the stage action they imagined for their play and, indeed, to propose scenes in which action rather than dialogue was the main means of communication. Bernard Shaw is well-known for stage directions that seem to be directed to the general reader rather than to the performer, and in his plays the secondary text is sometimes more extensive than the dialogue. In the modern theatre the distinction between primary and secondary text is sometimes unclear, the primary text may very well not consist of dialogue, and parts of the secondary text may seem to lend themselves to being spoken during the performance.

The stage directions, or *didascalia,* as contemporary theorists prefer to call them, are the most obvious site for information concerning the space and how it may function in the creation of meaning in performance, but this kind of information is not restricted to the *didascalia* and secondary text. Even a text with minimal stage directions contains a great deal of spatial information in the dialogue and in the basic organization of plot and dramatic action. The playwright's decisions in terms of the latter will determine the location of the fiction, whether there is more than one such location, and the way the action moves from one to the other (alternating, one replaced by the other, one embedded in the other, etc.); it will also specify the nature of this place or places (palace, forest, bedroom, kitchen, street, etc.), the number and nature of the offstage fictional places and their relation to the onstage (how near, how they are valorized, and perhaps even through which point of the presentational space they are accessed). The action and the dialogue provide more information, which practitioners may choose to work with or against, concerning the onstage fictional space (whether it is enclosed or open, indoors or outdoors, large or small, crowded or empty, etc.), how many (and which) characters will be onstage at any time, and the way in which they occupy the space (mobile or immobile, individuals or groups, confronting each other or united, in direct communication with the audience, etc.).

In traditional playtexts stage directions most commonly contain some indication of the fictional place (possibly only a rudimentary indication such as "Lady Sneerwell's dressing room" or "A room in Sir Peter Teazle's house" or a fuller description of pertinent features) and the entrances and exits of characters. They may also include reference to the necessary scenic features (e.g., two doors and a window), although this may not be specified in a direction but emerge from the mechanics of the action as the actors explore this in rehearsal. There is an example of such an omission in Genet's play *The Maids,* in which the opening stage direction mentions only a window and one door: "Rear, a window opening on the front of the house opposite. Right, a bed. Left, a door and a dressing table" (trans. Frechtman 1957, 7). It is not until page 24 that there is a direction indicating that in fact there must be two doors, one leading to the kitchen and one to the world outside the apartment: "Exit Solange, left. Claire continues tidying the room and leaves right." Some playwrights provide detailed descriptions of the fictional place as such; others have clearly imagined this in terms of the staging conventions of their day and describe aspects of the presentational space, such as the location of doors and windows. Some include instructions concerning actors' movements in relation to the dialogue, where they are situated in the presentational space, and may stipulate major actions such as "sits" or "kneels" and even business like "reads newspaper" or "pours drink."

In his book *Discourse as Performance* Michael Issacharoff devotes a chapter to stage directions. He divides Ingarden's *Nebentext* into four subcategories: extratextual (prefaces, commentaries, etc.), autonomous (manifestly intended for the reader), unreadable (technical instructions to practitioners, like the timed pauses in Beckett's later work), and normal (Issacharoff 1989, iii). The function of all this is, in his view, to "orient our reading of the playscript" but it is not entirely clear from his analysis who is covered by the first person plural umbrella. Is the playscript addressed to practitioners or to general readers, is it to be read in the context of a theatre practice or as pure fiction? Jeannette Savona speaks of "spectator-readers" and "practitioner-readers" in her analysis of stage directions in terms of speech act theory, and she claims that it is precisely this ambivalence about the addressee and about the illocutionary force of the speech acts in question that characterizes theatre texts as such:

> This ambivalence as to the very nature of the didascalic discourse, composed of semi-fictional, semi-serious speech acts, both representational and directive, must be considered a specific characteristic of all written theatre texts. (Féral, Savona, and Walker 1985, 242)

The printed, published playtext is read in many different ways by different readerships, but for the purposes of my analysis here I am concerned with how practitioners read and use written texts in the creation of performance. It is evident that indications concerning performance can be found in both primary and secondary text, and Aston and Savona speak of "intra-dialogic" and "extra-dialogic" directions (1985, 72–78). Observation of rehearsal process suggests that the most practical categorization of this information concerns the degree of precision (or constraint) involved. As I see it, there are at least four, and possibly five, levels of explicitness involved, but of course, as the director's theatre has so often demonstrated, the performance can ignore even the most explicit indication of action, frequently with compelling effect.

Extra-dialogic directions are the stage directions proper, usually, but not always, unambiguously separate from the dialogue, conventionally set in a different typeface or in brackets. Within this category of directions there seems to be a distinction between two orders of spatial indication. There is a primary level of spatialization that is indicated by the characters' entrances and exits, which, as has been argued in chapter 4, is also one of the major structuring elements. These indications regulate the characters' coming and going and determine the configuration of characters onstage at any time, clearly a critical factor in terms of use of the space. This level of the playwright's spatialization is very compelling to practitioners, although imaginative directors have even ignored directions of this type: for example, in Antoine Vitez's production of *Phèdre* the messenger Panope, who comes on only three times in Racine's play, each time to announce a death, was onstage throughout the action (Biscos, in Jacquot 1978, 195–277). The part was played by a singer, and she intervened at appropriate moments, chanting and vocalizing in such a way that her role as harbinger of doom was powerfully realized. In the same production Theseus, who in Racine's text does not enter until act 3, was also present throughout, prowling around the space between the performers and spectators, watching and listening to what was going on in his absence, a striking way of making manifest his power over all the other characters.

A secondary level of spatial indication in the extra-dialogic directions concerns movement within the presentational space ("he crosses down left" or "she moves to window and stands looking out"), and business such as "he pours champagne," or "he sits with coffee." This type of direction is frequently ignored by practitioners doubtless because it seems to relate so strongly to a particular mise en scène, one imagined by the playwright while writing but one that is necessarily incomplete, and certainly by no means always one actors and director wish to reconstruct. Some playwrights, like Beckett, Pinter, or Feydeau, are extremely precise in their mapping together of word and business, and performers ignore the second-level directions in plays by these writers at their peril. In general, however, it seems that this kind of partial description of mise en scène is a feature of playwriting from the period of naturalism onward. It functions in part to supplement the inexpressivity characteristic of naturalistic conversational dialogue, but it is probably no coincidence that playwrights began to specify aspects of mise en scène precisely at the same time that the director began to emerge as an artist in his own right.

The dialogue is a major source of spatial indications for the actors, and these are the so-called intra-dialogic directions. Here again we can distinguish between a number of orders of indication, largely in terms of how explicit they are, how obvious, and how constraining to the performers. An explicit intra-dialogic direction occurs in which a given action is clearly indicated and in which failure to heed the direction (always an option for the actor or, more commonly, the director) would be disconcerting or would add a significant overlay of new meaning. For instance, if a character says "What are you all staring at?" there is a strong presumption that the other characters onstage must be staring at something. When Solange says to Claire: "Be calm, my darling. Put your feet there. Close your eyes" (Genet 1957, 60), it would make a nonsense of the words if Claire were not doing as her sister tells her, permitting herself a brief moment of weakness.

A second order of performance indicator exists within the dialogue when a move or action is implied but not specified or made explicit. In the scene from *The Maids* just quoted Claire is lying on Madame's bed almost falling asleep while Solange watches over her, and after a long pause Claire says: "You've got beautiful hair. Such beautiful hair. Hers . . ." (62). Here it seems that something must motivate her comment, maybe she has reached up to stroke her sister's hair, or Solange may be rearranging her own hair or brushing it. Some gesture, however, seems to be required, although nothing is specifically indicated. It is one of the primary tasks of the actor to explore the text in order to pick up such moments and flesh them out, and the moves and business devised will have a decisive effect on the meaning conveyed. The text, at these points, seems to demand some move or gesture and to exert pressure on the performers to do something without specifying exactly what is to be done. Actors in rehearsal explore the text to find places where it is open to intervention, and the move, gesture, or action they choose then confers meaning upon the words in question and is instrumental in their construction of the character they are playing. Such moves, gestures, and actions also form part of the paradigmatic structures of that performance

and thus become fundamental to the meaning of the play in that production.

The following example of such a moment, which occurred in the
workshop production of Robert Lowell's translation of *Phèdre,* makes
clear that the implications can go far beyond the given moment. When
Phaedra comes to see Hippolytus, ostensibly to plead for her children
now that Theseus is dead but really to declare her passion to him, she
says among other things:

> Who else can understand a mother?
> I forget. You will not hear me!

(Lowell 1961, 40)

After the question Phaedra (Gillian Jones) paused, looking at Hippolytus
(John Howard), but he turned his head sharply away from her, refusing
to meet her gaze. It was thus his gesture that motivated her next words
"I forget . . . ," and this functioned to throw the focus briefly to Hippolytus and to foreground the interaction between the two; furthermore, it
suggested his hostility toward her and was instrumental in constructing
him as an assertive, aggressive character who might well reach for his
sword when angered.

There is a third level within the dialogue that is not clearly apparent
to the general reader but which emerges in rehearsal when skilled, professional actors "work" the text. In these moments there is no obvious
requirement for a move or gesture, no ambiguity crying out for clarifica-
tion, and yet once an actor has pounced and begun to explore different
possibilities it becomes evident that the text is indeed open and can be
made to serve different meanings. Over the years that I have been
observing actors in rehearsal I have frequently marveled at their ability
to find moments in texts that, on a superficial reading, seem perfectly
clear and unambiguous, to tease them out and use them to inflect, enrich,
or even radically transform the (apparent) textual meaning.

The Maids provides a striking example of precisely such a moment.
After Madame has left the stage, the two maids are in total disarray, realizing that their denunciation of Monsieur will be found out and that the
life they have lived in Madame's household is no longer possible.
Claire's response to their plight is to revert once again to the game they
act out every night, in which she puts on Madame's dress and becomes
the abusive mistress, so that Solange will "kill" her. On this occasion

Solange resists the onset of the game, rejects Claire's assumption of their guilt. Genet's text reads as follows (in my translation):

> *Claire:* I accuse you of the most horrific of all crimes.
> *Solange:* You're mad, or drunk! There has been no crime, Claire, I challenge you to accuse us of a specific crime.
> *Claire:* We'll invent one then, because . . . You wanted to insult me! Don't hold back! Spit in my face![1]

What does Claire mean when she says "because," what is the force of the pause marked by suspension points in the text, what connection is being made here?

Actors working with this text in the project described in chapter 5 treated the moment in a number of different ways. In the FR version Elaine Hudson (Claire) turned and looked pointedly at the teapot containing the poison they had prepared for Madame, and her meaning became clear: the maids are guilty because they wanted to kill Madame, because they actually tried to kill her, or perhaps, more profoundly, they are guilty because they tried but failed to kill her. Elaine Hudson was able to express the meaning she wanted through her use of an object that was already present in the space. The audience knows that the tea has been drugged, a certain amount of tension has surrounded Claire's attempt in the preceding scene to persuade Madame to have a cup, and the teapot remains onstage, normally unnoticed, until Claire in the role of Madame demands in the closing moments of the play that the maid (Solange in the name of Claire) bring her a cup. In this production, without departing in any way from Genet's script, the actor used the teapot to make a meaning that is not obvious on a straightforward reading of the text and yet one that was utterly compelling in performance. The moment did not require elaborate or time-consuming business, a half-body turn and a pointed look was all that was needed, and the meaning was there to any spectator in tune with Genet's perverse logic.

In the FS version of the scene it was Solange (Robyn Gurney) who looked fixedly at the teapot, crouching on the ground while Claire (Elaine Hudson) spoke of their guilt; in this version Claire whistled to attract Solange's attention after she said "because . . . ," and Solange turned to find her sister standing directly in front of Madame's white dress (hanging on the back wall) and speaking in Madame's voice. Here the meaning was different: Solange's look at the teapot conveyed her anguish at their failure to kill Madame before her departure or perhaps her anger at Claire who was entrusted to do this. Claire, on the other hand, was not interested in the real Madame at all and was using the moment as a means of inciting her sister into beginning the game again (for only in the game can there be a solution). In view of the fact that the two women produced such different meanings in each of their two versions, it is particularly noteworthy that in the versions of the scene produced by the two male actors the moment was not marked at all, there was no pause, and Claire's motivation for initiating the game was not explored.

The spatial indicators that I have been considering here range from the explicit to the implicit, from those that are binding on the performers to those that can be ignored without any change of meaning, but even the third-level intra-dialogic indications, which emerge only from the physically situated, interactive work of the rehearsal process, are nevertheless triggered by the text. A further major source of spatial information in the playtext is more deeply embedded in the structure of the language itself. English and other Western languages are full of spatial reference and spatial metaphor, and, as the phenomenologists have pointed out, the very way we think and articulate concepts is both profoundly spatial and dependent on the organic nature of our bodily existence. In Anne Ubersfeld's theorization of space in the playtext it is spatial reference at this level of linguistic abstraction that constitutes what she calls the "spatial matrix," and she proposes a method of textual analysis to bring to the surface the underlying system of space in the text (1977, 173–75).

Ubersfeld's method involves noting not only all textual references to place and space at the substantive level but also verbs of movement, adverbial phrases concerned with space and the occupation of space, all mention of objects that could potentially be present onstage, and all prepositional phrases whether or not they refer to place as such. She points out that it is necessary to examine the text of both dialogue and stage directions in this way, for the dominant ideas of spatiality permeate the text as a whole. Having listed every possible spatial reference, it is necessary to group them into paradigmatic groups and clusters and to examine how these relate to one another. From this will usually emerge oppositions of one sort or another (e.g., legitimate/nonlegitimate, personal/social, valorized/devalorized, etc.), and there will be connections with particular characters and particular fictional places.

While such detailed analysis may seem at first like a rather laborious academic exercise, it has been my experience that actors in rehearsal, working the text intensively, pacing around book in hand, mapping together words and actions, do in fact seem to respond to precisely the sorts of indications from which Ubersfeld constructs what she calls the spatial paradigms of the text. A designer might be interested primarily in spatial references at the substantive level ("Country public house or she-been, very rough and untidy" or "a large room in a house in North West London"), in the objects and furnishings needed, and in the requirements in terms of entrances and exits and specific actions. Actors, by contrast, through the bodily, physical exploration of the text to which I have just referred, seem almost to ingest it (many commentators resort to digestive metaphors when trying to describe this aspect of the actor's process, and actors themselves speak of "getting the lines down"). In studies I have carried out on productions of *Phèdre* and *Les Bonnes* (McAuley 1987a, 105–20; 1987b, 3–25; 1989, 113–44), there has been a striking correlation between the gestural and movement patterns evolved by the actors (what I have called "performance paradigms") and the textual paradigms that emerge from an Ubersfeldian analysis of the grammar of space in the text (oppositions such as up/down, mobile/immobile, inward/outward, distance/proximity). Actors would certainly not use terms such as performance paradigms and, in the productions I have analyzed, would probably have described their performances more in terms of psychological and emotional intentions than repeated spatial and gestural patterns. Yet that is what I saw as I watched the work taking shape day by day through the rehearsal process or analyzed it after the event with the assistance of video recordings.

It is evident from what has just been said that the text serves different agents in the creative process in different ways and also that each of these agents will read differently from the general reader or literary critic. Even in terms of the spatial content it is likely that actors, designers, and directors will read differently, will respond to different grammatical structures, different levels of spatiality, for they are using the text as the basis of very different creative practices. The designer is primarily concerned with space at the nominal level, the places to be constructed, the number of people who will occupy these spaces, and the actions they must accomplish. The actor is concerned with spatial reference at the level of prepositional phrases and verbs, because actors must first of all occupy the space and do things, both real and not real. They are also concerned with the text as a physical reality, as matter that occupies their bodily spaces, that forces tongue to touch palate and lips, and breath to pass in and out of their lungs, and for Jouvet it is this corporeal experience that is the actor's first level of working the text. The actor must move as well as speak, and here, too, there are indications for the actor deeply embedded in the text. The director is concerned with all these elements but also with what I have called the "thematic space" (see chap. 1). This involves the whole relation between onstage and offstage spaces, the system of space that emerges from the fiction and from the values associated with the fictional places (the opposition between court and forest in *As You Like It,* e.g., or the unspecified menace that seems to threaten the onstage place in Pinter's early plays). The sorts of text that appeal to theatre practitioners and that seem to demand to be produced over and over again, that are not exhausted by production, are ones that feed the creativity of actors and designers as well as directors, that provide the different creative agents with the different kinds of material each needs to set in motion their own production process.

There is another aspect of textual space that can be seen to impact upon the theatrical production process, and this concerns the play text as physical object, whether printed book, typewritten manuscript, or photocopy. Before the advent of print actors did not have access to the whole text but only to their own part, with a brief indication of their cues. In some places it was customary for the playwright to read the play aloud to the assembled actors, so that the first time the work as a complete entity was before them was as an oral presentation and in the writer's voice. Sometimes this task was performed by the company manager or later the director. Nowadays, with the ready availability of texts, each actor is provided with the whole text, and the rehearsal process usually begins with the whole company assembled around a table reading the text aloud together. Fragmentation is still, however, very much part of the process: rehearsal necessarily involves working on small segments, and not all actors are present throughout the whole process. Furthermore, actors tend to mark their texts in some way to indicate their own lines—either underlined or highlighted—and this functions to isolate or physically demarcate their own part. The text as a whole then takes on the appearance of "my bits" and "the rest." This text-centered approach may be in part responsible for the idea that the dimensions of a role are somehow to be measured in terms of the number of words to be spoken or the impression that the major focus of attention onstage must necessarily be the actors who are speaking. Molière has given the lie to that by writing many scenes in which he gives himself very little or even nothing to say and in which his character is nevertheless the comic focus of the whole scene. Modern actors and directors completely miss the potential of these scenes through their obsession with the word being the dominant sign in the theatre.

It makes a difference to the actors' attitude to the text and also to the work process in which it figures if this text takes the form of a printed book or a typed script. In fact, modern actors usually use the term *script* rather than *play* or *text,* even if they have been given a printed and bound book. The term *script,* while it may literally mean simply "that which is written," has connotations of openness or even of being incomplete in itself. It thus invites the actors to share in the production process, whereas the terms *play, text,* or *book* convey a certain idea of closure or completeness, which may suggest that the actor is engaged in the lesser task of interpretation rather than creation. Many actors find it very difficult to work from a book designed for silent reading, so they may cut it up and paste the sheets into a larger book or folder or photocopy it onto larger sheets. The aim is to provide themselves with room around the edges of each page of text to write notes concerning the work in progress (see, e.g., the page from Lyn Pierse's script for *The Three Sisters,* reproduced in chap. 4). When the text takes the form of a printed book, perhaps with preface, introduction, and explanatory notes, the actors must necessarily be affected with some sense of the work's cultural importance or at the very least its prior existence and independence from their work process. The book possesses a kind of sanctity that the stapled sheaf of photocopied pages does not: the latter enables the actor to feel more in control, pages can be marked, changes can be more easily introduced and noted, and the writer's authorial presence is somehow diminished.

During the phase of rehearsal when actors are working with book or script in hand the textuality of the text is paramount, and even factors such as the layout of the page and size of typeface can have an impact. Richard Foreman, who sees his role as a writer more as one of generating material for performance than of writing plays, insists that purely material factors such as the amount of space around the words on the page can be important in the performance-making process:

The scripts looked like open-field poems. I'd try to leave lots of empty space on the page, making it easy to scan, so there was a concrete, plastic feel, as if you were handling an object or participating in the blocking of a play on stage. (1992, 16)

Lindy Davies is so convinced that the material object constituted by the book or script impedes the actors that, although actors in her productions are of course given the text of the whole play, they do very little work with the book in hand. The dialogue for the scene or segment being rehearsed is copied out on large sheets of butcher's paper and pinned up on the walls of the rehearsal room so that the actors do not need to carry their scripts with them but can work with both hands free and their bodies unconstrained from the outset. The actors work sentence by sentence or phrase by phrase, glancing up at the wall to get the precise form of the words but focused in mind and body on the emotion and the circumstances from which they will find the impulse to say those words. They are thus physically liberated from the constraints of holding a script as well as from the subliminal influences of the printed page.

The invention of print, the development of publishing, and advances in the technology of word processing such as typewriters and photocopiers have all had an impact on the work processes of actors insofar as they determine the nature of the texts that are available and the material form in which they are available. The authority of the text, its sacrosanct or purely provisional status, its primacy or otherwise in relation to the performance, and even the work practices involved in rehearsal are affected by this material form.

From the earliest times theatre in the West has involved both a written text and body-centered, highly spatialized performance practices, and indeed theatre can be said to exist at the interface between the oral and the literate noetic worlds. The complex interaction between these two different forms of experiencing, knowing, and telling is one of the characteristic features of theatre as it has developed in the West, and it distinguishes Western theatre from some other great theatres of the world, notably some of the great Eastern performance traditions. It has become fashionable in this fin de siècle to decry the text-based theatre of our Western tradition and to see it as somehow irremediably constricted by the concerns of a dominant social class. As I see it, however, the great strength of the Western theatre tradition is precisely the fact that it is posited on creative interaction between the written and the embodied present of performance.

Writing and print may indeed effect a kind of closure, as Walter J. Ong has argued so cogently, insofar as that which is written is thereby removed from the context of the real (physical and social) world:

> By isolating thought on a written surface, detached from any interlocutor, making utterance in this sense autonomous and indifferent to attack, writing presents utterance and thought as uninvolved with all else, somehow self-contained, complete. (1982, 132)

While the play text is inevitably marked by this aspect of its textuality, the performance practice for which it is intended explodes any sense of closure or reification. The theatre work can never be reified for the play or performance piece never exists in any complete and definitive way but is always dynamically in process, from performance to performance and production to production. There is no single way to produce a play or performance text, and each production constructs new meanings, reveals new things, creates a new entity. Theatre is marked by a fundamental indeterminacy, and because it never produces a definitive object it avoids closure.

A further vitally important aspect of the dominant Western theatre tradition is the way the written text brings the past into the present, enables us to use the past to illuminate the present, forces us to think dialectically about past and present. Richard Bauman, in his book *Verbal Art as Performance,* uses the term *emergent* to refer to the fluidity of performance, its quality as event, and, like Ong, he sees this as a fundamental feature of orality. Theatrical performance is, thus, part of emergent culture, in which "new meanings and values, new practices, new significances and experiences are continually being created" ([1974] 1984, 38). Bauman also uses Raymond Williams's idea of "residual culture" to refer to traces of earlier practices and beliefs that remain in the lived culture of the present, and written texts of all sorts are clearly a significant aspect of residual culture. What I have been saying in this chapter about the relationship between written text and performance, and indeed what emerges from many of the examples with which I have illustrated my comments about the meaning-making process in theatre in preceding chapters, suggests that the theatre, precisely in its much-criticized text-based form, exists at the interface between residual and emergent culture and necessarily activates both. In the European tradition of theatre the text (i.e., the product of another time and place) must necessarily be reworked by performance, existing in a particular space and at the present time. This kind of theatre is, or can be, a site for the transformation of residual into emergent; it is (potentially) an active powerhouse, continually reflecting upon and radically transforming the past and opening up the future.

7

The Spectator in the Space

For we are where we are
Not
    —Pierre-Jean Jouve, *Lyrique*

You were in the picture, beholding, yet
    part of it.
    —H. A. Saintsbury, *We Saw Him Act*

If the performance event can be defined as what takes place between performers and spectators in a given space and time, then the spectator has to be seen as a crucial and active agent in the creative process. The spectators are physically present in the theatre space just as the performers are, and, if theatre is an event occurring "in the actors' organisms," as Grotowski claimed (1969, 86–87), then it is also occurring in the spectators' organisms. Aristotle was evidently aware of this when he chose such a heavily anatomical term as *catharsis* to describe the impact of the performance on the spectator. Critics and analysts have, however, been rather silent about the nature and practice of theatrical spectatorship, notwithstanding the intense interest in the role of the reader/receiver generated in recent years by reception theory, phenomenology, and postmodern critical theory and the excellent work done by film critics to theorize the spectatorial positions elicited by mainstream narrative cinema.

When Maurice Descotes, published his historical study of French theatre audiences in 1964, he could claim with some justification that, "from the point of view of theatre history, it is as though the spectator hardly exists" (1964, 2). Since the 1960s that particular gap has begun to be filled, and theatre historians have produced a number of very valuable accounts of the theatregoing public and the experience of theatregoing at various periods (Booth 1991; Hemmings 1993; Mittman 1984; Lough 1957; Arnott 1989), there have been demographic studies of contemporary audiences, and there have also been a number of empirical studies of how spectators make meaning in the theatre (Gourdon 1982; Sauter 1988; Fitzpatrick and Batten 1991). Notwithstanding these historical and empirical studies, which I have drawn on with great pleasure in writing this chapter, it is true to say that theatrical spectatorship is still relatively untheorized compared with film. Barbara Freedman (1991) is a brilliant exception here, even though her interest is rather more in how the theatre can assist in a rethinking of psychoanalysis and postmodern critical theory than vice versa. In this chapter I propose the basis for a theorization of the spectator in the theatre and discuss the role of space in providing both the fundamental condition for spectatorship and the major variable determining the nature of the theatre experience.

The first problem confronting anyone trying to theorize theatrical spectatorship is the ephemeral nature of the performance event. As in every other domain of performance studies, the analyst/critic/theorist is confronted with an absence: the performance is a plenitude, but, when it is over, nothing remains. When the question at issue is the spectator's experience, the material traces are even more tantalizingly absent than are those of the performance. The historical record contains some wonderful written accounts by sensitive spectators of aspects of the performance experience, some graphic artists have been interested in the spectator (the work of Daumier warrants particular mention here), some playwrights have included spectators in "play-within-the-play" scenes or have described the spectatorial process as they conceived it. I have drawn on such records because, as I see it, the theoretical enterprise involves a continual to-and-fro between the anecdotal (all that remains of the experience), the empirical, and the attempt to draw from both insights of general validity.

A further problem concerns the huge range of practices to be taken into account. In contrast to the cinema's hundred-year history theatre has played a central part in the cultural life of human societies for at least two and a half thousand years and in that time has fulfilled many different social functions and taken many different forms. It has moved from the open air to being a predominantly indoor activity, it has taken place in purpose-built venues and in the streets and public places of the community, it has been an integral part of a society's religious life and a purely secular activity; spectators have been mobile and immobile, standing and seated, in well-lit spaces and in darkness, women have been denied access and welcomed; attention has been focused on the stage and shared between stage and auditorium, and so on.

Such a range of practices makes it difficult to establish conditions of theatrical spectatorship in terms comparable to those proposed by film theorists in the 1960s and 1970s (see, e.g., Mulvey 1975). In the cinema, notwithstanding the significant improvements in the quality of sound and image reproduction and the changes in the social experience involved in going to the cinema (size and luxury/shabbiness of cinemas, audience demographics, composition of program), the actual method of delivery has not varied greatly over the past century. Today, as in the 1920s or the 1950s, film requires a certain technological apparatus: a projector, normally situated above and behind the spectators, beaming the image onto a screen placed in front of them, and spectators, now as then, sit in a darkened auditorium, their attention focused on the fixed space of the screen.

There have, of course, been attempts to account for the theatre spectator's experience, and, particularly in the twentieth century, there have been practitioners with a coherent philosophy, geared to elicit a specific kind of reaction. I have already mentioned Aristotle, whose theory of catharsis was the first significant attempt to theorize the spectator's experience. The ambiguities involved in the few textual references that have survived have provoked generations of scholars into their own interpretive speculations, but these have usually been more concerned to reconstruct the experience of Greek tragedy for an imagined audience than to explore in any detail how theatre spectators of the scholar's own day were actually responding to tragedy or to any other dramatic genre. From the Renaissance onward the most frequent theory advanced by critics and practitioners alike to account for the theatre spectator's experience involved some version of Horace's "profit and delight,"[1] Molière, for example, claiming that the function of comedy was to "correct men's faults while at the same time entertaining them" ([1669] 1962, 632). Brecht's critique of neo-Aristotelian theatre provided the first radical alternative in centuries to the moral/didactic view, and his theory of alienation posited a politically sophisticated audience, prepared to think as well as feel; the theatre was no longer to be simply an officially sanctioned place of entertainment but part of a broader social movement aiming at the revolutionary transformation of society.

Brecht's claims concerning the effect of his practice on spectators, like Aristotle's claims concerning the effect of tragedy, seem to be largely speculative (what it was hoped would happen rather than what did in fact happen); similarly, the "moral" argument put over the centuries following in the wake of Horace's *Ars poetica*, was probably prompted more by the need to defend the theatre from its ever-present enemies than by any evidence that it actually did fulfill such a moral or didactic purpose. Theatre practitioners, notably actors, gain a great deal of intuitive knowledge about audience response through their years of performance practice, but, as is so often the case in the theatre, this has rarely been written down or systematically collated.

Meyerhold was an exception in this regard. He was fully aware of the importance of the spectator, whom he termed the "fourth creator" in addition to the writer, the director, and the actor (Braun 1969, 58–64), and, as soon as he had the resources to do so, made a serious attempt to record in a systematic manner the perceptible responses of his audiences. According to Stourac and McCreery (1986), after he became the director of the State Institute of Theatre Art he used the services of teachers and students to carry out systematic research in the documentation of both performance and spectator response. Stourac and McCreery, quoting from Russian-language sources, give details of the code that was elaborated in order to record spectator response but sadly provide no further details as to the success or failure of the experiment, its duration, or the use made of the results.

> There were 20 categories of behaviour to be noted by the observers in the auditorium: a) silence; b) noise; c) loud noise; d) collective reading; e) singing; f) coughing; g) knocks or bangs; h) scuffling; i) exclamations; j) weeping; k) laughter; l) sighs; m) action and animation; n) applause; o) whistling; p) catcalls, hisses; q) people leaving; r) people getting out of their seats; s)throwing of objects; t) people getting onto stage. (1986, 20)

The code indicates something about the active nature of theatre audiences in the early years of Soviet Russia, and it points up the inadequacy of those models that reduce spectator response to either approval (applause) or disapproval (hissing).

Yet another factor that complicates the task of theorizing theatrical spectatorship is the way claims are made about the theatre that seem to be based not on the experience of actual performances but on either a kind of virtual performance imagined on the basis of reading playtexts or on the assumption that theatre functions like some other performance practice. For example, one frequently comes across claims that theatre is a place where the "monolithic male gaze" that is supposed to dominate mainstream film is equally dominant or that the spectator in the theatre can be seen as "an embodied eye" (i.e., the spectator's experience is primarily a visual one). My reflections on my own experiences in the theatre and my reading of the historical record lead me to doubt both assertions: it does not seem to me that the theatre has ever been a place for monolithic gazes of any sort, even at the height of the fashion for perspective decor, and, even if it can be argued that spectators in the contemporary theatre, sitting in a darkened auditorium, are aspiring to the condition of being a "viewpoint and nothing more,"[2] I would reply that the theatre always resists this reduction. In the theatre the scopic drive is always being subverted or displaced, either because the reality of the actors' bodies and the performance space intrude themselves, thereby disrupting the fiction, or through the periodic return to the social due to the physical presence of other spectators and the institutionalized breaks in the performance, or because the performance itself demands active participation. Furthermore, I would speculate that even in the cinema, where the victory of the scopic and the virtual is so much more complete, the increasingly widespread practice among spectators of consuming large tubs of popcorn during the film can be seen as a strategy of resistance whereby the spectators continually remind themselves of their bodily existence.

In a study of the televisual apparatus as it operates in MTV, Ann Kaplan introduces the very pertinent notion of the "decentered spectator" (Pribram 1988, 132–56), constructed from the rock video channel's constant flow of short segments and shifting points of view. She does not see that this notion has any relevance to theatre, which she sees as subject to the monolithic male gaze, but it seems to me that the conditions of spectatorship that have prevailed through much of theatre's history are likely to produce a decentered spectator (as will be discussed here in more detail). Indeed, the notion of decenteredness can be very useful in theorizing theatrical spectatorship, even though (or perhaps because) actors and the teachers of actors place so much emphasis on being "centred." It can be argued that the actor has to be strongly centered in mind and body because the spectator's attention is so decentered.

Another often repeated assertion is that the spectator in the theatre, or perhaps only in mainstream theatre, is passive. While it is certainly true that theatre audiences today are quieter and more compliant than they have been at some earlier periods and that the darkened auditorium brings the theatre experience closer to that of film, the question of passivity needs nevertheless to be treated with caution. Susan Bennett emphasizes (and perhaps exaggerates) the "passive and reactive" role of the spectator in traditional theatre, in order to distinguish it from "the productive and emancipated spectator" of the "emergent theatre of the last thirty years" (1990, 177). Accounts by spectators such as that by Kierkegaard at the Königstädter Theater quoted in chapter 3, the iconographic record left by observers like Daumier, and even the architectural configuration of the stage and auditorium in "traditional" theatres all suggest that theatre, even when performances were at their most pictorial, did not permit the spectator to be passive. Acknowledging that the audiences for mainstream theatre nowadays generally behave in a restrained manner, one may nevertheless question whether this necessarily denotes passivity: does being quiet equate with passivity? Is activity to be judged solely in terms of bodily mobility? In terms of encouraging the development of Bennett's "productive and emancipated spectator," factors such as the degree of manipulation and control involved in the relation between performance and spectator are probably more important than the conventions in force concerning appropriate behavior in a given theatre.

The historical record indicates that theatregoing has usually been a very energetic affair. The need to queue for places in pit and gallery (often a two-hour wait whatever the weather, and the jockeying for positions could get so rough that, in Paris at least, armed guards were deemed a necessity), the crush in the pit (seating was not introduced in the pit in French or English theatres until the latter part of the eighteenth century), fighting, eating (Hogarth's audience [see fig. 28] seems divided between those who are intent on the play and those who are busy procuring refreshment—and possibly other things—from the orange sellers), flirting, showing off one's fine clothes (Ben Jonson claimed that the only reason Londoners went to the theatre was to show off their clothes),[3] were the norm.

Even in the second half of the nineteenth century, when, according to contemporaries, the theatre was much more sedate than it had been in preceding generations, Daumier's lithographs show a great variety of active behavior among spectators. Audiences were avidly partisan, and the historical record contains many references to riots breaking out in theatres where audiences were confronted with radically new ideas or

Fig. 28. Hogarth, *The Laughing Audience.* (Photography courtesy
of the British Museum. Copyright © the British Museum.)

when ticket prices were increased too steeply. The term *pommes cuites*
(baked apples), still used in contemporary French to refer to a bad actor
or a bad performance, is a reminder of the baked apples hurled at the
stage by disgruntled spectators. Percy Fitzgerald, writing in 1882 against
the newfangled idea of darkening the auditorium, claimed that the auditorium "should be lit soberly enough to see faces and features and *to read
a play*" (Booth 1991, 84; my italics). The phrase provides another insight
into the theatregoing habits of some Victorian spectators: watching the

performance while reading the text suggests a kind of critical distance
rather different from the rapt attention Daumier depicts but by no means
evidence of passivity. Daumier's spectators watch the play with a kind of
avidity (see fig. 29) if they are in good seats; otherwise, they must
actively struggle to see the stage, but their absorption seems nonetheless
intense. He usually shows at least one spectator who is fast asleep, but
others are passionately involved, transfixed by what they are seeing and
vicariously experiencing, and so this seems to be more a comment about
the variety of spectator reactions provoked by any performance than evidence of general boredom or passivity.

In France the paid "claque," hired by playwright or theatre manager, was a further means of channeling spectator response. This was
often simply a crude means of stimulating applause, but its function
could be much more subtle. In the 1820s the leader of the claque at the
Comédie Française was a paid employee of the company; he distributed
his *chatouilleurs* (ticklers) at strategic points throughout the auditorium
to stimulate laughter at appropriate moments (much like the "canned
laughter" used in radio and television comedies), and, as F. W. J. Hemmings recounts, by the 1850s,

> he sat in on dress rehearsals, taking notes which would serve him to give
> instructions to his subordinates when the play came to face the all-impor-
> tant opening performance, and afterwards he would have a private con-
> ference with the director in which the play or musical comedy was
> analysed scene by scene in order to determine where it might need to be
> boosted a little, or where the chef de claque could safely rein in his men,
> confident that the scene would "carry" without their help. (1993, 116)

It sounds remarkably as though the *chef de claque* was becoming a "professional spectator," long before the emergence of the director as creative
artist and even longer before anyone would define this as part of the
director's task.

Gender and class are variables that, throughout nearly the whole of
theatre's history, have ensured that the theatre experience is very different for different members of the audience even at the same performance
in the same theatre. The class variable meant that, throughout the eighteenth and nineteenth centuries and for the first part of the twentieth
century, spectators had differential access to the theatre building and to
the performance, different conditions of visibility and audibility prevailed in different parts of the auditorium, and a different level of effort

Fig. 29. Daumier, *Act 5 at the Gaiety Theatre.* The avid gaze of the
nineteenth-century audience. (Photography courtesy of the
British Museum. Copyright © the British Museum.)

was required to participate in the event. The gender variable has meant
that, even within a given class, there was a further significant differential, for the performance met different desires, and viewing was constrained in different ways: for instance, from Ben Jonson's period
onward men's interest in the play seems to have been overlaid by a narcissistic desire to be seen and a voyeuristic desire to look at women in the
audience; at the same period for many women the desire was to see the
play without being seen, and they watched from behind masks or veils,
they sat in *loges grillées,* behind latticework shutters (as seen in Marcel
Carné's film *Les Enfants du paradis*), and in the eighteenth century they
might even look at the performance through holes pierced in their fans.
At later periods, when women had acquired the right to go to the theatre
without having their morals impugned, for them, as for male spectators,

the pleasure of going to the theatre was bound up with the pleasure of dressing up in fine clothes, being seen and seeing others, as well as watching the play (see Booth 1991; Hemmings 1993; Descotes 1964).

This multiplicity of practices makes it difficult to establish conditions of theatrical spectatorship necessary for any general theorizing, and, of course, it may be argued that the experiences of the past are irrelevant to today's spectators. To an extent this is true, but it seems to me that history cannot be so readily disposed of, for past practices leave their traces in the present. Moreover, in the theatre, in contrast to other art forms, the continued use of playtexts and theatre buildings dating from past eras means that these traces can, for good or ill, be very much part of the present experience.

Theorization of cinematic spectatorship has revolved around what Jean-Louis Baudry, writing in 1970, called "the basic cinematographic apparatus": the projector, beaming the image onto a screen and replacing the camera in a sort of relay process, thus makes possible what Baudry called the spectator's "double identification" with the screen image:

> the spectator identifies less with what is represented, the spectacle itself, than with what stages the spectacle, makes it seen, obliging him to see what it sees; this is exactly the function taken over by the camera as a sort of relay. (1985, 540)

Whether the identification has been considered within a theoretical framework deriving from psychoanalysis, feminist theory, or Marxist ideological critique, it has been through the material apparatus that produces and delivers the film image that the spectator's experience has been theorized. The question immediately arises about whether there is in the theatre a comparable basic apparatus and, if so, of what it might consist. It is obvious that theatre is not dependent on a technological apparatus like film, even though theatre practitioners have often made use of machines, optical illusion, and technical advances in areas such as lighting, and yet, in the theatre as in the cinema, any attempt to theorize the nature of spectatorship needs to be grounded in awareness of the physical and psychic conditions of the activity in question.

In the theatre there is no centralizing apparatus, no camera to select and frame the pro-filmic reality and to position the spectator in relation to what has been filmed, no projector to provide the illusion of a single source to the multiple fragments that make up a film, and no editing process to "suture" the spectator into the chain of discourse, to use Jean-Pierre Oudart's (1969) potent phrase. Instead of a screen there is a stage, horizontal in relation to the spectator rather than vertical, the auditorium provides a multiplicity of different viewing positions (good and bad) instead of the uniform vision of the cinema, instead of the virtual presence of the filmed image there is the real presence of the actor, instead of the reassurance of repeatability there is the knowledge that the performance is unique, can never be repeated, and furthermore that the spectators' presence, behavior, and response is part of the event, instead of completeness and closure there is an ongoing process whereby the work continues to evolve and change throughout the run of performances.

The Basic Apparatus of Theatre

Theatre consists of human beings in a defined space watched by other human beings, and it is this reality that constitutes the basic apparatus of theatre. The nature of the defined space has varied greatly from age to age and culture to culture, and, where there is no formal definition (e.g., as in street theatre), the spectators will make their own by virtue of the positions they choose to occupy. The primary fact of theatre is, however, the live presence of both performers and spectators, and from this flow two major consequences for the spectator: first, theatre involves an energy exchange among and between spectators and performers, and, second, the performance is necessarily embedded in a social event.

Comparison of theatre with cinema and television in this respect throws into relief the distinctive nature of the theatre experience. In the cinema the spectators are physically present, but the actors are a virtual presence only, unable to respond to the spectators or to adjust their performance to what might be occurring in the auditorium. They are images on a screen that remind us of the absence of that which is represented, as Susan Sontag has said of all photographic images: "A photograph is both a pseudo-presence and a token of absence" (1977, 16). With television both performers and audience have become pseudo-presence, and the absence of audience is only accentuated by shots of a studio audience, reminding those at home that they are not part of that audience. The current fashion for program presenters to sign off with phrases like "I'll see you at the same time tomorrow night" may be intended to create a sense of presence, but it is extremely doubtful that anyone is taken in.

Energy Exchange

Actors are energized by the presence of the spectators, and the live presence of the actors means that the spectators' relationship to them is very different from the relationship between spectator and dramatic fiction in the cinema. In the theatre, due to the live presence of both spectators and performers, the energy circulates from performer to spectator and back again, from spectator to performer and back again. The actor, while appearing to speak only with the character's words, is always also communicating directly with the audience, but (and this is where theatre differs from the other dramatic media) there are feedback loops in operation between actors and spectators in the theatre. John Gielgud speaks, in one of his volumes of memoirs, of the way the actor must heed the minutest signals emanating from the audience: "He learns to listen, to watch (without appearing to do so) to respond, to guide [the audience] in certain passages and be guided by them in others—a never-ending test of watchfulness and flexibility" (1974, 178). To say that the actor is responsive to the audience conveys so little of the intense concentration, alertness, and skill that are involved in performance. John Harrop's description of one of the pitfalls that can occur in playing comedy provides a further insight into the feedback loops and into this aspect of the actor's complex craft:

> One of the dangers of playing comedy is that the actor will begin to play last night's performance, with the rhythms and stresses that were successful then: playing for the laugh, rather than playing the action and the line in the present with an ear on how tonight's audience is responding. (1992, 49)

What worked on one occasion for one audience will not necessarily work the next night for another, and the actor, engaged in Gielgud's "never-ending test of watchfulness and flexibility," must be able to adjust to the minute signals emitted by the spectators.

It is evident that what is involved here is much more subtle than approval/disapproval or even the twenty types of signals notated by Meyerhold in his attempt to document audience response. Years ago I read an article by, I think, Louis Jouvet—a program note or a piece in one

of those ephemeral journals published for subscribers by the theatres of
the cartel. He was commenting on the differences between audiences,
and he used dozens of different adjectives to encapsulate the variety of
reaction from one audience to another. I have not been able to trace the
quotation but, from memory, he used words like absent-minded, intelligent, frivolous, boisterous, cold, thoughtful, lazy, inattentive, reverent,
irreverent, and the list went on for over a page. At the time I simply
thought the article a delightful piece of French whimsy, but now I realize
that it constitutes very useful ethnographic evidence. If actors can read
the mood of the audience with this degree of precision, then it must be
being signaled in some way.

Most spectators (and even reviewers) go to see a production only
once and so tend to take the audience response as a given unless it
becomes marked in some way, perhaps by being out of sympathy with
what the individual spectator is feeling. It is the actors, who perform
night after night, who perceive it as a variable, but actors, of course,
rarely write their knowledge down. This is why the testimony of people
like John Gielgud and Louis Jouvet is so valuable, for it provides insight
into the nature of the feedback loops that are activated in performance.
Simon Callow, performing in Martin Sherman's *Passing By* for Gay
Sweatshop in the early 1970s, was overwhelmed by the way the audiences of gay men responded to the play:

> The tiny Almost Free, smallest of all the fringe theatres, was packed every
> day with men who had never seen anything like it before. They were
> deeply moved. It was a touching story; but it wasn't that. It was as if a
> secret that had been kept for too long were finally being told to people
> who knew it individually but had never seen it acknowledged. The qual-
> ity of attention was transformed. It was their lives they were watching. For
> the first time since Belfast, I felt the energy coming *the other way*. Their
> appetite for the play was insatiable. (1985, 58)

Performance analysts have hardly begun to explore the factual basis
for such anecdotal evidence, and much work is needed to understand
how the complex and subtle interchanges occur, but what is evident
from the scattered references in published sources such as actors' memoirs is that spectators in the theatre are far from passive, that the live
presence of both performers and spectators creates complex flows of
energy between both groups, and that it is even questionable whether
what is going on can be discussed in terms of stimulus and response. At

the very least questions need to be asked about who is doing the stimulating and who is responding.

Primacy of the Social

A performance is something that takes place in space and time, it happens, and it will never happen in the same way twice. For spectators to
experience a play, they must go to the theatre, and the slippage between
the literal and figurative meanings of that phrase is highly significant.
Going to the theatre indeed involves *going to* the theatre, and the being
there is a major part of the experience. The performance is embedded in
a social event, and both the performance and the fiction it presents are
constantly at risk of being overtaken by the social.

The social experience enhances, even accentuates the individual's
response to the performance. One laughs more heartily and longer when
others are laughing too, which is one of the reasons why television comedy shows so frequently include a studio audience, and why producers
of radio comedy insert bursts of recorded laughter at appropriate
moments. Maurice Descotes points out that the extraordinary propensity
for audiences in the eighteenth century to weep copiously at affecting
moments can be better understood when we realize that it was a shared,
public weeping: "these tears were shed collectively" (1964, 190). People
went to the theatre prepared to weep, they laid their handkerchiefs out
on the balcony rail in front of them before the performance had begun,
and it seems that displaying one's emotional response was as much part
of the pleasure of theatre as displaying one's person.

The theatre has at some periods of its history provided the same sort
of social function as the pub or café: a place where people (mainly men)
went regularly to socialize and meet their friends. Subscribers who
rented a box or a regular seat in the stalls went to the theatre, not so much
to see a particular play as to have a convivial evening in the company of
friends and acquaintances. E. Genest describes a typical male subscriber
to the orchestra stalls in the latter part of the nineteenth century: "He has
fixed habits, he sees the same faces there, his friends, people he has
known for years; it is part of his life; the opera simply gives the evening
an extra charm" (1920; in Hemmings 1993, 16). It is evident why the early
modernists reacted so violently against the complacency of such spectators, against a theatre that had allowed itself to become, as Brecht
claimed, simply an aid to digestion. Nevertheless this dimension of the
theatre experience is still an important part of spectators' pleasure,

whether the group in question is made up of the moneyed middle class or radical intellectuals. In contemporary Western society factors such as gender, sexual preference, race, ethnicity, and political ideology come into play, and much of the most dynamic theatre today is produced in relation to such subgroups. For the individual spectator a significant part of the pleasure of the theatre event is experiencing it in the company of like-minded people, and, as Simon Callow found in his work with Gay Sweatshop in the 1970s, when play and production really address the concerns and desires of the people who make up such audiences, the experience can be much more powerful than anything occurring in the commercial domain.

In earlier periods the social dimension of theatre going seemed often to overwhelm the dramatic fiction, in other periods spectators have desired above all to lose themselves in the fiction, to be able to experience the fiction as completely as possible. The latter desire is, however, one that theatre is peculiarly ill equipped to fulfill and it is no coincidence that narrative film developed at the same time that theatre artists and spectators were discovering the limitations of naturalistic theatre. Film is the dramatic medium that can most successfully put the spectator's social presence under erasure, to use Derrida's term. In the theatre the spectator must always experience the dramatic fiction through the performance that presents it and in the context of the social reality of the event. The former has a fragile existence, always at the mercy of the latter, and it takes only a small error by an actor or technician, or an exhibitionist in the auditorium for the fiction to be disrupted, sometimes with disastrous consequences for the performance as a whole.

It is true that in the cinema, too, the spectators are present and that there is a social occasion. Their presence has not, however, led to the development of customs and conventions that facilitate the construction of a sense of occasion, or a sense of the group as a collective. On the contrary, practices that might lead to the formation of a such a sense have progressively been abandoned: for example, the serial (involving weekly attendance at the same cinema), or the program consisting of main feature, B feature, or newsreel and shorts, with periodic intervals for the purchase of refreshments. The cinema has become the ideal place for the individual to remain anonymous, the darkened auditorium minimizing the impact of other people's responses and facilitating the private and personal relation between individual spectator and the fictional world presented on the screen. Spectators are not encouraged to linger at the end of a screening, and as they leave by one door a new group is already queueing to come in at another. The turnaround time between screenings in the big city cinemas is in the order of fifteen minutes. People can no longer stay to "see the film round again," as happened in the cinemas of the 1950s, and current commercial practice accentuates the notion of the film audience as a temporary and arbitrary grouping of individuals.

Spectators go to the theatre as individuals, or more frequently as members of subgroups (couples, families, groups of friends, even teacher and students) and *through the process of responding* to the performance they become a collectivity, a group with a particular quality that can be perceived by the actors and differentiated from other similar groups. The architectural design of the auditorium can facilitate the formation of a sense of the group as collectivity, other theatre buildings militate against this. There are other aspects of the theatre event that also contribute to the transformation process: the socializing that may take place before the show and in the interval (in the auditorium itself or in the other social spaces in the theatre), the crush around the bar for drinks, the curtain calls at the end of the performance. Spectators leave the theatre in an energized state at the end of a really good performance, and they are energized and unified in part by their own actions in applauding and cheering, and this is the final "anagnorisis" of the performance: a revelation of the state that has been constructed by their interaction with the performance. As Herbert Blau put it:

> [The audience] does not exist before the play but is *initiated* or *precipitated* by it; it is not an entity to begin with but a consciousness constructed. The audience is what *happens* when, performing the signs and passwords of a play, something postulates itself and unfolds in response. (1990, 25)

Bernard Beckerman points out that the spectator in the theatre is being appealed to both as an individual and as part of a collective. As he sees it:

> The play projects doubly, to each member of the audience as an individual, sparking his or her private memories, and to the audience as a whole, in that distinctive configuration that it has assumed for a particular occasion. (1970, 133)

Beckerman's double projection frequently constitutes a third level that renders the psychic mechanism involved in being a theatre spectator even more complex. Spectators are, as he rightly states, first of all individuals whose experience of the play will be significantly inflected by a host of personal circumstances; but they are likely also to be attending the performance in smaller social groupings, so the individual spectator may form part of a subgroup within the whole as well being part of a collectivity, that of the audience for that particular performance at that particular place and time. The experience of the individual spectator, while always personal, is also occurring at group and collective levels.

The English language provides us with a collective noun *audience* but then rather confusingly tells us that an audience is made up of spectators, as though hearing were a communal act but seeing an individual one. Whether the popular usage reveals an interesting insight into cognition or not, the slippage makes clear that theatregoing involves both collective and individual experiences and that these may be of a rather different order. In French, too, the collective nouns (*l'assistance* or *le public*) are different from the concrete, and in French as in English, the individual member of the "le public" in a theatre is "un spectateur," one who sees. A similar divergence is present in other European languages (in German *das Publikum* is made up of individual *Zuschauer,* or onlookers, in Italian *il pubblico* is made up of *spettatore*), and it is interesting that the theatre experience has generated the need for differentiation between the collective and the individual in so many different cultural contexts. *L'assistance* is a much richer term than *audience* and more appropriate to the function involved: it refers primarily to the spectators' physical presence, to the being there, but the secondary meaning of *assister* (to help) is also relevant and suggests that in the theatre the collective presence of the audience provides something more than mere listening.

The fact that the dramatic fiction can be experienced only through the presentational reality of the performance, and that both are embedded within the social reality of the total event is crucial to the theatre function. In the theatre of the twentieth century, some practitioners have sought to accentuate one of these terms at the expense of the other two, for example in naturalistic theatre the dramatic fiction demands that awareness of the presentational be suppressed, in task-based performance such as that of the Wooster Group or Richard Foreman's Ontologic-Hysteric Theater the dramatic fiction is displaced by the presentational, and in happenings the emphasis is on the reality of the spectator's experience. The reality of theatre is, however, that none of these three terms can ever be totally suppressed, each always reasserts itself (to the detriment of any enterprise that requires suppression), and it is the tension between the three terms that constitutes the ground of theatricality.

If it is agreed that the primacy of the social and energy exchange are the immediate implications for the spectator of the theatrical "apparatus" (live presence of both performers and spectators in a given place/time), the next step in the process of theorizing the spectator is to tease out in more detail the general conditions that allow communication in relation to this basic apparatus. What are the factors that can be seen to constitute the fundamental conditions of experiencing the performance event? It seems to me that there are three principal factors that need to be taken into account in any theory of theatrical spectatorship.

Belief/Disbelief

The first of these I call Belief/Disbelief—the slash intended to bind the mutually exclusive terms into an insoluble unity—and it refers to the complex truth and reality status of what is experienced. Theatrical performance occurs live, in real space and time, and the fiction (to the extent that there is one) is always grounded in the lived reality of both performers and spectators. Within the performance event, spectators are always aware that they are watching a performance, they know that the dramatic fiction being presented is fiction, and they also know that the actors who are presenting this fiction are really present in the presentational space. One or other of these knowledges can be foregrounded, either momentarily or throughout a whole performance: for example, the device of the play within the play or something else that draws attention to the spectators' role as spectators will foreground the presentational, the choice of film or television stars or other celebrities as actors will foreground the actorial reality; the fictional (and with it the related notions of character and narrativity) can be foregrounded by being brought into question (as happens, e.g., in much postmodern performance with its refusal of acting and valorization of doing, or the insistence on authenticity and the autobiographical).

In the theatre these three levels are constantly interacting, constantly competing for attention, can be exploited in differing ways for different purposes, but the key fact is that all three are necessarily present in some form or other. What is presented in the theatre is always both real and not real, the actors are present and absent: I see Gérard Depardieu and Tartuffe, a figure who is both Gérard Depardieu and not–Gérard Depardieu. Furthermore, there is Gérard Depardieu (film star and celebrity), and Tartuffe (fictional character) and between the two there is what the Prague structuralists called the Stage Figure and what I call the presentational reality. So we have Depardieu and not–Depardieu and something else that is neither Depardieu nor not–Depardieu, and although the production style and factors such as the celebrity status of the actors can mean that one or other of these levels is foregrounded, they are always all three in action, and they cross over and interact with each other and infect the spectator's grasp on reality. Lear's grief at the death of Cordelia, when I know perfectly well that there is no death and no grief on the reality level, may nevertheless cause me to weep real tears. I experience within my own body a physiological response to something that is not in fact occurring.

The line from Pierre-Jean Jouve's poem ("Car nous sommes où nous ne sommes / Pas"), translated as one of the epigraphs to this chapter, perfectly sums up the spectator's place in relation to the fiction in the theatre. The spectators are aware of their own reality, and that of the performance itself, they dismiss or relegate to a lower level of awareness this knowledge in order to enter fully into the emotions of the fiction. At the same time they remain conscious that the actors are a real flesh and blood presence, conscious of the performance as performance—indeed Willmar Sauter's research has shown that the aesthetic appreciation of the presentational is one of the key factors in spectatorial pleasure (1988, 17–27). If an accident occurs on stage, spectators may assume it was intentional and integrate it into the fictional, if an actor is visibly injured the reality level will in all likelihood take precedence over the others. My recollection of the occasion when Georges Bigot sprained his ankle toward the end of the Théâtre du Soleil's *Henry IV* is of my concern for the injured actor, admiration for the way the other actors handled the situation and for his fortitude, and my apprehension that something else would go wrong. The disjunction between fiction and reality was accentuated, and as a consequence it is this that dominates my memory of that performance. The subtle balance and interplay between the different orders of reality that is an essential part of theatre's mode of operation was brutally disrupted.

As Octave Mannoni describes it, the psychological mechanism triggered in the spectator by theatrical performance is akin to Freud's notion

of *Verneinung* (negation or denegation) in that it engenders in the spectator a divided consciousness, or rather it permits a repressed idea to
return in relative safety to consciousness. In Freud's words:

> With the help of the symbol of negation [*Verneinungssymbol*], thinking
> frees itself from the restrictions of repression and enriches itself with
> material that is indispensable for its proper functioning. (1953, 19:236)

For Mannoni, just as negation provides the mind with knowledge that
would otherwise be denied, so in the theatre we are able to access levels
of our own being that in normal circumstances would be repressed, or
possibly activated only through dreams. He says that

> through conventions, through the symbolic, [theatre] permits us to
> repossess our own imaginary. In order to repossess and order the imag-
> inary, we first have to go and find it where it is located in the vicinity of
> the dream agency, and this can only be done by artificially recreating the
> presumed originary confusion between real and imaginary. (1969,
> 167–68)

Anne Ubersfeld has speculated that the refusal of illusion and "acting" in much modern and postmodern theatre, the emphasis on the presentational or on the reality of the actors' presence as ends in themselves,
may function to limit the spectator's capacity to interact at such a profound level with the performance:

> But limiting the role of the spectator to contemplation of the physical real-
> ity of the performance is perhaps to limit the psychic impact of the stage.
> For the uniqueness of the perceptive process in the theatre is that it
> involves a virtually instantaneous alternation between a) recognition of an
> image and its negation; and b) perception of the fiction and of the perfor-
> mance. To suppress or limit one of these two terms is at the same time to
> limit the productivity of theatrical practice. (1981, 317)

In agreeing with Ubersfeld, I am in no way denying the fascination of
"pure performance," nor the skill of its exponents, nor downplaying the
political and philosophical importance of postmodern performance in its
critique of bourgeois theatre practice. It is, however, important to understand that in turning away from the narrative/character/text-based
repertoire of the Western theatre tradition, practitioners restrict the role
of the spectator, in rejecting illusion and replacing acting by doing, they
give spectators less scope to play with *Verneinung* and less potential
access to their own unconscious.

Marjorie Garber, in her account of cross-dressing and the cultural function of the transvestite, notes that many literary and cultural commentators "look *through* rather than *at* the cross-dresser," intent on "subsuming that figure within one of the two traditional genders" (1992, 9). Her provocative thesis is that the transvestite constitutes a third term, and that like other third terms it functions to throw into question easy notions of binarity: "The 'third' is that which questions binary thinking and introduces crisis . . . The 'third' is a mode of articulation, a way of describing a space of possibility. Three puts in question the idea of one: of identity, self-sufficiency, self-knowledge" (11). Theatre, too, partakes of this "thirdness," theatre undermines the comfortable opposition between reality and illusion, or reality and unreality, absence and presence, here and not-here, now and not-now, and the spectator in the theatre enters into a game that stops this side of madness but that functions to throw into question our "normal" modes of apprehension of the real. Theatre takes place somehow between the opposing terms, as the great Japanese playwright Chikamatsu Monzaemon put it over three hundred years ago: "Art lies in the shadowy frontiers between reality and unreality. Art appears unreal but is not unreality; art has the appearance of reality, but it is not reality."[4] While the rationalist might say that things are either true or false, real or not real, and that there is no space between such terms, the theatre in its normal functioning subverts these certainties, transforms the subversion itself into play, and in so doing it has the potential of allowing the spectator to access normally suppressed levels of consciousness.

The Play of Looks

The second factor constituting the condition of theatrical spectatorship is the complex play of looks that is involved. The etymological derivation of the word *theatre* suggests that the theatre has always been a place of looking and that looking has always been central to the theatregoer's experience. The fact that we use the word "spectator" in English to refer to an individual member of a theatre audience may further suggest that what is involved is essentially a matter of seeing, that the theatre is primarily a visual experience. While looking and seeing are important (and, indeed, I am arguing that a particular kind of looking is one of the constitutive elements of the phenomenon of theatre), it is important to bear in mind that spectators in the theatre are engaged at least as much (and sometimes more) in listening and hearing. As Peter Arnott points out in his study of performance conditions in ancient Greece, the back rows of the Theatre of Dionysus were three hundred feet from the stage, so an actor would appear less than an inch high to a spectator sitting toward the back of the arena, but the acoustics were (and still are) excellent (Arnott 1989). Whatever else it might have been, this theatre was a place for precise verbal communication. In many other theatres at various times over the long history of theatre, the sight lines provided by the design of auditorium and stage and the available techniques of lighting the stage have meant that visibility has been greatly constrained for large numbers of spectators.

The stress on looking and seeing, the insistence on the visual, are problematical insofar as they may encourage a misleading elision between theatre and film spectatorship. Even when sight lines and lighting techniques are good, spectators sitting or standing in a theatre experience the space with all their senses, and it would be more appropriate in the circumstances to speak of a spatial than a visual experience. Gertrude Stein's wonderful descriptions of her earliest memories of theatre make this distinction very clear: "the general movement and light and air which any theatre has, and a great deal of glitter in the light and a great deal of height in the air" (Stein [1935] 1988, 112). Of her first outing to the theatre, probably a production of *HMS Pinafore* in London, she said: "but the theatre was so huge that I do not remember at all seeing a stage I only remember that it felt like a theatre that is the theatre did. I doubt if I did see the stage" (113). Experience of theatregoing teaches us to look at the stage, but the spectator in the theatre is always involved first and foremost in the phenomenological experience of being there, of the space in relation to oneself, of one's self *in* the place, of the "height in the air," of the "feeling" (whatever that is) of being in a theatre. For the spectator in the Theatre of Dionysus, the experience of being there together with fifteen thousand fellow citizens and the sense of occasion must have been overwhelming.

I refer to a play of looks because there seems to be a number of different kinds of looking going on. There is the spectator looking at the actors and at the presentational space more generally, there is the actor looking back at the spectators (and, as Claudel's Lechy Elbernon explains it in the passage from *L'Echange* that I shall quote at length later in this section, this returned gaze is central to the moral force of theatre), and there is the spectator looking at other spectators. The first of these looks is also a major factor in film and television, where, of course, it works in different ways due to the mediation of camera and screen, but the second and third are peculiar to theatre and are constrained in particular ways by performance conventions and by the design of the performance space. All three are dependent on the fact that in the theatre both performers and spectators are physically present to each other.

The actor/actor or character/character look needs to be mentioned here, although, as far as the spectator is concerned, it is subsumed into what I have designated the first look, being one of the things the spectator sees when looking at the actor. In the theatre, by virtue of the presence of actor and spectator in the same space, we see both the person looking and the person or thing that is being looked at. This means that the actor/actor look functions to make connections and to direct the spectator's attention within the theatre space. Another feature of the actor/actor look is that it is doubled by the character/character look and thus becomes the site for the active play of denegation that is such an important part of the spectator's pleasure. Feminist critics have emphasized the importance of the look in narrative film where the camera has made the actor's face the primary site of signification, but in film it is the editing conventions that enable us to read a sequence of images as someone looking at, or exchanging looks with, someone else. Tim Fitzpatrick's studies with the Eyemark recorder (1990, 9–22; Fitzpatrick and Batten 1991, 11–31) have shown that theatre spectators also concentrate their attention on the actors' faces, but their field of vision includes the whole body of the actor and its location in the presentational space.

The Spectator/Actor Look

The primary look in the theatre is that directed by the spectators to the actors, and in Claudel's description of the theatre that he gives to the actress, Lechy Elbernon, in L'Echange, it is this look that is constitutive of theatre itself. Lechy is describing the theatre to Marthe, who has never been to the city.

> Lechy Elbernon: There is the stage and the auditorium.
> Both are closed, people come there at night, and they sit in rows one
>   behind the others, watching.
> Marthe: What? What do they watch if everything is closed?
> LE: They watch the curtain in front of the stage,
> And what is behind it when it is raised.

And things happen on stage as though they were true.

Marthe: But if they are not true! It's like the dreams one has when one is asleep.

LE: That is why they come to the theatre at night.

([1893] 1967, 676)

People come to the theatre and sit in rows, one behind the other, to watch something that has no more reality than a dream, as Prospero reminded his spectators four hundred years before.

Daumier was a very acute observer of theatre audiences, they form one of his recurring subjects, and I think that in his images of spectators looking at actors he has revealed something profoundly true that goes beyond the particular Parisian moment he recorded. In his drawings, the spectators do not seem to be dreaming, but on the contrary gaze with avid attention at the actors, and there is something almost troubling about their avidity. One senses a kind of brutality, even cruelty underlying the rapt attention and the emotional investment that is clearly also there. François Périer, in his introduction to a collection of Daumier's lithographs, quotes a chilling comment by Balzac, reminding us that the events of the Terror occurred in Paris only a generation or so before Daumier's spectators devoured the actors with their gaze:

> In Paris everything becomes a spectacle, even the most authentic grief. There are people who will sit at their windows to see how a son weeps when following his mother's coffin. Just as there are those who want to be comfortably seated to watch how a severed head falls. No people in the world have looked with more voracious eyes. (Balzac 1833, 102)

The voracious gaze of Daumier's nineteenth-century audience has perhaps become a little more mellow today, but there is still an underlying aggressivity in the relation between spectator and actor that seems to me to be characteristic of theatre. The edge of tension that comes from live performance is always present, even in the bourgeois theatre of the late twentieth century.

An anecdote recounted by F. W. J. Hemmings about an event that took place in Le Havre in 1827 provides a most revealing example of the aggressivity that once marked the relations between spectators and actors: the curtain call was at that time becoming a widespread practice but actors felt it to be an imposition and many disliked having to return to the stage at the end of the performance. On this occasion, the star in the touring company's production of Boieldieu's *La Dame blanche*, refused to take a curtain call "and was chased by a furious crowd all the way back to her lodgings" (Hemmings 1993, 93). It is probably no coincidence that the actor in question was a woman, and the "furious crowd" was doubtless predominantly composed of men, for the actress has long occupied a very ambivalent place in the economy of sexual desire in Western societies. In contemporary society, however, a similar ambivalence marks the relations between the crowds of adoring fans and the singer or film/TV star of the moment: there seems to be a rather thin line between the frenzied adoration of the crowd and the lynch mob. The desire that is invested in the relationship between fan and star, or between spectator and the fictional being incarnated by the actor, can still lead to adulation turning to fury, and it is this quality that Daumier has perceived.

The actor needs and desires the spectators' watchful attention, and some actors are very explicit about the kind of attention they want. Greta Scacchi, talking about her performance in *Miss Julie* at the Sydney Theatre Company in which the stage design brought her within a few inches of the front row of seats, told students at Sydney University how difficult she found it to perform for matinee audiences. It appears that the elderly spectators who frequent matinee performances are more prone to doze off, consult the program during the performance, or even hold whispered conversations with their neighbors, all of which can be disconcerting to the actors, and even perceived as a kind of insult. Actors have also made it clear on occasion that they object to people taking notes during the performance, and although this kind of behavior does not spring from any lack of concentration on the part of the spectator, it is possibly troubling because it suggests a degree of critical distance rather than the rapt attention the modern actor desires. In the exchange of energy that occurs in a good live performance, the audience gives as much to the actors as they give back.

The Actor/Spectator Look

It is evident from the last paragraph that, in the theatre, the actors can see the spectators (or, rather, depending on the size of the auditorium and the levels of lighting, they can see some of the spectators), and the fact that the actor returns the spectators' gaze is absolutely crucial to the theatre experience. Naturalism brought in the fiction of the "fourth wall" and a style of acting in which actors had to feign ignorance of the presence of the audience, but in this, as in so many other ways, the theatre resisted what naturalism demanded.

Lechy Elbernon continues her description of the theatre with a detailed reference to the way the actor, in this case Lechy herself, looks back at the spectators, and in Claudel's view it is this look that stimulates the spectator to look into his own being:

> I look at them, and the whole house is nothing but well dressed living
>   flesh.
> They are hanging from the walls like flies, right up to the ceiling.
> And I see these hundreds of white faces.
> Man is bored, and ignorance is his lot from the day of his birth.
> And knowing nothing of how it all begins nor how it will end, so he goes
>   to the theatre.
> And he looks at himself, his hands placed on his knees.

Lechy Elbernon, when she sees the spectators, sees them first as a physical presence ("well dressed living flesh"), but her look triggers the introspective look of the spectator into himself, and her own look is then transformed and becomes a sort of moral searchlight:

> And I look at them too, and I know that out there is the accountant who
>   knows that tomorrow
> They are going to audit the books, and the adulterous mother whose
>   child has just fallen ill,
> And the man who has just committed his first theft, and another man
>   who has done nothing all day.
>
> (Claudel 1967, 676)

The actress shows herself on the stage, and through this showing the spectator sees what he carries in his own heart. I have quoted this extraordinary passage at some length for the insight it reveals into the physical and emotional reciprocity involved in the relation between actor and spectator. Claudel claims for the theatre the power to move people from seeing to knowing, from sight to insight, and this occurs through the play of looks around the absence that is the dramatic fiction ("something happens on stage as though it were true").

Without necessarily endorsing Claudel's metaphysics, Barbara Freedman's meditations on theatre, psychoanalysis, and postmodern theory lead her to a similar stress on the importance of the return look in the theatre. In her view it is the return look that constitutes theatricality, which she defines as: "a fractured reciprocity whereby beholder and beheld reverse positions in a way that renders a steady position of spectatorship impossible" (Freedman 1991, 1). The actor on stage, looked at by the spectators and in turn looking back at them, is a paradigmatic instance of what Lacan calls "the gaze," and Freedman insists on the importance of this in her brilliant analysis of the spectator's experience in the theatre:

> On the side of neither presence nor absence, theatre stages a continual posing and reposing of the interplay of regards and so plays out the desire to fix position in relationship . . . This strategic decentering challenges the distinction between observer and observed, eye and gaze, and so suggests the power of theatre as theory. (66)

Neither the spectator's nor the actor's desire can be fulfilled (which is, indeed, the nature of all desire), but the energy generated by the "interplay of regards" is fundamental to the theatre experience.

The aggressivity that I have already mentioned in relation to the spectators' mode of looking, is clearly reciprocated in the actors' attitude to the spectators. In Stephen Aaron's study of stage fright, he comments on the colloquial phrases used by actors to refer to their relationship with the audience: "lay 'em in the aisles," "knock 'em dead," "kill 'em"; one actor he knew would say, when the performance was going well, "I've got them by the balls," and another actually said "The audience is the dragon to be slain, the woman to be raped" (Aaron 1986, 68). Even John Gielgud, recalling the thrill of performing to a rapt audience, uses a rather warlike metaphor:

> The sensation of an audience suddenly concentrating, with not a murmur in the auditorium, is a great moment. It is very thrilling in a new play or a new part when you get that feeling for the first time, knowing that you are holding the audience completely, in total command of the battlefield. (1979, 213)

Images of wooing and seduction may also be common, but the underlying aggression and fear that is undoubtedly present is part of the energy exchange that is peculiar to theatre, and it exists because the actor looks back.

It is significant that Daumier's drawings of theatre audiences that reveal the spectators' gaze in all its troubling intensity are those where the artist has positioned himself to see from the actor's point of view. When he adopts a point of view from within the auditorium, to the side or at the back of a box, his focus tends to shift from the relation between spectator and stage to the social or domestic interchange going on between spectators. The actor receives the full intensity of the spectators' gaze, sees (desires/fears to see) the spectator looking at him or her, and the worst thing a spectator can do to an actor is to fail to look (hence Greta Scacchi's dislike of performing for the catnapping spectators at Sydney matinees). The spectators' gaze empowers and energizes the actor, but the reverse is also true: it is the live presence of the actor that channels this energy and, as Arthur Symons put it so memorably, "flings it back, intensified, upon itself" (1927, 151). Even if this level of experience is rare, the theatre always holds out the lure that it may happen, and theatre makes demands on its audiences in intangible ways to contribute to the energy exchange. Reflecting on my own experience, I would say that I go to a cinema with relief, in the pleasurable expectation that the trajectory of my experience (of my looking) has been planned in advance, that I have simply to surrender myself to the film. Going to the theatre, by contrast, always involves a kind of mental "gearing up," the knowledge that I have to take responsibility for my looking, knowledge that in some indefinable way I am a participant rather than simply an onlooker.

The "liveness" of live theatre, the energy exchange bound up with the play of looks is dependent on the material conditions of vision, but in many theatres throughout the major part of this century, the house lights are dimmed once the performance proper begins. For most of its history, theatre has been performed in conditions where the actors could see the spectators, and the spectators could see both the actors and each other. In the open air theatres of ancient Greece and Elizabethan England and in the medieval marketplaces, this was so, and in the candlelit theatres that were the norm from the renaissance until the discovery of gas lighting, the auditorium was actually better lit than the stage. Wagner is credited with being the first person to black out the auditorium, at his Festspielhaus in Bayreuth in 1876, his goal to force the spectators to concentrate their attention on the stage. It is no coincidence that directors such as Antoine, developing naturalistic staging and acting, should in the following decades have adopted the innovation with enthusiasm. The presence of the audience is inimical to the illusion of reality the naturalists were attempting to create on the stage, so "removing" the audience by blacking it out made good sense. Actors and audiences in other theatres were by no means convinced of the desirability of this development, and it was introduced very slowly and with considerable reluctance, not becoming the invariable custom in London until after World War I (Booth 1991, 62). Actors were aware from the beginning that their performances were in a sense diminished, not enhanced, and they missed the sense of direct communication that eye contact with spectators can bring. F. W. J. Hemmings comments with great perspicacity that this change marks a watershed in theatre history:

> Henceforth a chasm was to yawn between the world of the stage and the world the spectator inhabited; there was loss as well as gain, but whatever the balance of advantage might be, going to the theatre was no longer the same experience as it had been. (1993, 46)

It is interesting that when Claudel revised *L'Echange* for performance by Jean-Louis Barrault's company in 1951, he completely recast Lechy Elbernon's discussion of the theatre. He omitted all reference to the actor looking at the spectators and to the power of this gaze, but he made Lechy speak of "that huge jaw open to swallow you up" ([1951] 1967, 745). Between 1893, when the first version of the play was written, and 1951, when the second version was performed, there had been a major change in the conditions of vision in the theatre, and Lechy, like other French actors, must perform in front of a black hole, no longer able to see bank clerk or adulterous mother.

In fact many theatre artists resisted the practice, realizing that theatre needed the exchange of energy that could come only from the exchange of looks. Meyerhold wrote a fascinating paragraph about this in relation to his 1910 production of Molière's *Dom Juan:*

> And there is no need to plunge the auditorium into darkness, either in the intervals or during the play itself. Bright light infects the spectators with a festive mood as they enter the theatre. When the actor sees a smile on the lips of a spectator he begins to admire himself, as though looking in a mirror. The actor wearing the mask of Don Juan will conquer the hearts not only of the actresses in the masks of Mathurine and Charlotte, but also the heart of the owner of those beautiful eyes that he sees flashing in the audience in response to the smile he is acting. (Braun 1969, 103)

The spectator's flashing eyes are real, while the actor's smile is acted, and the seduction of the spectator is equated with that of the fictional characters (doubly, trebly fictional in that Don Juan tricks each girl at the expense of the other, and both are deceived into thinking he is promising marriage) but the spectator's (real) smile allows the actor to admire himself "as though in a mirror." The complex interplay of fiction and reality, the play of seduction and deceit is specifically dependent on both parties being able to see each other.

F. W. J. Hemmings was undoubtedly right to claim that once the auditorium is blacked out the experience of theatregoing is irredeemably changed. Not only is the two-way flow of energy between actor and audience impeded, but the spectators can no longer see each other, and while this has certainly led to quieter, more sedate audiences, it has also greatly diminished the working of what I see as the third look of theatre.

The Spectator/Spectator Look

The historical record reveals that spectators in the theatre have usually been involved in a good deal of interaction with each other, often incurring the wrath of playwrights who felt that their works deserved a more attentive reception. Ben Jonson complained bitterly about the behavior of spectators in many of his prologues and epilogues and even went so far as to dedicate one play, *The New Inn*, to "The Reader," on the grounds that at least readers of the play will pay better attention than those who were present at the first performance:

> What did they come for, then? thou wilt ask me. I will as punctually answer: To see, and to be seen: to make a general muster of themselves in their clothes of credit: and possess the stage against the play: to dislike all, but mark nothing. And by their confidence of rising between the acts, in oblique lines, make affidavit to the whole house, of their not understanding one scene. (1950, 426)

While Jonson may have had a rather jaundiced view, it is certainly true that audiences in the seventeenth and eighteenth centuries behaved in ways that would not have been tolerated in later periods, and the recurring theme of commentary on spectator behavior is that people went to the theatre as much to be seen as to see. What they went to see was not only the spectacle on the stage, but also the spectacle in the auditorium, and furthermore, at some periods the spectacle on the stage itself might include a substantial number of spectators.

In the seventeenth and eighteenth centuries spectators were regularly seated on the stage as well as in the auditorium and, as Barbara Mittman has shown in her study of this practice in the French theatre, by the time Voltaire had prevailed on the management of the Comédie Française to abolish seating for spectators on the stage (in 1759), there were occasions when over 300 spectators were accommodated in the area behind the proscenium curtain, 270 of them on the stage itself, the rest in the stage boxes (1984, 47–51). These spectators, petty nobility for the most part, were renowned for their disruptive behavior, coming in late, drawing attention to themselves, ogling the actresses, making witty but distracting comments, but even if their behavior had been impeccable the sheer weight of numbers must have proved an alternative attraction that could easily overwhelm the play. Mittman recounts that when 'princes of the blood' arrived, the performance would be suspended, all the spectators in the theatre would stand and bow, the marquises in the best stage seats would relinquish them, and then the performance would resume (33). It is obvious from this that the social events occurring in the auditorium outweighed the importance of the play on the stage, and that the most prestigious of these would take place on the stage itself, even to the extent of displacing the performance.

The lighted auditorium in indoor theatres from the seventeenth century until well into the twentieth century has meant that spectators were very much aware of the composition of the audience: celebrities attracted attention and their presence might indeed disrupt the performance while spectators applauded or booed them. If spectators on the stage could displace the performance in the eighteenth century, the presence of actors and actresses in the auditorium would attract a great deal of attention a hundred years later. John Gielgud tells some delightful stories in his memoirs about the way, long after they had retired from the stage, Ellen Terry and her sisters would ensure that their entrance into the auditorium to attend a first night would make the maximum impact: "[They] would be greeted with excited cries and enthusiastic applause which they would acknowledge gracefully, bowing to the audience as they took their seats" (1972, 5).

It is a commonplace that male spectators went to the theatre for the erotic pleasure of admiring the sexual charms of the actresses, but accounts of theatregoing by contemporaries throughout the eighteenth and nineteenth centuries make such frequent reference to the male spectators' habit of looking at pretty women in the audience that this, too, must be understood to constitute part of the theatrical experience for men. While much of this activity had little or nothing to do with the play that was being performed, it is evident that a significant part of some men's pleasure was bound up more precisely with watching women watch the play. Kierkegaard's pleasure at the Königstädter Theater in

1843, for instance, came as much from looking at the young girl in the box opposite him as from the performance, and indeed his absorption in the unknown girl's reactions led him to "half fall in love with her" even though he never spoke to her and she never knew he was looking at her:

> In a box directly opposite me was a young girl, seated in the third row, half hidden by an older lady who sat in the first row. The young girl evidently was not in the theatre in order to be seen—as in fact in this theatre one is in a great measure dispensed from the sight of these disgusting feminine exhibitions . . . When I had looked at Beckmann and let the laughter convulse my whole body, when I had sunk back in fatigue and suffered myself to be carried away by the stream of shouting and merriment, and when I stepped out of this bath and returned to myself, then my eyes sought her, and the sight of her refreshed my whole being by its friendly mildness. And when in the farce itself a more pathetic mood cropped up, then I looked at her, and her nature bestowed upon me resignation to bear the pathos, for through it all she sat with perfect self-repose, with her quiet smile of childlike wonder. (1941, 71–72)

Kierkegaard is not interested in women who want to be seen, indeed he claims that such women make "disgusting exhibitions" of themselves, but his experience of the farce is, as it were, moment by moment filtered through that of the unknown girl. It is not that her responses mirror his, on the contrary, but through her "mildness" and "self-repose," she helps him to bear the violence of his reactions to both the comedy and the pathos.

Women, too, could derive pleasure from watching male spectators, as is evident from the following anecdote. At the free performances that the Comédie Française occasionally offered to the working people of Paris, it was traditional for coal merchants and fishwives from the market to occupy the king's and the queen's boxes respectively. On one occasion, in 1778, the crush was such that wealthier spectators had taken all the seats in the king's box and the theatre management offered the coal merchants seats on the stage itself. The newspaper report of the occasion says that when this happened, the women "not wanting to lose sight of them," left their boxes and demanded benches for themselves on the stage opposite the coal merchants (Mittman 1984, 105). It seems that the women's pleasure was not so much to see the play, or even to look at the wealthy spectators in the boxes, but to see their fellow workers as they watched the play.

It is perhaps significant that the women in this incident are working class for they are able to be uninhibited about their looking. In earlier periods, as has already been mentioned, respectable women could not look at the stage openly, but had to mask their looking behind veils, screens, and fans. Even when women of all classes had gained the freedom to look openly at the stage, their looking could still become the object of men's gazes. This might be the importunate stare of the man with the opera glasses in the background of Mary Cassatt's 1888 painting *Woman in Black at the Opera,* which Griselda Pollock has analyzed with such acuity (Florence and Reynolds 1995, 2–38), or the more discreet, but no less troubling scrutiny to which Kierkegaard subjected the young woman at the Königstädter Theater. This raises the question of the extent to which women's looking might be constrained by the fact that they have so continually been made the object of other people's (men's) looks. It is perhaps only in the darkened auditoria of the twentieth century, that women have been able to look freely without themselves becoming the object of men's gazes, but this substantially reduces what they look at to the spectacle on the stage and, as we have seen, a great deal of the pleasure of theatre has traditionally come from the spectacle in the auditorium.

Architects and theatre specialists alike agree that, if the object of theatre design is simply to enable as many people as possible to see and hear clearly what is happening on the stage, then the traditional *théâtre à l'italienne* is manifestly inadequate (Zielske, in Arnott et al. 1977, 23–44). The fact that such theatres were the norm for over two hundred years and that theatre not only survived in them but flourished as an art form suggests that more is involved than simply providing optimal conditions for viewing the stage. Division of the auditorium into boxes provided personal and domestic space within the public arena, and the overall design, while certainly not providing clear vision of the stage from all parts of the auditorium, was very successful at enabling spectators to see one another. Scholarly emphasis on play, production, and performance has tended to downplay the importance of the social experience occurring in the audience space. Spectators go to the theatre to see a performance, but also to participate in a performance of their own, and dressing up, putting oneself on display, has traditionally been an element in this other performance. It is becoming apparent that in the remodeled theatres of the middle part of the twentieth century, with their excellent sight lines and acoustics, where spectators sit in the dark and cannot see each other, theatregoing loses a vital part of its appeal.

What I have called the "other" performance need not be in competition with the performance on the stage (although, admittedly at certain times in the past, it has been very much a distraction). When Tyrone Guthrie's dissatisfaction with the proscenium arch theatre led him to explore the possibilities of the thrust stage, he immediately realized that one of the strengths of this new physical arrangement was the way the spectators were, as it were, brought into the picture:

> The audience did not look at the actors against a background of pictorial and illusionary scenery. Seated around three sides of the stage they focussed upon the actors in the brightly lit acting area, but the background was of the dimly lit rows of people similarly focussed on the actors. All the time, but unemphatically and by influence, each member of the audience was being ceaselessly reminded that he was not lost in an illusion, was not at the court of King Humanitie in 16th century Scotland but was in fact a member of a large audience taking part, "assisting at," as the French very properly express it, a performance, a participant in a ritual. (Mackintosh 1993, 54)

Traverse staging, popular in the 1970s, achieved a similar effect, and a recurring feature of various alternative theatre movements of the last thirty years has been the attempt to get spectators out of their seats, to mobilize them physically and mentally, to disrupt their habits of viewing. Returning the initiative to the spectator has entailed, among other things, reviving the possibility for spectators to see each other during the performance, and it can be argued that the spectator/spectator look is as important as the other two in achieving a vital theatre experience.

Sydney Front, a performance group active in Sydney in the late 1980s and early 1990s explored the relationship between spectator and performer in numerous productions, creating increasingly challenging situations that reversed, subverted, and teased out the ideological implications inherent in the play of looks between spectator and performer. In their penultimate show, *First and Last Warning* in 1992, they focused their attention rather on the spectator/spectator look. One of the most memorable moments I have experienced in the theatre occurred in this production. Spectators were separated into two groups on the basis of gender and taken into the theatre by separate doors. On the women's side, as we filed in we were each given a large orange carrier bag and a black nylon slip and were told to undress, put on the slip and place our own clothes in the carrier bag. There was no stage or seating and the rectangular space had been divided down the center by a curtain hanging from the ceiling. We could not see the men on their side of the curtain, and after the initial shock and understandable resistance to the idea of taking off one's clothes in public, quite a pleasurable degree of camaraderie developed between the women spectators. When everyone was ready, women performers from the Sydney Front, also wearing identical black nylon slips, asked us to line up along the wall, facing the curtain. At a certain moment the curtain fell with dramatic speed to reveal, lined up opposite us, the male spectators, all dressed like us in black nylon slips, holding identical carrier bags in which their clothes were packed.

The gale of laughter that this moment of recognition provoked was exhilarating, but what still makes me smile as I recall it years later, is the way the men gradually stopped laughing, beginning perhaps to feel slightly uncomfortable, while the women continued to find the spectacle irresistibly comic. Our laughter was provoked in the first instance, of course, by the incongruity of men in women's clothes, heightened by the tacky connotations of the black nylon underwear, but this was not drag, almost a cliché in the performance scene of the 1990s. The humor came from glimpsing details such as the lawyer with brief case in one hand and carrier bag in the other, the academic with neatly trimmed beard and glasses, the nylon slip barely reaching to his knees, and the sheepish expressions on familiar faces as one caught their eye. The first impression that we were the mirror of each other, that there was identity was followed by the realization of difference. The realization that we did not look as comic to them as they did to us, the way the tables had been turned, men becoming the object of women's (slightly mocking) gaze, the way the cliché of sexual display had been turned back on its "normal" consumers, these were the elements that continued to feed the women's laughter. This was a very powerful moment and the energy it unleashed threatened to overwhelm the performance that followed it; I certainly felt a sense of anticlimax when the performers moved to the center to claim the spectators' attention.

In this discussion of the play of looks that I see as constituting a fundamental aspect of theatrical spectatorship, I have deliberately chosen examples from many different periods and performance genres. In drawing on actors' memoirs and the excellent historical studies of theatregoing that have been produced in recent years, my intention is, of course, not to claim that the conditions of spectatorship prevailing at particular times in the past still apply today, but to draw attention to the fact that present practices have their roots in the past, and that past practices can still resonate in the present. I want to demonstrate that spectators in the theatre are involved in a vast range of different looks—shared, private, collective, offered, stolen, forbidden, obtrusive, unobtrusive, and so on—and, most important of all, that the look in the theatre is always a process of looking, always complex, always multiple, always energizing, and never totally under the control of anyone.

Multiple Focus and Independence of Vision

The third condition of communication in the theatre concerns the multiplicity of sign systems and framing systems involved in performance, and the way the spectator works to process this multiplicity. Everything in the theatre is double, treble, multiple in its function: the stage is always stage and presentational space as well as fictional place, the character exists only through the real presence of the actor and in the constructed being of the Stage Figure, the real time of performance is displaced/subverted by the fictional time of the dramatic action, and so on. In addition to this necessary doubling and trebling, the theatre has traditionally foregrounded its own processes, for example in plots that turn on disguise, impersonation, pretense, and the device of the play within the play, so the theatrical situation itself is frequently duplicated from within. The spectator is caught up in this play, aware of multiple levels of reality simultaneously, or willingly duped into ignoring one level only to have the tables turned as the suppressed level returns to throw into question what had been accepted as reality or fiction.

Susan Bennett claims that there are two frames that constrain the spectator's experience of a theatrical performance:

> The outer frame is concerned with theatre as a cultural construct through the idea of the theatrical event, the selection of material for production, and the audience's definitions and expectations of a performance. The inner frame contains the event itself and, in particular, the spectator's experience of a fictional stage world. (1990, 1–2)

Including both the "event itself," and the "fictional stage world" in the same frame is problematical in my view in that it elides fictional *énoncé* and presentational *énonciation*, which belong to very different orders of reality. However, the more serious difficulty with Bennett's two frames is that they cannot account adequately for the multiplicity of perspective that is fundamental to the theatre.

As I have argued throughout this study, the performance event itself involves a triple level of awareness. The social reality, the presentational and the fictional interact at all times, and the fictional is always at the mercy of the other two levels of reality and in any given performance one or other can come to the fore, momentarily or permanently, intentionally or unintentionally. These three levels of awareness are contextualized by the spectator's knowledge and culturally conditioned expectations of theatre (Bennett's outer frame), and the heterogeneous nature of theatre audiences suggests that this context is itself very diverse. The various psychological and ideological forces at work within the culture, the ways (recognized and unrecognized) that the theatrical event enacts these, and the individual spectator's complicity with, and resistance to, them constitute further dimensions of the context. In the circumstances, it may be argued that the image of the frame, so heavily marked with its structuralist provenance, is in fact too rigid to account for something as fluid and dynamic as the spectator's experience of theatrical performance.

A consequence of the multiplicity of focus that is typical of theatre is that the spectator gains a certain independence of vision. Spectators in the theatre differ from spectators in the cinema in that what the former see and hear, and their experience of the performance, is very much under their own control. The actors can influence this up to a point, and the mise en scène provides cues to the kind of attention required and an overall rhythm that will channel response in certain ways. However, even the most charismatic actor knows that the moments when the whole audience seems to be "suddenly concentrating," as John Gielgud put it, are few and far between and, indeed, their impact derives precisely from the fact that they are exceptional. Spectators in the theatre have so many calls on their attention, conditions of visibility and audibility vary considerably from different points in the auditorium of even the most democratically designed theatre, there are so many things one can look at in the presentational space and in the performance space more generally, that it is not surprising that a moment when everyone present seems to be focusing on the same thing is relatively rare. The freedom to choose what to focus on is an important part of the risk of live performance, and an important part of that sense of taking responsibility for one's own experience that I have already mentioned.

In the cinema, by contrast, partly because everyone sees virtually the same thing (the differences between the view of the screen image from different seats in the cinema are minimal), and partly because of the centralizing function of the camera and editing process, the spectator's attention is very much under the control of the film. What the film shows the spectator at any moment (a close up of this character's face, that character's hands, a long shot of the car containing the hero speeding to rescue the heroine, a close shot of the heroine's anguish) is what every spectator will see, even though the way each person responds to this may vary. In the theatre each spectator must make his or her own montage of details, and each of these will be determined by that particular spectator's interests, knowledge, and experience. The theatre spectator looks from actor to actor, looks at this one's hands or that one's feet, notices or does not notice details that in film would either be brought to the attention of the viewer through a close up or may not be visible at all; in the theatre the fictional place as created in the presentational space is present in all its detail throughout the action of a given scene and, again, the spectator can choose at any moment to glance around the space, may pick up a detail in relation to something that is being said that another spectator may pick up at another time in relation to something else.

The studies of viewing patterns of theatrical spectators carried out by Tim Fitzpatrick at the University of Sydney using an Eyemark recorder (1990; Fitzpatrick and Batten 1991) have shown that visual perception in the theatre, as elsewhere, is made up of a combination of "fixations" (a moment lasting perhaps as much as three seconds in which the point of foveal concentration does not move significantly) and "saccades" (a swift movement of the eyes that brings another object into the center of foveal concentration). Fitzpatrick has shown that theatre spectators differ considerably in the frequency with which they saccade and in the duration of their fixations. The evidence indicates that the actors' faces are the major focus of attention, and that the verbal text is the most important element stimulating saccades (unsurprising given the nature of the performances used in the studies), but the actual process of scanning the presentational space, the amount of detail perceived, and the number of what Fitzpatrick calls "pre-emptive and interpretive saccades" (which "betray the subject's inferences about what will or might happen next") vary substantially from spectator to spectator.

When attending performances in large theatres, spectators have traditionally possessed themselves of opera glasses or lorgnettes, and this has meant that they are able to construct an even more elaborate montage, including what in film would be called "close-ups." The human eye can focus on one part of the space while remaining aware through peripheral vision of what is going on around this privileged space, or it can take in the whole space (I can focus on a single dancer in the *corps de ballet*, aware at all times that she is one of many, or I can look at the whole row of dancers); opera glasses enable one to obtain a closer view of a detail but this is then, as it were, removed from the context by virtue of the mechanical intervention of the magnifying instrument. The use of opera glasses creates within the spectator an awareness of watching, awareness that one is choosing this detail or that, and it foregrounds the presentational over the fictional. It is no coincidence that naturalists and others who want the illusion of the fiction to be dominant, prefer small performance spaces in which such devices are unnecessary.

These comments refer to the variations in the way any group of spectators will actually experience the performance, and to the way that, in the theatre, each spectator creates his or her own sequence of signs from the same performance. But spectators in the theatre are not just witnessing the performance, they are also experiencing the social event in the audience space. In earlier, more unruly days the alternation between attention to the performance and to the social space was more obvious, because people were less inhibited about indulging in the many activities that, as the iconographic record makes clear, were competing for their attention: orange sellers, prostitutes, pickpockets, arguments about the quality of the play or performance, not to mention the voyeuristic delights of spying on the reactions of one's neighbors, fantasizing about them, and "half falling in love" with complete strangers that Kierkegaard describes.

Spectators in the theatre have traditionally paid only intermittent attention to the performance in progress. While practitioners and other spectators have frequently complained about the distractions caused by these inattentive spectators, others have bemoaned the loss of energy that each "reform" of the spectator's condition brings with it. As long ago as 1783, when the Comédie Française first introduced seats in the parterre, Sébastien Mercier claimed that

> the circulation of thoughts and emotions is no longer apparent; the electric current has been broken, for benches impede that instant mental communication and exchange of impressions. Formerly, an incredible enthusiasm

> animated the pit, and the universal effervescence gave theatrical occasions
> an interest which they have now lost. ([1783], in Hemmings 1993, 36)

This sort of comment is frequent and, generation after generation of theatre lovers has regretted the loss of energy that the turbulent and apparently unruly houses of the immediately preceding period provided. It
seems that what is lethargy to one person may be perceived as enthusiasm by another, but the point nevertheless emerges that, while the spectators' attention was intermittent it was nonetheless acute, and that lack
of attention to the performance did not necessarily lead to a drop in the
overall energy level in the theatre. The "effervescence" Mercier so
enjoyed was produced by spectators interacting with each other as much
as with the performance.

Theatrical performances have traditionally taken place in such energized spaces, and even though the mainstream performances of the late
twentieth century take place in comparative calm, it can be surmised that
this has more to do with the habit of dousing the house lights than with
a fundamental change in the nature of theatrical spectatorship. Spectators must still work to construct what in the cinema is a given, and no
two spectators construct exactly the same sequence of signs, the same
combination of detail and overview. Furthermore, notwithstanding the
increased concentration of attention on the performance that is a feature
of the contemporary period, the theatre event still involves a combination of the fictional, the presentational and the real, and the spectator is
still responding to all three, experiencing each through the filter of the
other two.

Space in the Spectatorial Experience

The condition of spectatorship in the theatre thus involves the physical
presence of both performers and spectators, the complex play of fiction
and reality, the equally complex play of looks between performers and
spectators and between spectators, the multiple frames that enable this
complexity to be experienced and the freedom for the individual spectator to foreground one frame or another at different moments and to construct his or her own sequence of events and signs. The part played by
the space of performance in the spectator's experience is fundamental
insofar as space is the condition of the spectator and the performer com-

ing together, but also in that the place in which the performance occurs is a major variable that over time and across cultures has determined the precise nature of the spectator's experience.

The size of the theatre has a bearing on the visibility and audibility of the performer, and on the nature of the attention that the spectator is required to give. The size of the auditorium, too, has an impact on the social experience and on the function that theatre comes to fulfill in a given society. The visibility of spectators to each other and to the performers during the performance is another factor that, as has been argued in this chapter, is of vital importance in terms of spectators' focus of attention, and of the priority given to the performance over the social event in which it is embedded.

The design of the audience space, in particular the auditorium itself, is a major factor in predisposing spectators to move around or remain seated, to focus attention on the stage or on each other, to exert themselves or to wait for someone to entertain them. The physical design of the space can assist in releasing the spectators' energy, or it can make this more difficult. John Gielgud's description of the Old Vic Theatre has already been quoted (chap. 2); in his view, it is the theatre building itself, the particular configuration of space, the particular relationship between audience space and practitioner space that it bodies forth, that constructs the audience as audience. It is perhaps no coincidence that Gielgud should regard the audience as the instrument on which the actor plays, given his comment, quoted earlier in this chapter, concerning the acute reciprocity that exists between actor and audience during the performance. This is an important observation, for it indicates that the audience is participating in the performance as cocreators rather than receivers. They are not a collection of separate human beings, although that is how they come to the theatre, but an entity that has its own life, its own energy, its own idiosyncrasies (as Jouvet has shown), and it is the physical disposition of the space that sets in motion the transformation from collection of individuals to collectivity. The physical disposition of this space also determines the extent to which personal and domestic subgroupings can form, the extent to which such subgroups are encouraged to turn their energy inward to the group, outward to the stage, or around the whole space. It is thus the space that influences whether the performance will be lived as a private or a public event.

The relationship between stage and auditorium and between stage and off-stage, both significantly determined by the architectural design of the performance space, exercise a determining influence on the kinds of representation that performance can achieve, and on the degree of distance from or proximity with the world beyond the theatre. Even a feature such as the disjunction between the spectator's emotion and the dramatic fiction, that Gertrude Stein saw as so characteristic a feature of theatre is substantially dependent on the separation of stage and auditorium, signaled in spatial terms by the physical reality of the curtain: "In the first place at the theatre there is the curtain and the curtain already makes one feel that one is not going to have the same tempo as the thing that is there behind the curtain" ([1935] 1988, 95). In open spaces that do not have a curtain, the separation is felt very strongly nevertheless and it seems that the performer creates a kind of energized zone around him or her that the spectator, even when free to move anywhere at will, is loath to enter.

There is always a distance between spectator and performer, either physically set by the arrangement of stage and auditorium, or spontaneously arrived at moment by moment by the spectators and performers. In flexible performance conditions spectators leave space between themselves and the performers in part from fear of becoming part of the spectacle and in part because distance is in fact a necessary part of being able to see. The amount of distance is determined by the architectural design of the theatre and the cost of the ticket, and in traditional theatres is likely to be a constant. In the cinema, by contrast, the focal length of the image changes constantly, changing the viewers' relationship to the image without obliging them to move from their seats. In modern and postmodern performance, the spectators are frequently obliged to move bodily from place to place, to take responsibility for their own viewing, for their own experience, and thus find themselves differently situated in relation to different episodes of the action.

Bernard Beckerman points out that the distance between spectator and performer in the theatre is more than simply the condition of visibility, for it has a psychological function. As he sees it, there has to be some form of demarcation between performer and spectator, even if this is shifting, even if it is being brought into question by the nature of the performance, because demarcation is crucial in theatre if the oscillation of stimulus and response between presenter and presentee is to occur (1970, 10). This is to say that spectators are stimulated into beginning to make meaning with what they see due to the separation or demarcation between them and the performers, so the distance is the condition not only of sight but of the beginning of understanding. In fact what is going on in the theatre involves two different interfaces, two different demarcations, two different gaps. There is the interface between actor and character and that between performer and spectator, and both are in process throughout the performance, both occur simultaneously, and in both the production style can function to widen the gap, draw attention to the interface or to mask it. For example, Brecht's *Verfremdungseffect* opens up the gap between actor and character, while in naturalism the space between performer and spectator becomes a veritable gulf.

The phrases quoted as epigraphs to this chapter—"For we are where we are / not" and "You were in the picture, beholding, yet part of it"—refer to different aspects of the destabilizing, decentering experience that theatre provides for its spectators, and both give a very definite spatial reality to the crucial multiplicity of focus. Jouve's line sums up succinctly the spectator's relation to the dramatic fiction (although in his poem his concern is art more generally). The spectators' awareness that someone will die, and no one will die at the end of *Hamlet*, that the swords are real but not real, becomes in Jouve's phrase a spatial awareness that displaces the spectator even as it situates him or her: we are where we are not (in Elsinore but not in Elsinore because in the theatre; in the theatre but not in the theatre because in Elsinore). Saintsbury refers to what I have called the "other performance," namely the spectator's experience of being in the auditorium and the fact of being part of the spectacle one has come to watch. Here, too, the spatial reality is paramount, for it is only because the spectators are really present in the auditorium that they can enjoy the shifts and turns in their consciousness of themselves, other spectators, the actors, and the dramatic fiction. It is evident, then, that space is at work in every aspect of the spectator's experience of the theatre event.

Afterword

Starting from the incontrovertible fact that theatre is a mode of artistic expression that requires the live presence of both performers and spectators, this book has set out to explore the multiple functions of the spatial reality that makes such simultaneous presence possible. Space, it has been argued, is the medium of theatre, and it is the real space in which performance occurs that distinguishes theatre from other dramatic media such as film, radio, and television. From the physical reality of the theatre building, its location in relation to other buildings and the social activities they accommodate, the organization of the audience and practitioner spaces within this building, to the stage itself, the fictional worlds created on and around it, and the modes of representation it facilitates, space is crucial to understanding the nature of the performance event and how meanings are constructed and communicated in the theatre.

The actor is the dynamic agent responsible for energizing the performance space and for activating all the theatre's signifying systems, and, in exploring this reality, the emphasis has again and again fallen on spatial factors. Whether we are considering the text/narrative/character-based theatre of the mainstream Western tradition, or physical theatre, or postmodern performance, the actor is first and foremost a physical presence, occupying a particular space, endowing it with meaning and drawing meaning from it. During a performance in the theatre the spectator may be aware above all of the dramatic fiction and the emotional experience this triggers, but observation of the rehearsal process in many different productions reveals the vital role played in the construction of this fiction by spatial elements such as entrance, exit, movement, gesture, proxemic relations, orientation, and position. These are indeed so important to theatrical meaning making that I have suggested

278

it is kinesis rather than mimesis that is at the heart of the performer's communicative practice. Any performance is segmented at the macro level by the performers' movements into and out of the performance space, and at the micro level it is movement, position, and gesture that articulate the verbal component of the performance, constructing it as discourse and ensuring that no two productions utilizing the same text will produce exactly the same meanings. In the theatre spatial and verbal elements interact powerfully, and meanings are created from this interaction that go far beyond the written text. Furthermore, the physical reality of the performance and the energies it unleashes in spectators and performers may on occasion produce an experience that goes beyond meaning.

In claiming denegation as the theatre's most potent mode of operation, I have again drawn attention to the role of the performance space in maintaining the dual consciousness in the spectator that is essential to this psychic state. It is because the spectators are present in the theatre, physically located in a given place, subliminally aware at all times of their surroundings, the responses of their neighbors, and the materiality of stage, set, and performance, that the dramatic fiction is always undercut. At the same time, it is the reality of the actors' bodies and voices, and the energy released by their corporeal presence, that give the fiction its emotional charge and make it so compelling. Hamlet both is and is not present, the actor performing Hamlet both is and is not present, and the tension between the presence and the nonpresence is the theatre's playground and the source of the endless fascination it has exerted over players and spectators for centuries.

The theatre building frames what goes on inside it, ensuring that its status as performance (i.e., not real) is signaled but ensuring, too, that it comes under the control of civic authorities (a tacit acknowledgment that the "not real" has the power to contaminate or disturb the "real"). In the same way the stage frames everything placed within its confines, transforming every object into a sign and inciting all who witness what is there to attribute meaning to it. A whole chapter was devoted to objects in order to discuss their increasingly complex functions in contemporary theatre practice, all of which depend in some way on their material reality and visibility in the presentational space. Even their characteristic mobility or transformability, while dependent on the active agency of the human performer, is only possible due to the fact that a material object is physically present in the performance space.

Theatrical performance does not necessarily involve the use of verbal language, and not all theatre has its genesis in a preexisting written text. The dominant tradition in Western theatre does, however, involve actors working with a preexisting written text to construct their performance, and the text may emanate from a very different place and cultural moment from the performance. Texts, whether dramatized or not, contain multiple indications of spatiality that the performers and other practitioners draw on during the production process, and I have argued that a major strength of the Western theatre tradition is precisely the interface between past and present, the residual and the emergent, that is necessarily activated by this form of creative practice. While there has been much criticism in recent years of this dominant tradition, responsible for producing what has been described variously as deadly, Aristotelian, digestive, or alimentary theatre, it needs to be emphasized that in such practice it is not a question simply of interpreting something that already exists, for it is only in performance that the theatre work comes into being, and each production produces a different work with different meanings. The verbal component of performance does not have to exist in written form before the practitioners begin work, and another branch of the Western theatre tradition involves actors improvising in performance on the basis of a preexisting narrative or physical score. While the performers' training and skills and the production process in these forms of theatre are very different, the experience for the spectator is not necessarily so different, for meaning still emerges from the interaction of verbal and physical, from introducing division into space by means of dialogue, as Maurice Blanchot observed so pertinently.

My final chapter concerns the spectator, the unmarked term in so much critical and theoretical writing about theatre. The spectator is present in the performance space and is as crucial to a definition of the theatre event as the performer; here, too, space is of fundamental importance. It is because the spectators and the actors are both present in the theatre that the actor can return the spectators' gaze and that the spectators can see one another, thus setting off the play of looks and the energy exchange that I have argued are essential components of the theatre event. The characteristic layering of signs and the complexity of the meaning-making process are equally dependent on the fact that the spectators are physically present and free to experience the multiplicity of signs in relatively autonomous ways. Furthermore, it is this physical presence that ensures that the theatre is as much a social event as a mode

of artistic practice, and, although artists have throughout history complained when the social became too dominant, it is evident from the
strictures about passive audiences in mainstream theatre expressed by
contemporary alternative theatre practitioners that an energized social
space is of vital importance to artists and spectators alike.

I began this book with a definition of theatre as essentially a relationship between performers and spectators, and, as I reflect on the situation of this primary couple in contemporary theatre practice, it seems to
me that both are somewhat at risk. Spectators sitting in their serried
ranks in the darkness, discouraged from all but the most stage-managed
interactions with one another or with the performers, actors who are
marginalized in the creative process, presented with a set design on the
first day of rehearsals and expected to make it work, are equally disem-
powered. Henri Lefebvre makes a distinction between what he calls
"dominated" and "appropriated" space, defining the former as space
transformed and mediated by technology and controlled by the institutions of political power, while the latter is natural space, modified to
serve the needs and possibilities of a particular group in society (1991,
esp. 165). He claims that the highest expression of appropriated space is
the work of art; I would argue, however, that not only the contemporary
commercial theatre, dominated by designer and technology, but also the
art theatre, controlled by the director and the funding authorities, constitute dominated spaces that to a significant extent have been alienated
from their primary users (and it is perhaps for this reason that people of
the current generation must go to a rock concert or a football final to
experience the kind of performance energy that Kierkegaard found at the
Königstädter Theater in Berlin). Lefebvre goes on to say:

> Similar considerations apply to the body and to sexuality. Dominated by
> overpowering forces, including a variety of brutal techniques and an
> extreme emphasis on visualisation, the body fragments, abdicates respon-
> sibility for itself—in a word disappropriates itself . . . Any revolutionary
> project today, whether utopian or realistic, must, if it is to avoid hopeless
> banality, make the reappropriation of the body, in association with the
> reappropriation of space, into a non-negotiable part of its agenda. (166–67)

This was written in 1974, but the task is still ahead. The theatre, as the
place where the body and space come together most intensively, is one of
the few sites left in contemporary society in which the revolutionary
activity suggested by Lefebvre might occur, but this will only begin to

happen when the performance space is designed and ordered in such a way that genuine exchange can take place between the human beings on the stage and those in the auditorium and when the production process recognizes the centrality of the actors' role as coauthors of the performance.

Appendix

Artists involved in the productions, workshops, and experimental performance projects for which I observed the rehearsal process and which have been referred to in this book:

The Theatrical Illusion
Play by Pierre Corneille, trans. John Cairncross
Director: Rex Cramphorn
Set Design: Russell Emerson
Costume Design: Melody Cooper
Music: Peta Williams and Chris Wynton
Lighting: Derek Nicholson
Actors: Bruce Keller, Paul Brown, Ross Hill, Richard Healy, Gregg Levy, John Sheerin, John Baylis, Vanessa Downing, Gillian Allan, Neil Beaumont.

Britannicus
Play by Jean Racine, trans. Rex Cramphorn
Director: Rex Cramphorn
Set and Costume Design: Melody Cooper
Music: Sarah de Jong
Actors: Kate Fitzpatrick, John Howard, Deborah Kennedy, Tony Mack, Robert Menzies, Bill McCluskey, Kerry Walker.

Miss Julie
Play by August Strindberg, trans. Michael Meyer
Director: Richard Lawton
Set Design: Russell Emerson
Costume Design: Melody Cooper
Lighting: Derek Nicholson

283

Music: Robert Stephens, Sarah de Jong
Actors: John Howard, Lyn Pierse, Laura Williams

The Maids
Play by Jean Genet
Set Design: Derek Nicholson
Costumes: Ludmilla Knorles
Actors in the male versions: John Howard, Warren Colman
Actors in the female versions: Robyn Gurney, Elaine Hudson

A Doll's House
Play by Henrik Ibsen, trans. Michael Meyer
Workshop run by director Lindy Davies
Actors: Angie Milliken, Anna Looby

Phèdre
Text by Jean Racine; trans. John Cairncross, Tony Harrison, Robert Lowell
Director: Rex Cramphorn
Actors: John Howard, Gillian Jones, Anna Phillips

Dom Juan
Text by Molière, trans. Rex Cramphorn, amended by cast
Version 1
Director: Rex Cramphorn
Set and Costume Design: Melody Cooper
Actors: Kate Fitzpatrick, Rupert Burns, Suzette Williams, Joseph Clements
Version 2
Director: Beverley Blankenship
Costume Design: Melody Cooper
Actors: Brandon Burke, Drew Forsythe, Gillian Hyde, Christopher
    Truswell

Old Times
Text by Harold Pinter
Director: Aarne Neeme
Actors: Brandon Burke, Fiona Press, Susan Lyons

The Three Sisters
Text by Anton Chekhov, translation Elisaveta Fen
Director: Stuart Chalmers
Actors: Deborah Paull, Lyn Pierse, Jane Townsend

Notes

Chapter 1

1. "On a bare stage the actor is obliged to create everything, to draw everything from his own being" (note written in 1917; Copeau 1974, 1:220).

A note concerning translations: in quoting from foreign language sources, I have used published English translations where these are readily available, and I give full bibliographical references for both translation and original in the bibliography. I have used my own translations from French whenever I was unable to find a published English translation.

2. Of Aristotle's six constituents of tragedy (plot, character, diction, thought, spectacle, and song), he regarded spectacle as the least important: "Spectacle, or stage-effect, is an attraction of course, but it has the least to do with the playwright's craft or with the art of poetry. For the power of tragedy is independent both of performance and of actors, and besides, the production of spectacular effects is more the province of the property-man than of the playwright" (Aristotle, Horace, and Longinus 1965, 41).

3. See Richard Schechner's editorial comments in the *Drama Review* over the last ten years or Johannes Birringer, who writes of the "ambivalent fascination" theatre has for him "at a time when many among us would argue that theatre no longer has any cultural significance and is too marginal and too exhausted to intervene in contemporary cultural-political debates" (1993, x).

4. The phenomenon of the mega-musical may constitute an exception to this generalization insofar as the productions are imported as a total package, and the importing country has simply to provide local performers whose task is to present the package but not rework or rethink significant aspects of it. These productions have been extremely successful in attracting large audiences, but it remains to be seen whether such a mode of performance has any long-term place in the culture.

5. See, for example, the work of Willmar Sauter, Henry Schoenmakers, and other members of the International Committee for Reception and Audience Research, International Federation of Theatre Research; Roger Deldime at

the Centre for the Sociology of Theatre, University of Brussels; Tim Fitzpatrick at the Centre for Performance Studies, University of Sydney.

6. The term *scenography*, or *scenographic space*, is a good example of this. For Michael Issacharoff, for instance, the term refers to the stage itself as a physical entity (1989). Freddie Rokem, on the other hand, gives it a broader definition: the scenographic is for him the organization of the stage space that enables the spectator to experience the thematic concerns of the play (1986). Patrice Pavis, rather idiosyncratically, uses the term as a synonym for the more general theatre space (1980, 146).

7. My translation of these terms needs some comment. French has one word *scène*, whereas English has two, *stage* and *scene*, so there is always a certain ambiguity in French usage. Ubersfeld uses the distinction between *espace* and *lieu* (*space* and *place*, respectively), each qualified with the same adjective, *scénique*, to construct the first pair of related terms. In translating the words, I have retained her space/place distinction as well as using the appropriate English word in view of the meaning she ascribes. She continues to use the space/place distinction in a second pair of terms, qualified this time with the adjective *théâtral*, but this distinction cannot be neatly translated into English. In suggesting *theatre space* for the "lieu théâtral," or physical place where theatre occurs, and *theatrical space* for the global spatial function, I realize I have selected terms used by Hanna Scolnicov to convey a different distinction. This is a recurring problem in the minefield constituted by the terminology of spatial function in the theatre.

8. It should be pointed out, however, that until Ubersfeld introduced the distinction most French writers seemed to use *lieu théâtral* and *espace théâtral* as synonyms. See, for example, titles listed in the Arts du Spectacle collection published by the CNRS in Paris: *Le Lieu théâtral à la Renaissance; L'Espace théâtral médiéval;* and *Le Lieu théâtral dans la société moderne*.

9. Umberto Eco's famous discussion of ostension in the theatre remains one of the most cogent presentations of the fictionalizing power of the stage (1977, 107–17).

10. Willmar Sauter argues that our experience in the theatre is one of watching "the making of the fictional world as much as the fictional world itself," and his empirical studies show that the evaluative activity of spectators is most actively engaged in respect of what he defines as the artistic level of performance (Martin and Sauter 1995, 78–102).

11. The three levels of awareness in the spectator posited by Freddie Rokem (the stage as physical space, the fictional world, and the performance conventions in operation) are clearly a response to this same perception. So, too, is the tripartite system elaborated by Willmar Sauter in his analysis of theatre as an act of communication. His three "communicative levels" (sensory, artistic, and fictional) closely parallel Rokem's but have been theorized far more extensively as well as being situated within a broader theory of cultural experience. See Rokem 1986, 1–12; Martin and Sauter 1995, 78–102.

12. The distinction being made here between drama and theatre is not the

traditional one between plays as written text and plays in performance but drama seen as a genre involving enactment and representation and theatre as one (albeit the most ancient) of its modes of presentation. Martin Esslin addresses this question in *The Field of Drama* (1987, 22–35).

13. For example, the continuing series of studies contained in the *Voies de la création théâtrale* (published by the Centre National de la Recherche Scientifique, edited by Denis Bablet, Jean Jacquot, and others, since 1970) or the book-length accounts of the genesis of a particular production, such as David Selbourne's *The Making of* A Midsummer Night's Dream (1982).

Chapter 2

1. For example, it is thought that the Theatre of Dionysus in Athens was used by the Athenian Assembly on occasions when their usual meeting place at the Pnyx proved too small (see Frank Kolb, "Polis und Theater," in Seeck 1979, 504–45).

2. Luc Boucris (1993, 176–82) uses the terms *heavy* and *light* to make a distinction between performance spaces in relation to the constricting or intrusive nature of the technical apparatus involved.

3. It is important not to confuse negation with denial (Freud's terms are *Verneinung* and *Verleugnung*), for it is only the former that permits the contradictory beliefs to be held simultaneously. The French translation of *Verneinung* is "dénégation," and increasingly the word *denegation* is being used in English, too, in order to stress the double negative that is at work. See Mannoni 1969, 9–33, 161–83.

4. When the new opera house at the Bastille was opened, it was decided that, in view of the poor sight lines in the Palais Garnier, all opera performances would be located at the Bastille and the older theatre would be reserved for concerts and ballet. The pressure of public demand forced management to abandon this entirely rational policy and to program both opera and ballet in both theatres.

5. This phrase has been used by actors at the Wharf Theatre, where the auditorium is very steeply raked and spectators are in close proximity to the actors, to describe the experience from their perspective.

Chapter 3

1. This term has been variously translated as *transformability, mobility,* and *changeability,* and it was central to Jiri Honzl's analysis of the fundamental features of theatrical semiosis ([1940] 1976, 74–93).

2. Otokar Zich's book, *The Aesthetics of Dramatic Art,* was published in 1931; it is quoted frequently by the Prague School semioticians but has still not been translated into English.

3. This project has been analyzed in more detail in McAuley 1989, 113–44.

4. Tim Fitzpatrick used an Eyemark recorder to track a number of spectators during performances of this scene; preliminary results were presented by Paul Dwyer in a conference paper entitled "Overt Surveillance" at the Australasian Drama Studies Conference at the University of New England in July 1995.

5. In this 1941 translation by Walter Lowrie of Kierkegaard's essay, the theatre in question is referred to throughout as the Königstäter, but in the more recent translation by Howard and Edna Hong (Kierkegaard 1983) it is called the Königstädter, which is the name I have used here.

Chapter 4

1. The terms are taken from André Bazin's famous essays on the nature of montage in realistic film (1981).

2. Results of my study of spectator perception of structure undertaken in connection with the *Dom Juan* project (to which I refer on several occasions here) will be published in a book entitled *Rehearsal, Performance, Reception: The Production of Meaning in the Theatre*, which I am writing in collaboration with Tim Fitzpatrick and Terry Threadgold.

3. The performance notation consists of a transcription of the verbal component of the performance with a note of each displacement move and major gesture mapped onto this text. The rationale for such a notation is discussed further in the final section of this chapter.

4. Victor Turner has demonstrated in many brilliant essays that it is possible "to regard the etymology of key terms in major languages as a many-leveled system whose strata are composed of successively deposited layers of historical 'experience'" (1982, 16). Popular usage, too, can be very revealing of the dimensions of experience associated with a given term, and the specialist knowledge of generations of practitioners may be, as it were, layered onto the terminology they use.

5. Some theatres in these parlous times depend on bar sales to balance the budget and so an interval is compulsory. It is interesting to note that in Strindberg's time the sale of alcohol at interval paid almost half rent bill for many theatres, and his decision not to have a bar at the Intimate Theater was highly controversial (Strindberg 1964, 172).

6. The neoclassical dramaturgy of the seventeenth century and beyond, working with a fictional world that was rigidly constrained by the unities of place and time, established the entrances and exits of characters as key markers of dramaturgical structure. A graphic convention evolved of naming and numbering these units (known as "scenes") within each act; the structure is thus set out on the page, and the playtext obliges performers and readers to recognize it, but the operative principle clearly comes from the stage itself and not from

any literary values. The interest and tension created in the theatre by the entrance of a character, the perception that an exit or an entrance creates something new, is at the basis of the decision to found a whole dramaturgy on these shifts.

Chapter 6

1. This exchange does not appear in Bernard Frechtman's 1957 translation which differs in many important ways from the French text published by L'Arbalète in 1963 and considered by Genet to be definitive. The passage in question is as follows in French:

Claire: Je vous accuse d'être coupable du plus effroyable des crimes.
Solange: Vous êtes folle! ou ivre. Car il n'y a pas de crime, Claire, je te défie de nous accuser d'un crime précis.
Claire: Nous l'inventerons donc, car . . . Vous vouliez m'insulter! Ne vous gênez pas! Crachez-moi à la face!

Chapter 7

1. "Poets aim at giving either profit or delight, or at combining the giving of pleasure with some useful precepts for life" (Horace 1965, 77–95).
2. The phrase comes from Michel de Certeau's essay on "Walking in the City" ("The exaltation of a scopic and gnostic drive: the fiction of knowledge is related to this lust to be a viewpoint and nothing more"); see de Certeau [1980] 1984, 92.
3. See *The Devil Is an Ass*, the induction to *The Staple of News*, and *The New Inn*.
4. 1926, 47; Earle Ernst translates the "shadowy frontiers" as the "slender margin between the real and the unreal" (1959, 48).

Bibliography

Aaron, Stephen. 1986. *Stage Fright: Its Role in Acting.* Chicago: University of Chicago Press.

Alter, Jean. 1987. "Waiting for the Referent: *Waiting for Godot.*" In *On Referring in Literature,* ed. Anna Whiteside and Michael Issacharoff, 42–56. Bloomington: Indiana University Press.

Antoine, André. 1903. "Causerie sur la mise en scène." *La Revue de Paris,* 1 April, 596–612.

———. 1921. *Mes souvenirs sur le Théâtre Libre.* Paris: Arthème Fayard.

Appadurai, Arjun, ed. 1986. *The Social Life of Things.* Cambridge and New York: Cambridge University Press.

Argyle, Michael. 1988. *Bodily Communication.* 2d ed. London and New York: Methuen.

Aristotle, Horace, and Longinus. 1965. *Classical Literary Criticism.* Trans. T. S. Dorsch. London: Penguin Books.

Arnott, James. 1981. "An Introduction to Theatrical Scholarship." *Theatre Quarterly* 10 (39): 29–42.

Arnott, James, Joëlle Chariau, Heinrich Huesmann, Tom Lawrenson, and Rainer Theobald, eds. 1977. *Theatre Space: An Examination of the Interaction between Space, Technology, Performance and Society.* Munich: Prestel Verlag.

Arnott, Peter D. 1989. *Public and Performance in the Greek Theatre.* London and New York: Routledge.

Artaud, Antonin. 1958. *The Theatre and Its Double.* Trans. M. C. Richards. New York: Grove Press.

———. 1964. *Le Théâtre et son double.* Vol. 4 of *Oeuvres complètes.* Paris: Gallimard.

———. 1970. *The Theatre and Its Double.* Trans. Victor Corti. London: John Calder.

Aston, Elaine, and George Savona. 1991. *Theatre as Sign-System.* London and New York: Routledge.

Bablet, Denis. 1965. *Esthétique générale du décor de théâtre de 1870 à 1914.* Paris: Editions du CNRS.

————. 1972. "Pour une méthode d'analyse du lieu théâtral." *Travail Théâtral* 6:107–25.

Bablet, Denis, and Jean Jacquot, eds. 1977. *Les Voies de la création théâtrale*, vol. 5. Paris: Editions du CNRS.

————. 1988. *Le Lieu théâtral dans la société moderne*. Paris: Editions du CNRS.

Bachelard, Gaston. 1957. *La Poétique de l'espace*. Paris: Presses Universitaires de France.

————. 1964. *The Poetics of Space*. Trans. Maria Jolas. New York: Orion Press.

Balzac, Honoré de. 1833. *Scènes de la vie parisienne*. Vol. 8 of *Oeuvres Complètes*. Paris: Calmann-Lévy.

Bakhtin, M. M. 1981. *The Dialogic Imagination*. Trans. Michael Holquist and Caryl Emerson. Austin: University of Texas Press.

Barba, Eugenio. 1985. "The Dilated Body: On the Energies of the Actor." *New Theatre Quarterly* 1 (4): 369–82.

————. 1986. *Beyond the Floating Islands*. New York: PAJ Publications.

Barish, Jonah. 1982. *The Anti-Theatrical Prejudice*. Berkeley: University of California Press.

Barthes, Roland. 1963. *Sur Racine*. Paris: Seuil.

————. 1966. "L'analyse structurale du récit." *Communications* 8:1–27.

————. 1977. *Image Music Text*. Trans. Stephen Heath. London: Fontana Press.

Baty, Gaston. 1949. *Rideau baissé*. Paris: Bordas.

Baudrillard, Jean. 1968. *Le Système des objets*. Paris: Denoël/Gonthier.

Baudry, Jean-Louis. 1985. "Ideological Effects of the Basic Cinematographic Apparatus." In *Movies and Methods*, ed. Bill Nichols, 531–42. Berkeley and Los Angeles: University of California Press.

Bauman, Richard. 1975. *Verbal Art as Performance*. Illinois: Waveland Press.

Bazin, André. 1981. *Qu'est-ce que le cinéma?* Paris: Editions du Cerf.

Beckerman, Bernard. 1970. *Dynamics of Drama: Theory and Methods of Analysis*. New York: Alfred A. Knopf.

Beckett, Samuel. 1956. *Waiting for Godot*. London: Faber and Faber.

Bennett, Susan. 1990. *Theatre Audiences: A Theory of Production and Reception*. London and New York: Routledge.

Bentley, Eric. 1965. *The Life of the Drama*. London: Methuen.

Bergan, Ronald. 1990. *The Great Theatres of London*. London: Prion.

Bernard, Michel. 1976. *L'Expressivité du corps*. Paris: Editions Jean-Pierre Delarge.

Berry, Cicely. 1973. *Voice and the Actor*. London: Harrap.

————. 1987. *The Actor and his Text*. London: Harrap.

Bharata-Muni. [1951] 1967. *The Natyasastra*. Trans. Manumohan Ghosh. Calcutta: Granthalaya Private Limited.

Birdwhistell, R. L. 1970. *Kinesics and Contexts*. Philadelphia: University of Pennsylvania Press.

Birringer, Johannes. 1993. *Theatre, Theory, Postmodernism*. Bloomington: Indiana University Press.

Biscos, Denise. 1978. "Antoine Vitez à la rencontre du texte." In *Les voies de la création théâtrale*, ed. Jean Jacquot, 6:195–277.

Blanchot, Maurice. 1969. *L'Entretien infini*. Paris: Gallimard.

Blau, Herbert. 1990. *The Audience*. Baltimore: Johns Hopkins University Press.

Blonsky, M. ed. 1985. *On Signs*. Oxford: Blackwell.

Booth, Michael R. 1991. *Theatre in the Victorian Age*. Cambridge: Cambridge University Press.

Boucris, Luc. 1993. *L'Espace en scène*. Paris: Librairie Théâtrale.

Bradby, David, and David Williams. 1988. *Directors' Theatre*. London: Macmillan.

Brecht, Bertolt. 1964. *Brecht on Theatre*. Ed. and trans. John Willett. London: Eyre Methuen.

Brook, Peter. 1968. *The Empty Space*. London: Macgibbon and Kee.

———. 1970. "Introduction." *L'Architecture d'Aujourd'hui*. Special issue on "Les lieux du spectacle," n.p.

———. 1989. *The Shifting Point: Theatre, Film, Opera 1946–1987*. New York: Harper and Row.

Callow, Simon. 1985. *Being an Actor*. London: Penguin Books.

———. 1992. *Shooting the Actor or the Choreography of Confusion*. London: Vintage Books.

Carlson, Marvin. 1984. *Theories of the Theatre: A Historical and Critical Survey from the Greeks to the Present*. Ithaca and London: Cornell University Press.

———. 1989. *Places of Performance: The Semiotics of Theatre Architecture*. Ithaca and London: Cornell University Press.

Casey, Edward S. 1993. *Getting Back into Place: Toward a Renewed Understanding of the Place-World*. Bloomington: Indiana University Press.

Chaudhuri, Una. 1995. *Staging Place: The Geography of Modern Drama*. Ann Arbor: University of Michigan Press.

Chikamatsu Monzaemon. [1652–1724] 1926. *Masterpieces of Chikamatsu: The Japanese Shakespeare*. Trans. Asatora Miyamori. London: Kegan Paul Trench Trubner.

Claudel, Paul. [1893, 1951] 1967. *L'Echange*. In *Théâtre 1*. Paris: Bibliothèque de la Pléiade.

Clifford, James, and George Marcus, eds. 1986. *Writing Culture: The Poetics and Politics of Ethnography*. Berkeley: University of California Press.

Communications. 1977. Special issue on "Sémiotique de l'espace," 27.

Connor, Linda, and Patsy Asch. 1995. "Subjects, Images, Voices: Representing Gender in Ethnographic Film." *Visual Anthropology Review* 11 (1): 5–18.

Copeau, Jacques. 1974. *Registres*. Vol. 1 of *Appels*. Paris: Gallimard.

Crohn Schmitt, Natalie. 1990. *Actors and Onlookers: Theater and Twentieth Century Scientific Views of Nature*. Evanston, Ill.: Northwestern University Press.

Dagognet, François. 1989. *Eloge de l'objet: pour une philosophie de la marchandise*. Paris: Librairie Philosophique J. Vrin.

Daumier, Honoré. 1982. *Les gens du spectacle*, ed. Jacqueline Armingeat. Preface by François Périer. Paris: Editions Michèle Trinckval.

de Certeau, Michel. 1980. *Arts de faire*. Paris: Union Générale d'Editions.

———. 1984. *The Practice of Everyday Life*. Trans. Steven Rendall. Berkeley and Los Angeles: University of California Press.

Descotes, Maurice. 1964. *Le Public de théâtre et son histoire*. Paris: Presses Universitaires de France.

Diprose, Rosalyn, and Robyn Ferrell, eds. 1991. *Cartographies: Poststructuralism and the Mapping of Bodies and Spaces*. Sydney: Allen and Unwin.

Durand, Régis, ed. 1980. *La Relation théâtrale*. Lille: Presses Universitaires de Lille.

Duvignaud, Jean. 1977. *Lieux et non-lieux*. Paris: Editions Galilée.

———. 1993. *L'Acteur*. Paris: Editions Ecriture.

Eco, Umberto. 1977. "Semiotics of the Theatrical Performance." *Drama Review* T73:107–17.

———. 1976. *A Theory of Semiotics*. Bloomington: Indiana University Press.

———. 1979. *The Role of the Reader*. Bloomington: Indiana University Press.

Elam, Keir. 1980. *The Semiotics of Theatre and Drama*. London: Methuen.

Eliade, Mircea. 1958. *Patterns in Comparative Religion*. London: Sheed and Ward.

Erikson, Jon. 1995. *The Fate of the Object: from Modern Object to Postmodern Sign in Performance*. Ann Arbor: University of Michigan Press.

Ernst, Earle, ed. 1959. *Three Japanese Plays from the Traditional Theatre*. London and New York: Oxford University Press.

Esslin, Martin. 1987. *The Field of Drama: How the Signs of Drama Create Meaning on Stage and Screen*. London: Methuen.

Featherstone, Mike, Mike Hepworth, and Bryan Turner, eds. 1991. *The Body: Social Process and Cultural Theory*. London: Sage Publications.

Féral, Josette, Jeannette Savona, and E. Walker, eds. 1985. *Théâtralité, écriture et mise en scène*. Quebec: Editions Hurtubise.

Fischer-Lichte, Erika. 1992. *The Semiotics of Theatre*. Trans. J. Gaines and D. L. Jones, of 3 volume *Semiotik des Theatres*, 1983. Bloomington: Indiana University Press.

Fitzpatrick, Tim. 1989a. "The Dialectics of Space-Time: Dramaturgical and Directorial Strategies for Performance and Fictional World." In *Performance from Product to Process*, ed. Tim Fitzpatrick, 49–112. Sydney: Frederick May Foundation.

———. 1989b. "Flaminio Scala's Prototypal Scenarios: Segmenting the Text/Performance." In *The Science of Buffoonery*, ed. Domenico Pietropaolo, 177–98. Toronto: Dovehouse.

———. 1990. "Models of Visual and Auditory Interaction in Performance." *Gestos* 9:9–22.

———. 1997. "Shakespeare's Exploitation of a Two-Door Stage: Macbeth." *Theatre Research International* 20 (3): 207–30.

Fitzpatrick, Tim, and Sean Batten. 1991. "Watching the Watchers Watch: Some Implications of Audience Attention Patterns." *Gestos* 12:11–31.

Florence, Penny, and Dee Reynolds, eds. 1995. *Feminist Subjects: Multimedia Cultural Methodologies*. Manchester: Manchester University Press.

Foreman, Richard. 1992. *Unbalancing Acts: Foundations for a Theatre*. New York: Pantheon Books.

Freedman, Barbara. 1991. *Staging the Gaze: Postmodernism, Psychoanalysis and Shakespearian Comedy*. Ithaca and London: Cornell University Press.

Freud, Sigmund. 1953. *Complete Works*. Vol. 19. Standard edition. New York: International Universities Press.

Frow, John, and Meaghan Morris, eds. 1993. *Australian Cultural Studies: A Reader*. Sydney: Allen and Unwin.

Fuchs, Elinor. 1985. "Presence and the Revenge of Writing: Rethinking Theatre after Derrida." *Performing Arts Journal* 26–27:163–73.

Garber, Marjorie. 1992. *Vested Interests: Cross-dressing and Cultural Anxiety*. London: Penguin Books.

Garner, Stanton. 1994. *Bodied Spaces: Phenomenology and Performance in Contemporary Drama*. Ithaca and London: Cornell University Press.

Garvin, Paul, ed. 1964. *A Prague School Reader on Esthetics, Literary Structure and Style*. Washington, D.C.: Georgetown University Press.

Genest, E. 1920. *L'Opéra connu et inconnu*. Paris: E. de Boccard.

Genet, Jean. 1957. *The Maids*. Trans. Bernard Frechtman. London: Faber and Faber.

———. 1958. *Les Bonnes*. Paris: L'Arbalète.

Genette, Gérard. 1972. "Discours du récit." In *Figures III*, 71–227. Paris: Seuil.

———. 1980. *Narrative Discourse: An Essay on Method*. Trans. Jane Lewin. Ithaca: Cornell University Press.

Gielgud, John. 1939. *Early Stages*. London: Macmillan. Reprint, London: Heinemann, 1974.

———. 1964. *Stage Directions*. London: Heinemann.

———. 1972. *Distinguished Company*. London: Heinemann.

———. 1979. *An Actor and His Time*. London: Sidgwick and Jackson.

Goffman, Erving. 1959. *The Presentation of Self in Everyday Life*. New York: Doubleday.

———. 1964. "The Neglected Situation." In *Language and Social Context*, ed. Pier Paolo Giglioli, 61–66. London: Penguin Books.

———. 1974. *Frame Analysis: An Essay on the Organisation of Experience*. Boston: Northeastern University Press.

Gourdon, Anne-Marie. 1982. *Théâtre, Public, Réception*. Paris: Editions du CNRS.

Greimas, A. J. 1976. *Sémiotique et sciences sociales*. Paris: Seuil.

Grotowski, Jerzy. 1969. *Towards a Poor Theatre*. London: Methuen.

———. 1995. "From the Theatre Company to Art as Vehicle." In *At Work with Grotowski on Physical Actions*, ed. Thomas Richards, 113–35. London and New York: Routledge.

Hall, Edward T. 1959. *The Silent Language*. New York: Doubleday.

———. 1966. *The Hidden Dimension*. New York: Doubleday.

Halliday, M. A. K. 1973. *Explorations in the Functions of Language*. London: Edward Arnold.

———. 1978. *Language as Social Semiotic*. London: Edward Arnold.

Halliday, M. A. K., and Ruqaiya Hasan. 1976. *Cohesion in English*. London: Longman.

Harrop, John. 1992. *Acting*. London and New York: Routledge.

Helbo, André, ed. 1975. *Sémiologie de la représentation*. Brussels: Editions Complexe.

Helbo, André, J. Dines Johansen, Patrice Pavis, and Anne Ubersfeld, eds. 1987. *Théâtre: modes d'approche*. Brussels: Editions Labor. Trans. as *Approaching Theatre*. Bloomington: Indiana University Press, 1991.

Hemmings, F. W. J. 1993. *The Theatre Industry in Nineteenth-Century France*. Cambridge: Cambridge University Press.

Hess-Luttich, Ernest W. B., ed. 1982. *Multi-Medial Communication*. Tübingen: Gunter Narr Verlag.

Holland, Peter. 1989. "Space: The Final Frontier." In *The Play out of Context*, ed. Hanna Scolnicov and Peter Holland, 45–62. Cambridge: Cambridge University Press.

Holub, Robert C. 1984. *Reception Theory: A Critical Introduction*. London: Methuen.

Honzl, Jiri. [1940] 1976. "Dynamics of the Sign in Theatre." In *Semiotics of Art*, ed. Ladislav Matejka and Irwin R. Titunik, 74–93. Cambridge, Mass: MIT Press.

Horace. 1965. *On the Art of Poetry*. In *Classical Literary Criticism*, trans. T. S. Dorsch, 77–95. London: Penguin Books.

Huizinga, Johan. 1949. *Homo Ludens: A Study of the Play Element in Culture*. London: Routledge and Kegan Paul.

Huston, Hollis. 1992. *The Actor's Instrument: Body, Theory, Stage*. Ann Arbor: University of Michigan Press.

Ingarden, Roman. 1931. *Das Literarische Kunstwerk*. Halle: Max Niemeyer.

Ionesco, Eugène. 1962. *Notes et Contre-Notes*. Paris: Gallimard.

———. 1964. *Notes and Counter Notes*. Trans. Donald Watson. London: John Calder.

Iser, Wolfgang. 1980. "Interaction between Text and Reader." In *The Reader in the Text*, ed. Susan Suleiman and Inge Crosman, 106–19. Princeton: Princeton University Press.

Issacharoff, Michael. 1989. *Discourse as Performance*. Stanford: Stanford University Press.

Jacquot, Jean, ed. 1978. *Les voies de la création théâtrale*. Vol. 6. (Productions by Vitez, Planchon, Sobel and Strehler.) Paris: Editions du CNRS.

Jansen, Steen. 1968. "Esquisse d'une théorie de la forme dramatique." *Langages* 12.

———. 1973. "Qu'est-ce qu'une situation dramatique?" *Orbis Literarum* 20–28.

———. 1982. "L'espace scénique dans le spectacle dramatique et dans le texte dramatique." *Revue Romane* 17:3–20.

————. 1984. "Le rôle de l'espace scénique dans la lecture du texte dramatique." In *Semiotics of Drama and Theatre*, ed. Herta Schmid and Aloysius
van Kesteren, 254–79. Amsterdam: John Benjamins.

Jonson, Ben. 1950. *The New Inn. The Complete Plays of Ben Jonson* (1573–1637).
London: J. M. Dent and Sons.

Jousse, Marcel. 1974. *L'Anthropologie du geste*. Paris: Gallimard.

Jouvet, Louis. 1952. *Réflexions du comédien*. Paris: Librairie Théâtrale.

————. 1965. *Molière et la comédie classique*. Paris: Gallimard.

Kaplan, E. Ann. 1988. "Whose Imaginary? The Televisual Apparatus, the
Female Body and Textual Strategies in Select Rock Videos on MTV." In
Female Spectators Looking at Film and Television, ed. E. Deidre Pribram,
132–56. London and New York: Verso.

Kierkegaard, Søren. 1941. *Repetition: An Essay in Experimental Psychology*. Trans.
Walter Lowrie. New York: Harper Torchbooks.

————. 1983. *Fear and Trembling: Repetition*. Trans. Howard and Edna Hong.
Princeton: Princeton University Press.

Kirby, Victoria Nes. 1974. "The Creation and Development of People Show
#52." *Drama Review* T62:48–66.

Kitto, H. D. F. 1939. *Greek Tragedy: A Literary Study*. London: Methuen.

————. 1956. *Form and Meaning in Drama: A Study of Six Greek Plays and Hamlet*.
London: Methuen.

Kowzan, Tadeusz. 1975. *Littérature et Spectacle*. The Hague and Paris: Mouton.

————. 1992. *Sémiologie du théâtre*. Paris: Editions Nathan.

Kristeva, Julia. 1969. *Semiotike: recherches pour une sémanalyse*. Paris: Seuil.

————. 1977. "The Modern Theatre Does Not Take (a) Place." *Sub-Stance*
18–19:131–34.

Lakoff, George, and Mark Johnson. 1980. *Metaphors We Live By*. Chicago: University of Chicago Press.

Langhoff, Matthias. 1996. "Le Rapport Langhoff." *Nanterre Amandiers* 12:9.

Lassiter, Laurie. 1995. "David Warrilow: Creating Symbol and Cypher." In *Acting (Re)considered*, ed. Philip Zarilli, 313–21. London and New York: Routledge.

Leacroft, Richard, and Helen Leacroft. 1984. *Theatre and Playhouse*. London:
Methuen.

Leder, Drew. 1990. *The Absent Body*. Chicago: University of Chicago Press.

Lefebvre, Henri. 1974. *La Production de l'Espace*. Paris: Editions Anthropos.

————. 1991. *The Production of Space*. Trans. Donald Nicholson-Smith. Oxford:
Blackwell.

Liddell and Scott. [1889] 1961. *Greek-English Lexicon*. Oxford: Oxford University
Press.

Longman, Stanley. 1987. "Fixed, Floating and Fluid Stages." In *The Theatrical
Space*, ed. James Redmond, 151–60. Cambridge: Cambridge University
Press.

Lough, John. 1957. *Paris Theatre Audiences in the Seventeenth and Eighteenth Centuries*. Oxford: Oxford University Press.

Lovelace, Carey. 1995. "Orlan: Offensive Acts." *Performing Arts Journal* 49:13–25.

Lowell, Robert. 1961. *Phaedra*. London: Faber and Faber.

Mackintosh, Iain. 1993. *Architecture, Actor and Audience*. London: Routledge.

Mannoni, Octave. 1969. *Clefs pour l'imaginaire ou l'autre scène*. Paris: Seuil.

Marinis, Marco de. [1982] 1993. *The Semiotics of Performance*. Trans. Aine O'Healy. Bloomington: Indiana University Press.

Martin, Jacqueline, and Willmar Sauter. 1995. *Understanding Theatre: Performance Analysis in Theory and Practice*. Stockholm: Almqvist and Wiksell International.

Matejka, Ladislav, and Irwin R. Titunik, eds. *Semiotics of Art*. Cambridge, Mass.: MIT Press.

Mauss, Marcel. 1950. *Sociologie et anthropologie*. Paris: Quadrige/Presses Universitaires de France.

McAuley, Gay. 1974. "Language and Theatre in Molière's *Malade Imaginaire*." *Australian Journal of French Studies* 11 (1): 4–18.

———. 1983. "The Spatial Dynamics of Britannicus: Text and Performance." *Australian Journal of French Studies* 20 (3): 340–60.

———. 1987a. "Movement within the Scenic Space and Segmentation of the Performance Continuum." In *Approches de l'opéra*, ed. André Helbo, 105–20. Paris: Didier Erudition.

———. 1987b. "Paradigmatic Structures in Text and Performance: Movement and Gesture in Four Performances of *Les Bonnes*." *Kodikas/Code* 10 (1–2): 3–25.

———. 1989. "Body, Space and Language: The Actor's Work on/with Text." In *Performance: From Product to Process*, ed. Tim Fitzpatrick, 113–44. Sydney: Frederick May Foundation.

———. 1994. "The Video Documentation of Theatrical Performance." *New Theatre Quarterly* 38:183–94.

———. 1998. "Towards an Ethnography of Rehearsal." *New Theatre Quarterly* 53: 75–85.

Meyerhold, Vsevolod. 1969. *Meyerhold on Theatre*. Ed. and trans. Edward Braun. London: Methuen.

Minchinton, Mark. 1996. "Towards a Minor Theatre? Theatre Making Processes in Three Australian Theatre Groups and Their Directors." Ph.D. diss., University of Melbourne.

Mittman, Barbara G. 1984. *Spectators on the Paris Stage in the Seventeenth and Eighteenth Centuries*. Ann Arbor: UMI Research Press.

Moles, Abraham. 1969. "Objet et communication." *Communications* 13:1–21.

Molière. [1669] 1962. *Tartuffe*. In *Oeuvres complètes*. Ed. R. Jouanny. Paris: Editions Garnier.

Morris, Desmond. 1994. *Bodytalk: The Meaning of Human Gesture*. New York: Crown Trade Paperbacks.

Mulvey, Laura. 1975. "Visual Pleasure and Narrative Cinema." *Screen* 16 (3): 6–18.

Ong, Walter J. 1982. *Orality and Literacy*. London: Methuen.

Passow, Wilfried. 1981. "The Analysis of Theatrical Performance: The State of the Art." *Poetics Today* 2 (3): 237–54.

Paul, Arno. 1971. "Theatrewissenschaft als Lehre vom Theatralischen Handeln." *Kölner Zeitschrift für Soziologie (und Sozialpsychologie)* 23:55–77.

Paul-Lévy, Françoise, and Marian Segaud. 1983. *Anthropologie de l'espace*. Paris: Centre de Création Industrielle.

Pavis, Patrice. 1976. *Problèmes de la sémiologie théâtrale*. Montreal: Presses Universitaires de Québec.

———. 1980. *Dictionnaire du théâtre*. Paris: Messidor/Editions Sociales.

———. 1986. *Marivaux à l'épreuve de la scène*. Paris: Editions de la Sorbonne.

———. 1996a. *L'Analyse des spectacles*. Paris: Nathan Université.

———, ed. 1996b. *A Reader in Intercultural Performance*. London and New York: Routledge.

Payne, Michael. 1993. *Reading Theory: An Introduction to Lacan, Derrida and Kristeva*. Oxford and London: Blackwell.

Picon-Vallin, Béatrice. 1985. "L'espace et le temps." In *Les voies de la création théâtrale*, ed. Georges Banu, 273–92. Vol. 13 on Peter Brook. Paris: Editions du CNRS.

Poetics Today. 1981. Special issue on "Drama, Theatre, Performance: A Semiotic Perspective." Vol. 2, no. 3.

Pollock, Griselda. 1995. "The 'View from Elsewhere': Extracts from a Semi-Public Correspondence about the Politics of Feminist Spectatorship." In *Feminist Subjects, Multi-media Cultural Methodologies*, ed. Penny Florence and Dee Reynolds, 2–38. Manchester: Manchester University Press.

Potts, C. M. 1995. "What Empty Space? Text and Space in the Australian Mainstream Rehearsal Process." M.Phil. thesis, University of Sydney.

Pradier, Jean-Marie, ed. 1996. *La Scène et la terre: questions d'ethnoscénologie*. Paris: Babel (Maison des Cultures du Monde).

Pribram, E. Deidre, ed. 1988. *Female Spectators Looking at Film and Television*. London: Verso.

Price, Norman. 1989. "Writing in the Space: The Development of a Play from Conception to Performance." Master's thesis, University of Melbourne.

Prince, Gerald. 1973. *A Grammar of Stories*. The Hague: Mouton.

Quinn, Michael. 1990. "Celebrity and the Semiotics of Acting." *New Theatre Quarterly* 22:154–61.

Rabkin, Gerald. 1985. "Is There a Text on This Stage? Theatre/Authorship Interpretation." *Performing Arts Journal* 26–27:142–59.

Read, Alan. 1993. *Theatre and Everyday Life: An Ethics of Performance*. London: Routledge.

Redmond, James, ed. 1987. *The Theatrical Space*. Themes in Drama, vol. 9. Cambridge: Cambridge University Press.

Reinelt, Janelle. 1995. "Theatre on the Brink of 2000: Shifting Paradigms." *Theatre Research International* 20 (2): 123–31.

Reinelt, Janelle, and Joseph Roach, eds. 1992. *Critical Theory and Performance.* Ann Arbor: University of Michigan Press.

Richards, Kenneth, and Peter Thomson, eds. 1972. *Essays on the Eighteenth-Century English Stage.* London: Methuen.

Richards, Thomas. 1995. *At Work with Grotowski on Physical Actions.* London and New York: Routledge.

Robertson, Tom. 1980. *Six Plays.* London: Amber Lane Press.

Rokem, Freddie. 1986. *Theatrical Space in Ibsen, Chekhov and Strindberg.* Ann Arbor: UMI Research Press.

Rosenfeld, Sybil. 1973. *A Short History of Scene Design in Great Britain.* Oxford: Blackwell.

Rowell, George. 1981. *Theatre in the Age of Irving.* Oxford: Blackwell.

Rozik, Eli. 1993. "Les gestes métaphoriques de la main au théâtre." *Protée: Théories et Pratiques Sémiotiques* 21 (3): 8–17.

Sartre, Jean-Paul. 1973. *Un théâtre de situations.* Paris: Gallimard.

Sauter, Willmar, ed. 1988. *New Directions in Audience Research.* Utrecht: Institut voor Theatrewetenschap.

Savona, Jeannette. 1985. "La didascalie comme acte de parole." In *Théâtralité, ecriture et mise en scène,* ed. Josette Féral, Jeannette Savona, and E. Walker, 231–43. Quebec: Editions Hurtubise.

Sayre, Henry M. 1989. *The Object of Performance: The American Avant-Garde since 1970.* Chicago: University of Chicago Press.

Scarry, Elaine. 1985. *The Body in Pain: The Making and Unmaking of the World.* New York: Oxford University Press.

Schechner, Richard. 1977. *Essays on Performance Theory, 1970–1976.* New York: Drama Book Specialists.

———. 1985. *Between Theatre and Anthropology.* Philadelphia: University of Pennsylvania Press.

———. 1992. "A New Paradigm for Theatre in the Academy." *Drama Review* T136:8.

Schechner, Richard, and Willa Appel, eds. 1990. *By Means of Performance: Intercultural Studies of Theatre and Ritual.* Cambridge: Cambridge University Press.

Schmid, Herta, and Aloysius van Kesteren, eds. 1984. *Semiotics of Drama and Theatre.* Amsterdam: John Benjamins.

Scolnicov, Hanna. 1987. "Theatre Space, Theatrical Space and the Theatrical Space Without." In *The Theatrical Space,* ed. James Redmond, 11–26. Cambridge: Cambridge University Press.

Scolnicov, Hanna, and Peter Holland, eds. 1989. *The Play out of Context: Transferring Plays from Culture to Culture.* Cambridge: Cambridge University Press.

Seeck, G. A., ed. 1979. *Das Griechische Drama.* Darmstadt: Wissenschaftliche Buchgesellschaft.

Selbourne, David. 1982. *The Making of* A Midsummer Night's Dream. London: Methuen.

Serpieri, Alessandro, et al. 1981. "Toward a Segmentation of the Dramatic Text." *Poetics Today* 2 (3): 163–200.

Sher, Antony. 1985. *The Year of the King: An Actor's Diary and Sketchbook.* London: Chatto and Windus.

Sieffert, René. 1960. "Introduction." In *La tradition secrète du Nô,* by Zeami. Paris: Gallimard/UNESCO.

Sommer, Robert. 1969. *Personal Space: The Behavioural Basis of Design.* Englewood Cliffs, N.J.: Prentice-Hall.

Sontag, Susan. 1977. *On Photography.* London: Penguin Books.

Souriau, Etienne. 1950. *Les Deux cent mille situations dramatiques.* Paris: Flammarion.

Southern, Richard. 1962. *Seven Ages of Theatre.* London: Faber and Faber.

Spinks, Kim, and S. Baird, eds. 1995. *Walking on Water: Sydney Theatre Company at the Wharf.* Sydney: Currency Press.

Stanislavsky, Konstantin. [1926] 1967. *An Actor Prepares.* London: Penguin Books.

———. 1968. *Building a Character.* London: Methuen.

———. 1981. *Creating a Role.* London: Methuen.

States, Bert O. 1985. *Great Reckonings in Little Rooms: On the Phenomenology of Theatre.* Berkeley: University of California Press.

Stein, Gertrude. [1935] 1988. *Lectures in America.* London: Virago Press.

Steinbeck, Dietrich. 1970. *Einleitung in die Theorie und Systematik der Theatrewissenschaft.* Berlin: Walter de Gruyter.

Stourac, Richard, and Kathleen McCreery. 1986. *Theatre as a Weapon: Workers' Theatre in the Soviet Union, Germany and Britain, 1917–1934.* London: Routledge and Kegan Paul.

Strindberg, August. 1955. "Author's Foreword." *Miss Julie.* Trans. Elizabeth Sprigge. New York: Doubleday.

———. 1964. "Letters to the Intimate Theatre." In *Théâtre cruel et théâtre mystique.* Trans. Marguerite Diehl. Paris: Gallimard.

Suleiman, Susan, and Inge Crosman, eds. 1980. *The Reader in the Text.* Princeton University Press.

Suvin, Darko. 1987. "Approach to Topoanalysis and to the Paradigmatics of Dramaturgic Space." *Poetics Today* 8 (2): 311–34.

Symons, Arthur. 1927. *Eleonora Duse.* New York: Duffield.

Tavernier, Bertrand. 1996. "Un Immense supplement d'imaginaire." *Le Journal du Théâtre* 1:23–24.

Threadgold, Terry. 1993. "Performing Genre: Violence, the Making of Protected Subjects and the Discourses of Critical Literacy and Radical Pedagogy." *Changing English* 1 (1): 2–31.

———. 1995. "Postmodernism and the Politics of Culture: Chekhov's *Three Sisters* in Rehearsal and Performance." *Southern Review* 28 (2): 172–82.

Trewin, J. C. 1976. *The Edwardian Theatre.* Oxford: Blackwell.

Turner, Victor. 1982. *From Ritual to Theatre.* New York: PAJ Publications.

———. 1987. *The Anthropology of Performance.* New York: PAJ Publications.

Ubersfeld, Anne. 1964. *Le Roi et le bouffon.* Paris: Corti.

———. 1977. *Lire le théâtre.* Paris: Editions Sociales.

———. 1981. *L'Ecole du spectateur.* Paris: Editions Sociales.

———. 1984. *L'Objet théâtral: diversité des significations et langages de l'objet théâtral dans la mise en scène contemporaine.* Paris: Centre National de Documentation Pédagogique.

———. 1991. *Le Théâtre et la cité.* Brussells: Association International pour la Sémiologie du Spectacle.

———. 1996. *Termes clés de l'analyse du théâtre.* Paris: Seuil.

Van den Heuvel, Michael. 1993. "The Politics of the Paradigm: A Case Study in Chaos Theory." *New Theatre Quarterly* 35:255–66.

Veltrusky, Jiri. 1940. "Man and Object in the Theatre." In *A Prague School Reader on Esthetics, Literary Structure and Style,* ed. Paul Garvin, 83–91. Washington, D.C.: Georgetown University Press.

Villeneuve, Rodrigue. 1993. "La Concordance du corps et du sens." *Protée* 21 (3): 86–95.

Vitez, Antoine. 1991. *Le Théâtre des idées.* Paris: Gallimard.

Wekwerth, Manfred. 1972. *Theater und Wissenschaft.* Berlin: Henschel. Deutsche Akademie der Künste zu Berlin, Arbeitsheft 3.

Whiteside, Anna, and Michael Issacharoff, eds. 1987. *On Referring in Literature.* Bloomington: Indiana University Press.

Willett, John. 1986. *Caspar Neher: Brecht's Designer.* London: Methuen.

Williamson, David. 1986. *Collected Plays.* Vol. 1. Sydney: Currency Press.

———. 1997. "David Williamson Talks about Australia's Most Famous Party." *State Theatre Scenes* (Newsletter of State Theatre Company of South Australia) 9.

Wilshire, Bruce. 1982. *Role Playing and Identity: The Limits of Theatre as Metaphor.* Bloomington: Indiana University Press.

Worthen, William. 1984. *The Idea of the Actor: Drama and the Ethics of Performance.* Princeton University Press.

Zarilli, Philip, ed. 1995. *Acting (Re)considered: Theories and Practices.* London and New York: Routledge.

Zeami. 1960. *La Tradition secrète du Nô.* Trans. René Sieffert. Paris: Gallimard/UNESCO.

Zielske, Harald. 1977. "Box House and Illusion Stage-Problem Topic in Modern Theatre Construction." In *Theatre Space: An Examination of the Interaction between Space, Technology, Performance and Society,* ed. James F. Arnott et al., 23–44. Munich: Prestel Verlag.

Index